BK 780.924 K86J 1970
JOHN CAGE /KOSTELANET
1970 .00 FP
3000 262301 20011
St. Louis Community College

INVENTORY 1985

780.924 K86j 1970 FP
KOSTELANETZ SEP 1 72
JOHN CAGE
12.50

INVENTOR

INVENTORY 1985

JUNIOR COLLEGE DISTRICT
of St. Louis - St. Louis County
LIBRARY
5801 Wilson Ave.
St. Louis, Missouri 63110

BRODART PRINTED IN U.S.A.

John Cage

Documentary Monographs
in Modern Art

general editor: Paul Cummings

Also by Richard Kostelanetz

As author:

The Theatre of Mixed Means

Master Minds

Visual Language

Metamorphosis in the Arts

As co-author and editor:

The New American Arts

As editor:

On Contemporary Literature

Twelve from the Sixties

The Young American Writers

Beyond Left and Right

Imaged Words & Worded Images

Moholy-Nagy

Social Speculations

John Cage

edited by

Richard Kostelanetz

Praeger Publishers *New York • Washington*

Frontispiece: John Cage with pipe.

BOOKS THAT MATTER

Published in the United States of America in 1970
by Praeger Publishers, Inc.
111 Fourth Avenue, New York, N.Y. 10003

© 1968, 1969, 1970 by Richard Kostelanetz
© 1970 by John Cage

All rights reserved

Library of Congress Catalog Card Number: 77–121714

Printed in the United States of America

for
Buckminster Fuller

contents

Chapter titles for previously untitled writings have been supplied by the editor and are enclosed within brackets.

IV 1950–54

V 1955–59

VI 1960–65

VII 1966–70

VIII SOME RANDOM REMARKS

IX DATA

list of illustrations

Unless otherwise credited, illustrations are from John Cage's personal collection.

preface

This monograph about John Cage is told mostly in his own words and writings, although pieced together by another hand; and, because the editor's theme is that Cage is not just a composer but one of the century's seminal minds who has burrowed through many arts and "fields," materials of all kinds are included here—essays and reviews, scores and sketches, notes, and even designs by Cage himself, as well as photographs, reportage, and criticism of his diverse work. To divide one kind of activity from another would be contrary to the Cagean spirit; so this book is organized in roughly chronological order, produce of various kinds falling into their more or less proper sequential place. Otherwise, the book opens with, after an introduction, my own extensive interview with Cage, originally done in the summer of 1966 for both the chapter on him in *The Theatre of Mixed Means* (1968) and the profile published in several periodicals before its use in my *Master Minds* (1969); so that the lines from this conversation have previously appeared in both these volumes. Only one selection, "The Future of Music," has appeared in Cage's own books. *John Cage* closes with my own comprehensive critical essay, written in 1968; but criticisms of both past work and a career still in progress are incorporated in their appropriate chronological places, even if written sometime afterwards. In the beginning is a chronology of Cage's activity; at the end is a bibliography, a discography, and an index. Need one say that this book hardly brings Cage's explorations to an end?

John Cage has been a supremely cordial subject; he has my gratitude for considering all material within his copyright in a truly Ivesian spirit, in addition to his guidance and help in ferreting out forgotten and arcane matter. Without him, need I say, there would be no book. Hanns Sohm, Hans G. Helms, Dick Higgins, Scott Hyde, and many others graciously gave me important advice and/or lent rare materials; Marjorie Trenk helped both Cage and myself in innumerable ways; and the book's dedication to Buckminster Fuller reflects the great admiration of us both. John Hochmann deserves my thanks for commissioning this book; he, Nancy Reynolds, Regina Cohen, and their associates at Praeger Publishers guided the manuscript through many editorial problems.

Grateful acknowledgment is made to the individuals and organizations who granted permission to reprint selections appearing in this book. All possible care has been taken to trace the ownership of every excerpt and reproduction included here and to make full acknowledgment of its use.

New York, New York
14 May, 1970

RICHARD KOSTELANETZ

How do you choose a Ready-Made?

It chooses you, so to speak. If your choice enters into it, then taste is involved—bad taste, good taste, uninteresting taste. Taste is the enemy of art, A-R-T. The idea was to find an object that had no attraction whatsoever from the aesthetic angle. This was not the act of an artist, but of a non-artist, an artisan if you will. I wanted to change the status of the artist or at least to change the norms used for defining an artist. Again to de-deify him. . . . The idea of the artist as a superman is comparatively recent. This I was going against. In fact, since I've stopped my artistic activity, I feel that I'm against this attitude of reverence the world has. Art, etymologically speaking, means "to make." Everybody is making, not only artists, and maybe in coming centuries there will be the making without the noticing.

Do you feel that the act of creating a Ready-Made is an act of art?

I wouldn't say so, no. The fact that they are regarded with the same reverence as objects of art probably means I have failed to solve the problem of trying to do away entirely with art. It is partly because I have only a few Ready-Mades. I can count ten, twelve gestures of this kind in my life, that is all. And I'm glad I did not because this is where the artists of today are wrong, I think. Must you repeat? Repetition has been the great enemy of art in general. I mean, formulas and theories are based on repetition. —MARCEL DUCHAMP, in an interview (1963)*

Is it only that Mr. Cage does things that Europeans do not dare do and that he does them naturally and innocently, not as self-conscious stunts? Whatever the answers, no sleight of hand, no trap-doors, are ever discovered in his performances: in other words, no "tradition" at all, and not only no Bach and no Beethoven, but also no Schoenberg and no Webern either. This is impressive, and no wonder the man on your left keeps saying *sehr interessant*.—IGOR STRAVINSKY, in conversation with Robert Craft

* Copyright *Art News*. Reprinted by permission.

I introduction, conversation, chronology

Opening the Cage: 14 Variations on 14 Words

I have nothing to say and I am saying it and that is poetry.
—JOHN CAGE

I have to say poetry and is that nothing and am I saying it
I am and I have poetry to say and is that nothing saying it
I am nothing and I have poetry to say and that is saying it
I that am saying poetry have nothing and it is I and to say
And I say that I am to have poetry and saying it is nothing
I am poetry and nothing and saying it is to say that I have
To have nothing is poetry and I am saying that and I say it
Poetry is saying I have nothing and I am to say that and it
Saying nothing I am poetry and I have to say that and it is
It is and I am and I have poetry saying say that to nothing
It is saying poetry to nothing and I say I have and am that
Poetry is saying I have it and I am nothing and to say that
And that nothing is poetry I am saying and I have to say it
Saying poetry is nothing and to that I say I am and have it
—EDWIN MORGAN (1965)

From *The Second Life* (Edinburgh University Press), copyright © 1968 by Edwin Morgan and Edinburgh University Press.

Introduction

Richard Kostelanetz

The first time I saw John Cage, at a concert of avant-garde music in the early 1960's, I was immediately struck by his amazingly youthful appearance. All his features contributed to a deception of at least twenty years less than his official age. His black hair, cut in the spikey style we used to call "long crew," has neither thinned nor receded; only since then has he seen some gray around the temples and begun to grow it rakishly long. He is slightly under six feet tall, thin in build; and although long troubled by arthritis, he moves with the grace of a far younger man. Only the deep lines running down the sides of his face would betray his age. Actually, Cage presents two distinct faces, one hardly resembling the other. The "serious" face is long and narrow, with wide and attentive brown eyes, unusually long ears, and vertical lines sloping down to his heavy chin; in contrast, Cage's "comic" face, which graces most of his public pictures, is horizontally structured, his eyes nearly closed, his wide mouth exposing two even lines of teeth.

He talks easily and contagiously, laughing freely at his own jokes; and his voice is so singular it would be instantly recognizable on the radio or telephone. Animated and stylized in demeanor, he is an extremely skillful performer, both as a musician and as a lecturer or conversationalist, with sufficient presence to upstage nearly everybody in any situation. Usually, he is so infallibly elegant that everyone around him, particularly a purposeful interviewer, feels rather gauche. Probably because he knows that his ideas slide without self-conscious effort far beyond conventional thought, he constantly attempts to elicit agreement—indeed, his passion for persuasion is positively Jesuitical. A serious philosophical intelligence, Cage continually relates life to ideas, and vice versa; and, as the extended interview reprinted ahead demonstrates, his thinking is both integrated and continually developing. Indeed, he has been interviewed so many times before that he knows well what he thinks; so answers, gestures, and jokes come quickly to him. Like his friend McLuhan, Cage can flood his listeners with an endless supply of truly unusual ideas and perceptions—he is, as we say, a natural original; but implicit in the following discussion is the theme that his personal attitudes have yet to catch up with his espoused positions. For instance, although opposed in principle to evaluations, he is still both incorrigibly opinionated (as every unconventional artist must ultimately be) and a tough critic of his own creative endeavors.

Born in 1912, in Los Angeles, California, the son of an imaginative and versatile inventor, Cage grew up in Ann Arbor and Detroit, but largely in Los Angeles, where he attended the local public high school—becoming class valedictorian—and then Pomona College. He soon dropped out, however, to tour Europe and study art and architecture, before returning to Los Angeles, where he decided to make music his primary concern. Cage studied with the composers Adolph Weiss and Henry Cowell, as well as with Arnold Schoenberg, who had emigrated to Los Angeles in the early 1930's. Late in that decade, Cage became resident accompanist at the Cornish School in Seattle, Washington, where he first met the choreographer Merce Cunningham (then a student of the dancer Bonnie Bird), who has remained to this day one of Cage's closest friends and professional associates. In 1935, he married Xenia Andreyevna Kashevaroff, the daughter of an Alaskan Russian-Orthodox priest; and they traveled together for about a decade. After an entire year spent trying to found a center for experimental music, Cage took a job in 1942 teaching music at László Moholy-Nagy's Chicago Bauhaus, then called the Institute of Design. The following year, the Cages came to New York; and, thanks to the aid of newly acquired friends, he managed, in 1943, to present, at the Museum of Modern Art, the crucial concert that initiated his reputation as an adventurous figure on the New York musical scene. Since then, there has been no end to his originality and development, as well as his association with and influence upon a multitude of artists in various fields.

The following conversation with the editor of this book and Susanna Opper took place in the summer of 1966, mostly in the bedroom-study of Cage's home, a small three-room cottage in the Gate Hill cooperative community in Stony Point, New York, where he has permanently resided since 1954. The room itself is, like the house, awesomely modest—about twenty feet by ten. Low along one wall is Cage's narrow bed with a thin mattress; in the middle lies a small dining-work table, around which are three chairs. One wall is entirely glass; and just in front of it is a television set, which sometimes puts Cage to sleep at night. Books, papers, and magazines are haphazardly strewn about; and the place is conspicuously free of valuable possessions, such as works of art or electronic equipment. In the front room is a jagged rock wall, adjoining the neighboring house and offering protrusions for candles; another "wall" was that evening entirely open to the summer air; and its noises filled the house. Cage lives alone, cooks his own food, cares for his own place, and participates in community affairs when he is home. During our talk, he wore dungarees and a blue denim shirt, and he frequently stuffed cigarettes into a black holder. Obtaining an interview with him involved tiresome correspondence and several telephone calls; but, once we settled down, Cage was, aside from occasional unpredictable testiness, a congenial host.

Conversation with John Cage

Richard Kostelanetz

John Cage: I'm sorry I was so short with you before, but the season has been long and tiring. This activity that you are now doing is done by so many people that it takes up an enormous amount of time, the total result of which is that I don't have time to do my work. This problem is getting worse, and it's just that you happen to come at a point where I'm irritated about it. I'm normally very, very patient, you know, and so forth; but the situation is getting too much. People are terribly presumptuous. They call me at midnight—total strangers—just to hear my voice. They have nothing on their minds, nothing.

Richard Kostelanetz: *Why do you keep your name in the phone book?*

I consider it a part of twentieth-century ethics, you might say. I think that this thing I speak of about fluency is implied by the telephone, and that is partly why I have these ideas I have. If I were to have a totally determined situation in my own conception, then of course I could be unlisted.

Well, if you want to close yourself off, it is the easiest way.

Yes, but I would fail. Morris Graves, an old friend of mine, is searching for a place to live that is removed from the twentieth century; but he can't find it, even in Ireland. The airplane flies overhead. If he finds a beautiful property, he has to bring a bulldozer in.

You want very much yourself to live in the twentieth century?

I don't see that it would be reasonable in the twentieth century not to.

I'm interested in your notion that modern man is becoming more omniattentive—capable of perceiving many things. The pianist Glenn Gould tells me that he learned Schoenberg's difficult piano pieces while listening to the AM and the FM simultaneously.

When David Tudor practices anything, he always turns the radio on, sometimes several.

Can you compose to it?

Well, this building is very poor acoustically. If there's any music

Some passages are reprinted from *The Theatre of Mixed Means,* by Richard Kostelanetz. Copyright © 1967, 1968 by Richard Kostelanetz and used by permission of the publisher, Dial Press, Inc. New material copyright © 1970 by Richard Kostelanetz.

in the next part of the house, I can hear it here, not quite as well as they do.

Does it bother you?

I think now and then it seems intolerable; but mostly I can go on working through these things.

Do you watch that television often?

Not right now, it's not working very well. But I generally go to sleep with it on, because it has a timing device so that the thing turns itself off. I use it as a lullaby.

What do you watch?

The old movies.

Did you get a television early?

I announced my desire to have a television set in my article on Rauschenberg [1961] where I say that we are not so interested in poetry as we are in getting a TV set. I didn't have one at that time; but, having written that, shortly I found myself in a discount house buying one.

Do you watch cultural programs?

Sometimes I do. I'm getting more and more interested now in politics and economics and such subjects. If there is some discussion of one of these subjects announced and I have the time, I'll look at it.

You're still an anarchist?

I would say so, yes.

A communitarian anarchist? As opposed to apocalyptic? Or philosophical? Or an individualist anarchist?

Like who?

Like Max Stirner or Benjamin Tucker?

Oh, those people in the nineteenth century. I'm very impressed by all that.

However, their views are quite different from those of communitarian anarchists. Benjamin Tucker, for instance, believed in the necessity of free enterprise.

But you must remember that there is a real difference between the situation relevant to nineteenth-century anarchists and now.

Technology.

Exactly.

And what technology's impact is and its potential implies.

Exactly, exactly. An article I've written on this was published in *Joglars,* a little magazine in Providence, Rhode Island. In that article, called "Diary: How to Improve the World (You Will Only Make Matters Worse)," I bring together the ideas of Bucky Fuller and Marshall McLuhan and Robert Theobald, with my own views about services, utilities, and so on made global; so that economics and politics as we knew them would disappear and people would be in a position, so to speak, to live anarchistically.

Yet technology's possible pervasiveness implies the necessity for an anarchism of small communities, particularly because the media can control us in such a large way.

True. Many people are thinking in these terms. I'm all for multiplicity, unfocused attention, decentralization; and so I would be on the side of individual anarchy with minimal government. Small communities—what does that mean? It means, doesn't it, decentralization. Now if you have a small community, as we have here [Stony Point, N.Y.], does not the principle of decentralization continue? What do you come to—the Individual. I would also want a global situation that would confront what Fuller implies when he says, as long as one human being is hungry, the entire human race is hungry. This is the same utopian view as is to be found in Norman O. Brown and, I think, implicitly, in McLuhan, although he doesn't promote causes. Nevertheless, McLuhan has illuminated the whole situation of twentieth-century living.

Now some behavioral psychologists are saying the same thing, too—and economists. There is a vast chorus of people now, in different fields, all saying these things. I just discovered at Aspen a psychologist named Richard E. Farson, who has been developing notions along these lines. The way these ideas are getting about is extraordinary. One used to think—and know, as a matter of fact—that twenty years ago, if you got an idea, that if anybody had the same idea it would be a real coincidence, something you'd be astonished about; but now when you get an idea, you are almost certain that somebody else has it too and, furthermore, is doing something about it.

These students at Yale who edit the architectural magazine *Perspecta* are devoting an entire issue to Fuller, McLuhan, and Theobald. I gave a speech up there, and they will include the question-and-answer period in an issue of their magazine. If you take my ideas and Fuller's and McLuhan's and Brown's and Theobald's and Farson's—if we do a bit of reading—we discover that there are a large number of people who are really interested in how our lives are changing to the point where people may have their own lives rather than lives that society has given them secondhand. And a totally ordinary piece of music is a secondhand experience. Remember the title of that book of Fuller's—*No More Secondhand God* [1963]. What does it mean? It means just what I said. Or what does this statement of Artaud's mean—*en finir avec le jugement de Dieu*? We should be finished once and for all with the judgments of God.

Pursuing our earlier theme about common ideas further, I was going to say that in talking with McLuhan you'll come to a point where he'll refuse to agree. Similar to this is an idea in *Love's Body* [1966], Norman Brown's new book, where he denies, if you please—and it's amazing to read it—the Buber I-Thou business. Brown says that we must have a situation in which, when we speak, there is no answer. Now, how are you going to get him to agree with someone like Farson, who is involved with behavioral psychology and who favors a society which includes greater intimacy, more sexuality, and all kinds of cultural connections between people? What is Farson going to say to a statement like that of Brown's?

Well, if Brown once believed that union with one's brother is mankind's deepest desire, he then said, when I heard him at Columbia in 1963, that the error in his first book, Life Against Death *[1959], was attributing an ultimate reality to this desire, because it was, instead, just another symbol of even deeper forces. He seemed to be entering the world of* Finnegans Wake, *where everything is a symbol for something else. That was as far as I followed him. Now, from what you say, he seems to be favoring total atomization.*

Yes, it's incredible. It's just amazing.

But that's just the opposite of McLuhan.

You think, over and over again as you go through these pages, that you're right with McLuhan. In fact, McLuhan is cited and cited with agreement all the way through.

Do you see, as this suggests, a failure in the logic of the book?

No, one of the great things these books suggest—and I think you will agree—is that opposites have to be seen as nonopposites. I say, in the "Diary" I mentioned, that we have to see that chaos and order are not opposed. I feel, for instance, with regard to my own work with indeterminacy and so on, as related to the work of Buckminster Fuller, who wants to see tetrahedrons under every leaf, that there is no opposition between those two. I even went so far as to ask Bucky and his assistant John McHale whether I was wrong in thinking we were really not opposed. It would look as though, for instance, Bucky's notion of a comprehensively designed global village would correspond, say, to Milton Babbitt's notion of a totally organized composition. However, I met in London an architect named Keith Critchlow, who has integrated Oriental philosophy (in terms of the *I Ching* and the sixty-four hexagrams) with Bucky's structural principles by constructing a geodesic dome and identifying its units with individual hexagrams. He has made, in other words, a *model* of the nonopposition of chaos and order.

Where do the serial composers stand?

The question of the relation of this music to themselves and to society never enters their minds. They just assume that a musical composition is made by starting out and doing what the teachers told you to do, and they never even find out what that could mean. They never think, for instance, of the meaning of this business of development and recapitulation—what it would mean to start out with something and then to have a far-reaching series of variations and then return to the beginning, which is no longer expressed in two keys but in one key. What could that mean?

About their own personal experience?

Right. Now if they decide they know what it means, do they believe that? Now, say they believe it and they understand what it means. Does it occur in their lives? Is it something of any use to them?—that belief and that meaning? Now, in this day and age, that music is obviously of no use whatsoever. Now that business of owning your own home, which that might be thought to mean, is simply no longer a concern. We are involved not in ownership but in use.

The difference then between your music and say, Milton Babbitt's music is that he is very much concerned with finished products and you are more concerned with processes.

Yes, and they want to have a result which will be in accord with the things they do, to bring it about. Everything is determined to bring about what would presumably be the best result. I'd imagine that notions such as unity and precision might enter into their minds.

True, I've heard them use those words often.

Now an indeterminate piece, even though it might sound like a totally determined one, is made essentially without intention, so that, in opposition to music of results, two performances of it will be different. There's a beautiful statement in Fuller's *Education Automation* [1963] in which he says that the whole idea of things being fixed is a notion that we no longer need; and he applies this to his notion of the university, namely that it would be a big area with no fixed walls, an area which could quickly be used one way or another. This is typical of flexibility, changeability, fluency, and so forth. These are parts of the meaning of indeterminacy; and you can't say that those things have to do with totally determined music. On occasion, though, the two kinds of music might have a similar superficial resemblance.

A story I tell sometimes in relation to this is about visiting Hamada the potter in Japan. I arrived while he was still making the pot, sitting at the wheel, and he said, "I'm not interested in results. I'm just interested in going on." Now, what this nonintentional music wants to do is, by that means and other means, which can be theatrical or architectural or whatnot, to make it clear to the listener that the hearing of the piece is his own action—that the music, so to speak, is his, rather than the composer's; for the composer was not in the same position as he was, in respect to it—on the most mundane level, not in the same part of the room. If there is a plurality of sound sources distributed in space, he actually heard something different from what someone else heard.

As when you look at some modern buildings, you see something different depending upon where you stand in relation to it.

And what reflections and so forth, and transparencies and what not. So that, as Joe Byrd in a recent interesting manifesto said, it signifies a change from conception, which the totally determined people can get, to perception, which is what the listener can have.

Would you allow anyone to assimilate both your music and Babbitt's without accusing him of contradictions?

Unless you have, as I do and I think more of us must have, a sense of cause without which one's simply a dilettante, an aesthete. As Joe Byrd says, we will certainly listen to this other music—this totally determined music, or Beethoven, or whatever—but we'll never again take it seriously.

What does one take seriously?

Our social situation, you see, is so very urgent that quarrels between two musicians couldn't be very interesting; what could be more frivolous? The question really now—the most urgent thing—is getting us to shift from an economy of scarcity to an economy of abundance; and this is going to mean an utter change of our minds with regard to morals and everything. If we say, "Don't do that," then it doesn't matter whether Nero is fiddling or not, or what kind of music he's playing.

What you're saying then is that music has become less important to you.

On the contrary, music has served to introduce me to the very world we're living in.

Is it still introducing you to the world?

Of course, of course. Look at all these things we've been talking about. I don't get interested in these things out of disinterest in music, rather out of an intensified interest in music.

If you want to know the truth of the matter, the music I prefer, even to my own or anybody else's, is what we are hearing if we are just quiet. And now we come back to my silent piece. I really prefer that to anything else, but I don't think of it as "my piece."

Isn't it an extension of your 4′ 33″?

No, it's my experience now. I wrote that piece in 1952. This is now 1966. I don't need that piece today.

In a sense, though, you are fortunate enough to hear it all the time.

True, now it no longer has three parts, as it did originally. You remember it has three movements, which were determined by chance operations. Now I don't have to use those chance operations, for we don't have to think in terms of movements any more.

Would you say, then, that in your own life you have come to appreciate your environment more through your work in music?

Of course. Now do you want to know something interesting? Music did this for Charles Ives, too, before it did it for me. In the *113 Songs,* he envisages that any man—not a community—that any man, sitting on his porch looking out toward the mountains with the sun setting, could hear his own symphony. You might say that I misunderstand that; that this is a misinterpretation. Well, he might have meant that there were sounds in his head; but I mean that there are sounds in the environment.

Do you then favor anonymous art?

That question is not quite appropriate, because you can have art without even doing it. All you have to do is change your mind. You don't even have to have any skill.

Does this bother you—the assumption that anyone can be an artist, regardless of his skill?

No. No, not at all. Not at all. That's a European question, you know, not an American question, this whole thing of hierarchy—of wanting to make the most the best. And it took us ages, relatively speaking, to get out of that European thing. Many people are now out of it.

I certainly think that the fact that you live here, rather than somewhere else . . .

I'm thinking of leaving. Or say I'm not thinking of leaving. I leave anyway, because in this present business I'm so rarely home. This next year I'll be at the University of Cincinnati; but I won't even be there. While I'm there, I'll be going elsewhere.

If you say that music is random sound experience, then why do you compose music?

Well, the first thing you have to do is not ask the question "why." Look at your environment, which you are enjoying, and see if it asks why. You'll see that it doesn't. This custom of asking "why" is the same as asking which is the most or which is the best. They are very closely related questions that enable you to disconnect yourself from your experience, rather than to identify with it. That's the true answer. The practical answer is, when I was young and didn't know any better, I decided to devote myself to music. The "why" was answered way back then, historically. I promised Schoenberg that that was what I would do. He gave me lessons free of charge. He wouldn't have done it, if I hadn't promised.

If you had to do it over again right now, would you devote yourself to music?

Oh no, certainly not. I once said to Alexander Smith, who is one of the world's authorities on mushrooms, that if I had my life to live over again, I would be a botanist. He said, "Why?" I said, that way I would avoid the jealousies and the competitions and so forth that plague the art world. He said, "Well, that shows how little you know about botany." Presently, I mentioned the name of another mycologist; and he got quite angry and said, "Don't mention his name again in my house."

In all fields you find the same conflicts?

Not only that, but you'd get the same perceptions, for all the boundaries now are being obscured between the various disciplines. The primary question then is going to be how it is that one achieves the state of being disciplined. What the meaning of discipline is has then to be understood. The way I was educated I was not given the meaning of discipline. I was told that if I were going to be a composer I should know harmony, counterpoint, and all those things. You are told that you have to study those things, although they are of no use to you ultimately, and that you learn those things in order later to give them up when finally you get around to self-expression. But this isn't the nature of discipline. True discipline is not learned in order to give it up, but rather in order to give oneself up. Now, most people never even learn what discipline is. It is precisely what the Lord meant when he said, give up your father and mother and follow me. It means give up the things closest to you. It means give yourself up, everything, and do what it is you are going to do. At that point, what have you given up? Your likes, your dislikes, etc. When it becomes clear, as it now becomes to many people, that the old disciplines need no longer be taken seriously, what is going to provide the path to the giving up of oneself?

Don't hallucinogenic drugs encourage this giving up of oneself?

As they focus the attention, I'm opposed to them. I drink wine and I smoke, and so on. That's as far as it goes for me. There are many people who would disagree with me on this subject. Wherever I go, there is a great interest in dope, and then I find out from my closest friends that, although I didn't think so, they themselves are taking dopes. It is a common phenomenon now.

Is that because you find enough pleasure in life now not to want to turn on to something else—to escape from it?

The notion of escape seems pointless to me, just as the notion of an art which would be an escape from life would seem pointless to me. This I learned years ago from the *I Ching,* where art is viewed, in the hexagram on Grace, as a light shining on top of a mountain penetrating to a certain extent the surrounding darkness. Therefore, art can't answer the important questions, for those important questions will be asked in the darkness where art does not penetrate.

Does this mean that you are trying to get away from art?

No, this means we are trying to identify life with art, and we begin in the darkness.

What does the artist become, if he is not someone who seeks light?

He becomes a listener.

Then he becomes his own artist.

Of course. Now we get to a point of agreement with Brown, McLuhan, Fuller, and Farson. Now all of their disagreements have disappeared.

Would you accept, then, McLuhan's notion of the artist as seer into the environment?

Oh, yes.

Then you are a seer?

But I would say listener, because of music.

But is Milton Babbitt a seer?

No, because he's making something that then is part of our environment—an object which he puts outside of himself, which he puts outside of us, and which he then has to write long articles about, and so forth; and then to have that *Perspectives of New Music* and all that mathematical business in order to convince us that, if we didn't agree on an ear level, we will be obliged to agree on a mathematical level.

Yet, in Silence, *you speak of Babbitt as "the most accomplished and adventurous representative" of serial composition in America.*

Yes. Circumstances have made him the leader of that particular direction, which is what they have done to me, really. I'm not really so important, in and of myself. Both of us could disappear, and all these views would still be held.

But isn't this a result of your influence?

What is my influence on all these people we've been mentioning? Virtually nothing. Farson never heard of me before June, 1966, I'm sure.

Surely your influence upon the avant-garde practitioners in all the arts has been extraordinary.

I'll agree and disagree; but I would like to minimize the personalities involved and emphasize the fact that change was inevitable. I would go along utterly with McLuhan on this point—that the media we're involved in did it.

Do you accept then McLuhan's primary presupposition that shifts in the predominant media of communication can be so totally determining?

True, for how else can you explain a phenomenon like this? In 1933, '34, '35—somewhere along there—it took seventy-five rehearsals to put on Edgard Varèse's *Ionisation* [1930]. Right now, with students out of the Middle West at the University of Illinois, with two rehearsals we can get a better performance. Things do change.

Look at the difference between my life as a composer and La Monte Young's life. He never lived without some kind of support. Look what I had—nothing but opposition until 1949 and 1950.

What did you do before then?

Oh, I did everything. I had jobs as an art director for a textile company, also washing dishes, washing walls, doing library research, accompanying dancers. Not until 1960 was I able to live as a musician, so to speak—lecturing and concerts and so on.

Are you reasonably well-fixed right now?

I would be, but several years ago my mother suffered a serious stroke.* I am her sole support. The result is, I live as I've always lived.

What has been your schedule, say, this past year?

I'm never home more than two weeks at a time; and I run from one place to another like a chicken with its head cut off.

When do you work?

* She died in October, 1968.—Ed.

I don't have the time. I do remarkably little new work. Last year, starting from, say, this time [middle of summer], I wrote the review of the Schoenberg letters, which was in the *Kenyon Review,* the text on teaching for *Canadian Art.* I did *Variations V* and *Variations VI.* I wrote the article "How To Improve the World." That's just about it. That's not much work.

So you've been living, so to speak, off your earlier capital.

That's what people would prefer, you see—that I do nothing.

Except what you've done before.

That happens to everyone. I was speaking with Jasper Johns recently. I mentioned that some collector I had seen complained that there was no picture of his available on the market just now. He said in fact there is; it was not immediately purchased because it is not what people expect him to do.

What would you like to have happen then?

Oh, I would like to be unemployed. I think we all should be, and then we would all do our own work.

On sufferance from the government.

Well, this is the Theobald idea; it's La Monte Young's idea; it's everybody's idea. We all want that. We want credit cards without having to pay the balance at the end of the month; and, furthermore, we're going to get them. If we don't get them, there will be a catastrophe. The money comes from credit, which is nine times the money in circulation. Credit is the money which is loaned, which profit is made on, and so forth. Besides, this whole thing (money) is a fiction. It is a convention. You can simply have other conventions which would allow people to have the things they need. We have the machines to produce more than we can use. We invented the machines in order to reduce our work. Now that we have them we think we should just go on working. We're just being stupid. Before, we connected virtue and money with work; now, we must have a whole other morality based upon unemployment and the importance and responsibility of using this freedom. If we pass through this critical period, which Fuller says ends in 1972, we shall very rapidly be getting to a utopian situation. I forget the exact figures, but they go something like this: In 1900, 9 per cent of the world's population were "haves," and the other 91 per cent were "have-nots." And then at the end of World War I, 14 per cent; and then 27 per cent. Now it is something like 44. We are approaching 50 per cent; and then it can go zip up to 100, providing that we recognize the possibility.

Doesn't this imply a revolution in thinking on the part of the forces in power—a changed awareness by people who don't want this to happen even though it is happening?

Right. Theobald says, in a recent article, that our government had a commission to study economics, automation, and employment. Theobald, who was on the commission, says that they all knew what was going on—that all the information was available to them. When it came time for a vote, however, upon whether we needed employment or needed unemployment, all but two voted in favor of employment.

Amazing and shameful. I agree with Fuller when he puts the burden of recognizing the reality of the need for change, not upon the technologists, but upon the politicians.

He says that we will not be able to bring about the change through politics or economics, that these dimensions can't improve matters.

Here we come to a point of disagreement between Fuller and Theobald, for Theobald would like to change the economics within the existing economic structure; he is convinced of the need for Protestant ethics. But when you put all these minds together and get a little bit of Brown into Theobald, then you're not so worried about Protestant ethics.

* * *

How long have you had such a vociferously enthusiastic following?

I'm not sure. When I played in Europe in 1954, as late as then, David Tudor and I were thought to be idiots.

Well, you've always been controversial.

No, clowns. I think in 1958 there was a marked change. We were taken quite seriously, for the most part.

When did you have the nucleus of a following?

Well, we were ourselves a group to begin with—Morton Feldman, Earle Brown, Christian Wolff, myself, and Tudor.

Which dates back to 1950 . . .

. . . or 1949, even. I had met [Pierre] Boulez as early as then. We had had an interesting correspondence, which would be interesting reading if he would permit my letters to be printed, but he won't. He has either destroyed them or refused to allow others to see them. People have wanted to print that correspondence, which would have shown agreement between us at the beginning, and then divergence exactly on this point of total control and renunciation of control. We were using the same techniques, which were charts. He had turned the series into a chart arrangement, and I had turned to charts first as magic squares and then later in relation to the mechanism of the *I Ching* for chance operations.

Let me deal with a particular piece, for the moment. May I ask how you composed, say, Rozart Mix [1965] *for thirteen tape machines and six live performers?*

Did you ever see the score? It's just my correspondence with Alvin Lucier, a composer who teaches at Brandeis University. He wanted a concert of music in the Rose Art Museum. Because of engagements here and there, I had very little time to work on it, and he had purposefully separated me from the pianist David Tudor by engaging him to give a concert the previous month, so that this time I had to go without Tudor's assistance. I thought to make a tape piece, which I described in my letters to him. It would consist of loops, and we would have at least as many loops as there are keys on the piano—eighty-eight—which would be made by anybody, since I didn't have the time to do it. They could use any materials. We would have at least a dozen machines, and the loops would vary from the shortest viable length to something like forty-five feet long. I had been told that the Museum had a pool of water and a stairway, that it had an interesting architecture. So we would put the machines all over the building. Then the loops would get tangled up with themselves, and that would be part of the performance. Now if the loop broke at any point, it would be first priority to fix it; and once it was fixed, it was to be put back in the reservoir of loops, and another one would be put on that machine. The piece was also to begin without the audience knowing it had begun, and it was to conclude when the last member of the audience had left. When only twelve people were left, we had arranged to serve refreshments; all those people had a party.

Wasn't there another party the night before?

Well, I went up there ahead of time thinking that they might not have made all the loops, which turned out to be the case. They only had about thirty, I think; so I worked like a devil and made the rest of them. What you want, you see, is to get a physically confused situation.

Why the eighty-eight as a minimum?

The reason for that multiplicity is that you would not then be able to exercise choice. If you're making eighty-eight loops, you very quickly get uninterested in what it is you are doing.

What sound was on the loops?

It didn't really matter. That's part of the piece. I don't know what was on their loops.

If there were nothing on those tapes, would the piece be valid?

Well, that was not the piece that I wrote. In this case, I specifically said there should be something on the tape.

Could you run a tape recorder for twenty-four hours somewhere, or in the middle of New York City, and then cut it up and make the slices into loops? Would that discount the situation?

I don't suppose so. I mostly used material I had around; materials I had made years ago for the library of the *Williams Mix* [1952]. It was a collection of sounds that had been divided into six categories—country sounds, electronic or synthetic sounds, city sounds, wind-produced sounds, and sounds so small they required amplification.

That tape-collage piece on the record in your twenty-fifth anniversary album . . .

Yes.

May I ask how that earlier piece, Williams Mix, *essentially a tape collage, was put together, after you made a library of sounds?*

Through elaborate chance means, I predetermined which of those categories had to go together, and which parameters had to be modified. The categories were called A, B, C, D, E, F; and how these elements went together was determined by chance operations from the *I Ching*.

This is what you have to do if you are going to write by means of chance operations. You have to envisage exactly what are the questions you ask when you write music, and then toss coins to help you answer each question. Once I finish this, the results become a recipe for a recording to be made. I must then find, say for one moment, a vocally produced sound whose amplitude has been altered from what it originally was in nature. Then we go into an electronic studio, and we know what we are doing. All the cutting, all the splicing of the *Williams Mix* is carefully controlled by chance operations. This was characteristic of an old period, before indeterminacy in performance, you see; for all I was doing then was renouncing my intention. Although my choices were controlled by chance operations, I was still making an object. For that reason, this piece, I later said, in an article called "Indeterminacy," was equivalent to producing a Frankenstein. I denounced my own work.

But will you allow it to be played?

Of course. I made it perfectly clear what I think it is; so if people use it, they know what they are up against. I've gone through so many changes in my work that if I tried to cover my tracks and obscure what I have done, it would have been, I would say, immoral. Besides I'm not interested in whether any of my works are good or bad.

If you were not to renounce an earlier thing that expressed what you had formerly believed, then you would be accepting the legitimacy of contradiction or paradox.

What I really believe is made perfectly clear by my actions. For instance, I don't do a given piece any more.

What is the most recent stage in your development, which is to say, what was the most recent renunciation of conventional practice?

Measurement of all kinds. I attempt to make an action without any measurement.

In that respect, you couldn't write 4′ 33″ *now, because it has a fixed time.*

As you know already, I have discarded the idea of three movements. I did say in the notes treating the silent piece, as you may know, that those movements could be of any other length, because they were only that length through chance operations. I didn't want to set up chance as a—what-do-you-call-it?—a fetish that you would worship, so to speak.

What pieces are you working on now?

There's a commission from the Koussevitzky Foundation, which will be called *Atlas Borealis* with the *Ten Thunderclaps.** For the first part, I'll be using a map of the stars; and the second is from *Finnegans Wake*. Marshall McLuhan suggested my using the Joyce texts, and his son Eric, who is writing a book on the subject, is helping me with an understanding of the Thunderclaps.

Are these two separate pieces?

They are like *Atlas Eclipticalis* [1961–62] and *Winter Music* [1957]. One is a work for orchestra, and the other will be a concerto for string sextet. The "Thunderclaps," of course, are voice or voices.

* * *

How long have you been associated with Merce Cunningham?

I became musical director of his company in 1943, but I knew him in the 1930's in Seattle.

How have you worked together?

We work in various ways. He chooses an existing piece of music

* Still incomplete in 1970. The Koussevitzky commission will be fulfilled by *Cheap Imitation*, an orchestration of a piano solo (1969) of the same title.—Ed.

and makes a choreography, or he makes a dance and I either compose for it or choose an existing piece, or invite some other composer to write for it. Our collaboration has been such that neither one of us is at a fixed point. We started at a time when dancers were very proud. They made the dance first, and then a musician came in like a tailor. From about 1952 on, our music was no longer fitted to the dance. The music could go on for any length of time; so there no longer needed to be rehearsals of the dance and music together.

Can someone else perform your role in the concerts? Or do you have to go on all the tours?

I'm not always present.

Who is the author of Variations V?

It is published under my name.

Did you conceive all the parts, or were they written independently?

Well, the score is *a posteriori*—written after the piece. Do you see the implications of this? That changes . . .

But then that's not the score.

Nonsense, that changes our idea of what a score is. We always thought that it was *a priori* and that the performance was the performance of a score. I switched it completely around so that the score is a report on a performance. These are remarks that would enable one to perform *Variations V*.

That would make the score a surrogate for a critical review.

No, these are not critical remarks. They are explanatory remarks. Critics are never explanatory. These are remarks that would enable one to perform *Variations V*.

Well, how did you produce the score?

Well, I tossed coins again, setting as the limit then sixty-four remarks to be written. I got, I think, the number thirty-five—I forget. Then I tossed coins again to see how many words would be in each remark. I got five. Then I was faced with the problem of writing five words on *Variations V* that would be helpful for someone else if he wished to perform it. It then became what you might call a poetic problem—to think of something in five words that would be useful to another person if he were going to perform *Variations V*. Then I wrote them down. Then I did each of thirty-five things like that, and that's the score.

Did you also choose the media involved—dance, film, sounds?

Oh, one of the remarks is that there shall be dancers involved. And then there's a remark saying that at the first performance it was the Merce Cunningham Company. It could be other dancers.

So the selection of the basic elements—sound, dance, and film is fixed.

If you want to say that, yes. There could be other films, though, than those particular ones.

What would you say about something that happened like . . . Would you say that our talking here this evening is fixed or unfixed?

It might be fixed because of the notes I have before me here.

No, the fact that we're sitting here. It's an extremely realistic situation, terribly fixed.

Oh.

Really, in space, in time, you'll never be able to repeat it. We don't know precisely what we're going to say, but the moment we've said it, you've even got it fixed on your tape. So can we say then that *Variations V* is fixed, and the score of it is these remarks about these things that happened, which envisage that somebody else might also do this?

Has anyone else done it?

Yes, a group organized by Robert Moran in San Francisco.

Did you see it?

No.

Did you hear reports? Was it different?

Of course, it was different. How could it not be? Greatly different.

Say we wrote a score where two people come and want to interview a composer, and they bring a transistorized tape recorder. They meet at seven o'clock, etc. We could give lots of remarks about it. Then they could do this, say, in Ann Arbor, and you know it would be different.

Would you consider this—now, here—a theatrical situation?

Certainly. There are things to hear and things to see, and that's what theater is.

If you were blind, would it be a theatrical situation for you?

I imagine so, because I would visualize from what I hear.

Therefore, the radio is not theatrical.

How are you going to separate it from the environment that it's in? That's really the way to get interested in recording—to include the environment. You'll find more and more in one of these situations that nobody closes his eyes as much as he used to.

Would you say, then, that all life is theater? That all theater is life?

It could be seen as such, if we change our minds.

When did this occur to you?

I don't know when I gave conscious expression to it. The year 1952 begins to be very. . . . If you look in my catalogue, you'll be amazed at the number of things that happened in 1952. The *Water Music,* for instance, begins then, and then I had already given that happening at Black Mountain College. All these things began to be apparent, and I began to relate them to things I had observed in my life. This testing of art by means of life was the result of my attending the lectures of [D. T.] Suzuki for three years. I think it was from 1949 to 1951. It was in the Department of Philosophy at Columbia, and anyone could simply walk in. A few people actually took the course, but they sat around the table. The rest of us sat along the wall.

Did you feel uncomfortable, as an eminent man in his late thirties, taking courses at Columbia?

No, I wasn't registered. I still am a student. I'm studying chess now with Marcel Duchamp.

That explains why you have all these chess books around here. Is chess theater?

Well, you have to ask yourself what is theater. I would answer that theater is seeing and hearing.

Here's a very good statement by Joe Byrd, a composer now on the West Coast.

> What should we expect of these arts? Shouldn't we expect dance today to concern itself with movement in all forms, including the kinetic quality of football or stock-car races? Music to explore the psycho-physiological potentials of sound, the peculiar rhetoric of machines, the anxieties produced by low-frequency vibrations in sync with one's own nervous system? Poetry to fulfill [Gertrude] Stein's semantic implications to reawaken the sound and sight of a word and their relation to its meaning, to gloriously destroy the context, adjectival, and syntactical inhibitions that make all poetry verbiage? And theater (!) we might expect to become a catholic, experimental aesthetic extended to functional existence. Here the psychedelic experience is an example, but ultimately, because of its artificiality, a crutch. More, the obligation—the morality, if you wish—of all the arts today is to intensify, to alter, perceptual awareness and, hence, consciousness. Awareness and consciousness of what? Of the real material world. Of the things we see and hear and taste and touch.

Do you regard that as the purpose of the theater—to increase our perceptual awareness of the world?

Yes.

Before you came to that recognition about life as theater, what kind of theater did you appreciate?

I was among those dissatisfied with the arts as they were, and as Europe had given them to us. I infuriated Paul Goodman at Black Mountain by speaking against Beethoven. Paul Goodman, bright in other respects, swallowed European thinking hook, line, and sinker. I just looked at my experience in the theater, realized when I bought a ticket, walked in, and saw this marvelous curtain go up with the possibility of something happening behind it, and then nothing happening of any interest whatsoever. The theater was a great disappointment to anybody interested in the arts. I can count on one hand the performances that struck me as being interesting in my life. They were *Much Ado About Nothing*, when I was in college; it was done by the Stratford-upon-Avon players. Nazimova in *Ghosts* of Ibsen. Laurette Taylor in *Glass Menagerie*. The Habima Theater's *Oedipus Rex* in 1950 or thereabouts [Pause]. I run out. . . .

What qualities animated these performances?

That isn't an interesting question. The situation is complex. I was four different people, for those performances were widely spaced in time. It just happened. What can we say? We don't any longer know who I was. They somehow struck me so that I was, as we say, bowled over—really amazed.

Take this sort of thing, for instance, to show you what I mean: In the 1940's at some point—'43, '44, '45—I heard those short string quartet pieces by Webern. I was sitting on the edge of my seat. I couldn't have been more excited. Play the same music for me now, and I won't even listen to it. If you oblige me to do so, I'll walk out of the hall, in fact.

Do you see any theater at all now?

Never. Well, I go to happenings. That strikes me as the only theater worth its salt. We aren't having art just to enjoy it. We are having art in order to use it. Those things that we used have been consumed. We have to have fresh food now. You wouldn't ask me in the case of a steak I ate ten years ago somehow to regurgitate it and eat it over again, would you?

It would be a great scene, though.

This concern with the consumption of art and the consumption of ideas is very close to Norman Brown. He sees art as food going right through the body, and so forth, and then you can see that you use it up and you need something new. He insists on this in his new book. I was so glad to see this insistence upon freshness and newness and change in him, because over and over again recently we've had people attacking the avant-garde on the very notion that the new was something we should not want. But it is a necessity now.

In what sense? Intellectual? Physical? Moral?

Consumptual.

In other words, we have used up the other.

Yes. It's gone. It's finished. We must have something else to consume.

We have now, we've agreed, the new techniques. We have a grand power that we're just becoming aware of in our minds.

Technology.

Not only technology, but our minds themselves, which we dimly know are in advance of the technology. And our education has kept our minds stunted, and we are going to change that situation. Our minds are going to be stretched. We are going to stretch ourselves to the breaking point.

Still, a lot of people are going to go on being caretakers of the past. The past has no trouble, no lack of people who are going to make love to it.

Bucky Fuller doesn't want Times Square destroyed. He says we should keep it. We should keep everything so that we know what it used to be like.

Then one of the things you like about mixed-means theater, as opposed to old theater, is that performances are so lifelike. Now, is a happening more successful to you if it is lifelike?

Not that it should be lifelike, but that we should be able to consume it in relation to our lives. So that it would introduce us to the other things in our lives which we consume.

I assume you agree this is the ultimate educational purpose of the new theatrical art.

Yes, yes.

Constance Rourke has the thesis that a prime characteristic of American arts is indefinite identity—they don't particularly fit forms we know, like novel or epic.

That could be like breaking down the boundaries, certainly taking away the center of interest, emphasizing the field.

These are all American characteristics. This would make Ives your ancestor.

I'm flattered to say, yes. But I'm inclined to point out that your comment is a linear one, which is a Renaissance question, which is a European question, which is a non-electronic question.

Let me deal, if I may, with the critical questions the new form poses. I saw you at the Cinemathèque one Friday night in Decem-

ber [1965]. There were three events—Robert Whitman's, Robert Rauschenberg's, and Claes Oldenburg's. May I ask you to evaluate them?

You mean that you want me to criticize them—to say which one I liked the most and so on, or what?

As you prefer.

Well, I liked the Whitman best [*Prune. Flat.*] because it was the most complex. Even though he had an idea and was doing something he intended to do—this is true of all three of them—I liked it. They were not doing something I would do, because I am interested in non-intention, and I think that life is essentially non-intentional. Let me put it this way: You can only approach it effectively when you see it as non-intentional. In a sense, then, I criticize all three of them, but, of the three, the Whitman strikes me as most useful simply because it was the most complex. This connects it with life, which is also complex.

It also struck me as the one that filled its space and time most interestingly.

Right. That goes along with it.

In other words, it was almost as good as life. Would you say, then, that a basic critical comment about a happening stems from whether or not you wish to stay and look at it? If life outside the situation is more interesting than the happening, then the happening has not at all succeeded. Or would this be a purely subjective criteria?

For one thing, I would like the happening to be arranged in such a way that I could at least see through the happening to something that wasn't it. We'd be out of the La Monte Young fixation ideal. We'd be in the Duchamp-Fuller-Mies van der Rohe business of seeing through.

Didn't Claes Oldenburg's Moviehouse *piece impress you in this sense?*

Yes. But it was a police situation. It was politically bad—telling people not to sit down. I refused, so I sat down, and so did Duchamp.

Were you uncomfortable standing up?

No. I refuse to be told what to do.

When you go to a conventional concert, do you sit in the seat?

No one tells me that I can't get up and walk around. They do give me a ticket for a seat, and if I use it, that's my own business. That was my objection to the Kaprow [the original *18 Happenings in 6 Parts* (1958)]—being told to move from one room to the other.

Have you learned things from the new theater?

I think certainly.

Let me go back to the Black Mountain piece. Who authored that? Under whose name is it?

It isn't published. I planned the thing. Without my deciding to do it, it wouldn't have happened.

Could you remember what was in your mind when you did that?

It was the making of theater—to bring all these things together that people could hear and see.

What kind of intention were you dealing with at that time?

Non-intention.

Once you chose the elements, everything was improvisatory?

No, there were time-brackets during which these people were free to do what they were going to do.

Thus, at minute four someone was instructed to do something?

Not at minute four, but between minute four and minute eight, say, someone or a group of people had that time-bracket free. What they were going to do I didn't know. I knew roughly, but not specifically. I knew that Merce would be dancing, but I didn't know what he'd be dancing.

How long did that piece last?

Forty-five minutes.

Did the audience receive it well?

Yes, that was a very good situation at Black Mountain College. The cups were introduced [placed upon each seat] so that the audience had something to do. That is, when they encountered cups on their seats, what could that mean? It meant, of course, that they would be served coffee toward the end of the piece.

Did you give this piece any name?

No.

Why didn't you develop anything in this area yourself?

I have been doing nothing else since.

So all your work since has been "theater" in your mind?

Surely.

Are some pieces better than others?

Why do you waste your time and mine by trying to get value judgments? Don't you see that when you get a value judgment, that's all you have? They are destructive to our proper business, which is curiosity and awareness.

Yet you can answer the basic question of whether I like this or I didn't like this.

You asked me, and I got involved in making remarks about

that Cinemathèque performance. While I'm making them, I'm annoyed that I'm doing so. In playing chess, there's an expression of "losing tempo." I don't know if you know it. If you put your opponent in such a position that he's obliged to move back from where he was, then he loses time. We waste time by focusing upon these questions of value and criticism, and so forth, and by making negative statements. We must exercise our time positively. When I make these criticisms of other people, I'm not doing my own work; also, the people and their work may be changing.

But why don't you go yourself to every happening?

I've been telling you how busy I am. I barely have time to do my own work.

What I meant is, why do you go to one and not another? Because you happen to be in New York at that time?

Purely.

Do you walk out of one feeling happier that you went to that one rather than another?

The big thing to do actually is to get yourself into a situation in which you use your experience no matter where you are, even if you are at a performance of a work of art which, if you were asked to criticize it, you would criticize out of existence. Nevertheless, you should get yourself into such a position that, were you present at it, you would somehow be able to use it.

But does that alter the fact that you might have preferred going to a different happening?

That's not an interesting question; for you are actually at this one where you are. How are you going to use this situation if you are there? This is the big question. What are you going to do with your time? If you use it negatively, you really are not consuming. You're rather doing some other kind of thing which, as I've explained just now, loses tempo. You have somehow to use it positively. We have illustrations of how to get at this, and it would be part and parcel of the new ethic or new morality or new aesthetic.

Kierkegaard, for instance, in *Either-Or*, speaking of conversing with a bore, pointed out that he finally noticed perspiration was dripping off the fellow's nose and that he could enjoy that. By focusing his attention there, he could ignore all the rest of the business.

I've noticed that I can pick up anything in the way of a periodical or a newspaper—anything—and use it, not in the [William] Burroughs sense, but in its content sense—in terms of its relevance to positive action now.

Are there some happenings you can use better than others?

Let's say that that's true. Now let's ask this kind of question: Which is more valuable—to read *The New York Times* which is a week old or to read Norman Brown's *Love's Body*? If we face this issue squarely, we'll see that there's no difference.

Because you can get something out of both.

Right. Now a really difficult problem for you, which now brings us back to the question of discipline, would be this: Listen, if you can, to Beethoven and get something out of it that's not what he put in it.

Is that relevant?

We must get ourselves into a situation where we can use our experience no matter what it is. We must take intentional material, like Beethoven, and turn it to non-intention.

Is it a better way to apportion one's time? Aren't some things a better way to spend your time than other things?

Look what you did. Accepting the notion of non-intention, you then said, "Can you intend to be non-intentional?" That would mean you would go around choosing.

What you are saying, then, is that any happening is acceptable. I could have two people sit and stare at each other for three hours; but I don't think I can do that and still hold an audience. I just don't believe it. Do you?

Why do you speak of holding an audience? I think that these notions imply dropping the idea of controlling the audience, for one thing. We have spoken of wanting to turn each person into an artist, have we not? We've spoken of individual anarchy, etc. So, in the case of a performance, we would think of it, wouldn't we, as a celebration of some kind; and we would certainly not think of holding those people to us. If somehow they weren't enjoying the situation or consuming it, then would we be more pleased if they left? Not that we want them to go, but we don't want them to stay either. We have a certain freedom at the same time that we question the notion of freedom; this is very curious.

* * *

I get the impression that this evening we're talking less about theater or music than about philosophy.

That's because the boundaries have gone.

One sees a lot of parallels with existentialism.

Suzuki recognized that, too. I've not really read much in existentialism, but I gather that the big difference between it and Zen is one between pessimism and optimism. If you were to have a utopian existentialism, then you would have McLuhan and Fuller and. . . .

If you can't say bad and good about theatrical pieces, then there is no basis for criticism at all.

The best criticism will be, you see, the doing of your own work. Rather than using your time to denounce what someone else has done, you should rather, if your feelings are critical, reply with a work of your own.

Let's say I'm not a critic, and I merely attend a happening and decide that I simply don't like it.

Well, use that fact by doing something of your own.

In the new morality, then, criticism must turn into creation.

Formerly, we had boundaries between the arts, and you could say then, if you are saying what I am saying now, that the best criticism of a poem is a poem. Now, we have such a marvelous loss of boundaries that your criticism of a happening could be a piece of music, or a scientific experiment, or a trip to Japan, or a trip to your local shopping market.

So then my criticism is an expression of myself and my milieu.

Not an expression of yourself. This is something that is gone, too.

My criticism, then, is to take something I got out of a happening and then do something else.

I think it should be. Do you know, for instance, any criticism now which you can use? I find myself more and more questioning the professional function of the critic. I don't find what they have to say is interesting. What they do doesn't seem to change what I do. What I do changes what I do. What artists do changes what I do. I don't know of any instance where what a critic has done has changed what I do.

You don't, then, consider McLuhan a critic.

If you do, then I'd have to change my mind, because I find him very illuminating.

He used to be a critic. As a younger man, he contributed to literary quarterlies essays that looked and read like criticism.

Well, let's say he is a critic. Then he gives us the notion of what a critic really should be. Say that Norman O. Brown is a critic; then we'll have to say that Fuller is a critic.

What you are saying, then, is that most criticism is limited to a sweeping operation that deals within too fixed an area.

Well, what words would you use in regard to McLuhan? He uses the words "probe," "insight," "relation." He shows connections where we haven't dreamed there were any connections. Those are the kinds of contributions that the artist makes. McLuhan, you know, thinks of himself as a detective—someone who perceives patterns.

All of which shows that we're getting to the point where all sciences are Science, all arts are Art, and all thought is Thought; there's not much difference between philosophy and detecting. You can work out of a certain context, but this doesn't necessarily characterize, or even limit, all your activities.

Fuller has a good way of expressing this, to make fields of activity big or comprehensive. Dick Higgins uses the word "intermedia."

All say that we must avoid becoming too specialized, in both our intellectual interests and our sensory responses.

Recently, I had some conversations with Barney Newman, and he knew that, back in the forties and the early fifties, I was involved with Zen Buddhism. He said to me, "If you were talking now at the club [Eighth Street Artists], you certainly wouldn't talk about Zen Buddhism, would you?" He suggested that I had, so to speak, finished with that window shopping and that it no longer had any significance for me. The incident was of profound significance for me. Take the text of Zen that has been so meaningful for me, the *Huang-Po Doctrine of Universal Mind*, and consider that magnificent statement, "Imitate the sands of the Ganges who are not pleased by perfume and who are not disgusted by filth." This is almost the basis of Oriental philosophy and could be the basis of any useful ethic we are going to make for a global village. We are going to have to get over the need for likes and dislikes.

It is going to be difficult, say, in the case of the German people as a group. Though we always know we can deal with German individuals, when we come right down to it, lots of us don't like the German people. We don't like to be in Germany, we don't like to work in Germany; and the ideals that we have are not appealing to the Germans. You know that rule they made about any music that involves the performer in choice-making—they charge twice as much. They are really impossible, and they do things like this: You make arrangements to give a performance in a German city and then carry on a lengthy correspondence in which you straighten out what you are going to need when you get there. When you get there, you see that you have asked for a table and two chairs, but you also want a glass, which you had not mentioned in the correspondence. So you say, "May I have a glass?" They say, "But you didn't mention it in your correspondence."

Then they'll spend half an hour trying to put obstacles in the way of your having something you need, simply because you haven't preordained it. I obviously dislike that kind of situation, and I do connect it with Germans. When I have to go to Germany, I know ahead of time that I shall dislike it. What in heaven's name am I going to do? I am going to have to take an attitude of self-discipline. I'll suffer, but through that suffering—as we've always known—I will change, hopefully.

But you can still say now that you don't like those attitudes?

I could say I'd be much better off going to Germany if I didn't dislike the German people.

Yes, but you can also say right here and now that you dislike those attitudes, and that's a valid statement.

Yes, but I can also make a judgment against myself that I ought not to have that dislike. In other words, we're in a complex situation.

You see, the human condition, as Hannah Arendt calls it, is a complex affair, and it is not solved through conversations such as this we are having. We can set up ideals as I do—and I do really believe them—about getting rid of likes and dislikes; and, after every moment I say it, I have to confess that I still have them. I do try to get rid of them, but they pop up all the time.

And this will all be part of that new morality you're talking about. Not only you, who believe in this new morality, but all those people out there who are hardly tuned in are going to have to change.

We see it changing now. Look at the remarkable changes with regard to the Negroes on the part of society as a whole. They are happening right under our noses, not only here, but in the South. It's just amazing now how well we're getting along and how quickly we're getting along better than before. It's really a great step, and even greater than steps that have been made in Europe.

How long will it take to effect these changes you foresee?

Well, we have the optimism of Bucky Fuller that things are happening faster, which is also the optimism of Max Ernst, who said that formerly things took three hundred years to happen, then a hundred years, then twenty years, and so on.

How would you educate people to live in this new world we're talking about?

This is the most interesting question, and one which is being approached by all the people we've discussed—Buckminster Fuller in *Education Automation* and McLuhan; and they all seem to agree that the least important aspect in education is the teacher. I was just talking with a very bright fellow who was recently going to college, but he dropped out. When he went to college, he thought that people would be interested in him and what he could do, but he only discovered that they had no interest in him at all. We're not yet at the point where education, particularly higher education, has changed. It has only changed, I would say, in the case of individual teachers, and this is why people throng around those teachers. If I were going to college myself now, I would only go because of a person who was there.

The most advanced place seems to be Antioch, with its freshman year of no curriculum, where it is entirely incumbent upon the freshman to decide how to spend his time, because there are no regular classes, and there is nothing being taught to him. There are only library and faculty present, and he is asked to use them only in ways that he discovers.

Fuller, you know, also envisions a society where there will be nothing but education throughout one's life. That means education would have to be far more interesting than it is now.

You did pretty well in the educational system yourself. Weren't you valedictorian of your high school class in Los Angeles?

Yes, but I dropped out of college. My grades dropped, and several things disillusioned me about it; so I decided to go off to Europe. Then I studied just with people whose ideas interested me, and I'm still doing that.

When you study with a person, what does that mean?

Well, studying with Duchamp means being with him once or twice a week, having dinner, or playing chess, or seeing the environment. Or studying mushrooms means walking in the woods with Guy Nearing or with Alexander Smith.

You look upon learning as a one-to-one ratio, which we know to be ideal.

Nowadays, you can proceed by getting other people involved. You notice that solitary activity, as a composer formerly worked, only meets with obstacles. Just ask any conventional composer how he's getting along in this society. He'll tell you that he doesn't have enough performances, that people don't understand his work, that he's not making enough money, that he doesn't have enough time to compose, etc. In fact, among the letters I get from composers, I notice that more of them sense there is absolutely no reason for doing what they are doing; and, in order to escape from the possibility of a change of consciousness, they blame Babbitt and me for having created a musical world in which they have nothing but a dilemma.

I got a fantastic manuscript for my collection [published as *Notations* (1969)] from Suzanne Bloch of her father Ernst Bloch, who, toward the end of his life, would study a Bach fugue, and then sit down with a timing device and write the whole thing out by memory and see how fast he could do it. He would then go over it and mark with "X's" the errors he had made.

Why?

Exactly.

Do you want to ask us any more questions?

What do you think about eugenics? This is one of the things that's going to happen. It means the control of birth—not "birth control," but the removal of sex from reproduction and the controlling of what particular people shall have the privilege of living.

This sounds straight out of Aldous Huxley's Brave New World.

Not necessarily, because there's been a lot more thinking and experimenting since then, and we also know now that where the social controls are placed at present need not be where they will be placed in the future. Though I myself would want a place where there is no control, I can nevertheless envisage a utility which would have to do with the reproduction of the species. We are very near Letchworth Village, which is an institution for the mentally retarded. On the one hand, you might say that we shouldn't give any thought to this question of eugenics, for life, no matter how pinched, is life and is beautiful. I think, however, that people should have what we think are normal minds with normal bodies. Now I'm making value judgments, but in this area it would appear that one would need to, just as one would, when you go to the supermarket, choose fresh fruit rather than rotten fruit.

Don't you think that a woman and her husband should have a right to sign a little piece of paper when she goes into a hospital that would say, in effect, that if it has two heads or four arms or something like that, they should do away with it.

But what if there were a more invisible defect?

Perhaps we will develop our science and technology to detect these things at an early age.

We know that we use so little of our minds. What is the percentage? Something like a fraction of the mind; so that we really don't know much about what we could be. We also, I think, could be capable of putting eyes in the back of our heads, literally. There's a man at Washington University in St. Louis, Dr. Viktor

Hamburger, who works, of course, with animals, putting things (arms, eyes, etc.) where they haven't previously existed.

What you've been continually suggesting this evening is that the future will undergo more changes, in more dimensions of both life and art, than we can possibly envision right now. I find that reassuring, don't you? For our lives will always be consumptually new.

Chronological Table of John Cage's Life

Ellsworth J. Snyder

1912	Born, September 5, Los Angeles, California
1928	Graduated from Los Angeles High School, was class valedictorian
	Entered Pomona College, Claremont, California, remained for 2 years
1930 (spring)	Sailed for France; six months in Paris (studied architecture with Goldfinger; piano with Lazare Levy, etc.)
1930–31	"Wandering"—Biskra, Majorca, Madrid, Berlin (wrote poetry, painted, and, in Majorca, first composed music)
1931 (fall) to 1933 (spring)	Returned to California, continued writing, painting, and composing; supported himself by working as: 1) gardener in auto court (Santa Monica) 2) local lecturer on modern painting and music to housewives
	Studied composition with Richard Buhlig; developed method of composition employing two twenty-five-tone ranges (example: *Solo with Obbligato Accompaniment of Two Voices in Canon and Six Short Inventions*)
1933 (spring) to	Went to New York at suggestion of Henry Cowell to study harmony and composition with Adolph Weiss
	Also studied modern harmony, contemporary music, and Oriental and folk music under Cowell at New School for Social Research
1934 (fall) to	Returned to California and studied counterpoint with Schoenberg at his home, took Schoenberg's courses in analysis at University of Southern California; also took

Ellsworth J. Snyder finished, in 1970, his doctoral dissertation, *John Cage and Music Since World War II: A Study in Applied Aesthetics* (University of Wisconsin).

courses in counterpoint, analysis at UCLA
Married Xenia Andreyevna Kashevaroff

1937 Joined modern dance group at UCLA as accompanist and composer

to Studied bookbinding with Hazel Dreis, formed quartet of bookbinders for playing of percussion music

Moved to Seattle as composer-accompanist for Bonnie Bird's classes in dance at the Cornish School

Organized percussion orchestra, collected instruments, made tours throughout Northwest

Summer of 1938, on faculty and worked as composer for Marian Van Tuyl, Mills College, California

Fall of 1938, composed music for *Bacchanale* (dance by Syvilla Fort), the first prepared piano piece

1939 Moved to San Francisco, gave concerts of percussion music with Lou Harrison, worked as recreational leader for WPA

1941 Moved to Chicago to teach a class in experimental music at the Chicago Institute of Design (invited by László Moholy-Nagy)

Also accompanied dance classes of Katherine Manning

Gave concert of percussion music at Arts Club

Commissioned by CBS ("Columbia Workshop") to do radio show, in collaboration with Kenneth Patchen, *The City Wears a Slouch Hat*

1942 (spring) Moved to New York

Wrote music for Cunningham's *Credo in Us*

1943 (February) Cage's concert at Museum of Modern Art, first in the series of New York concerts and recitals that established his reputation as a prominent avant-gardist

1945 Divorced, moved to New York's Lower East Side

to	Beginning of study of Eastern philosophies with Gita Sarabhai and Zen with Dr. Daisetz T. Suzuki at Columbia
	Toured with Merce Cunningham Dance Company, finally becoming Musical Director
1947	Commissioned by Ballet Society to write score *The Seasons*
1948 (summer)	Taught at Black Mountain College in North Carolina
	Organized Satie festival there
1949 (January)	First New York performance of *Sonatas and Interludes* by Maro Ajemian at Carnegie Hall
	Received $1,000 award from National Academy of Arts and Letters
	Received grant ($2,400) from Guggenheim Foundation
	Spent three months in Europe, befriended Pierre Boulez, gave concerts and dance recitals in Paris with Cunningham
1950	Moved into "chance operations"
	Monroe Street Days
	Bozza Mansion
	Came under influence of the *I Ching*
	Helped edit *Possibilities* through its one-issue life
	Participated in *Artist's Club* started by Robert Motherwell and other artists
	Lectures: "Lecture on Nothing" and "Lecture on Something"
1951	Score for Herbert Matter's film, *Works of Calder,* awarded First Prize for Music by the Woodstock Art Film Festival
1952	*Music of Changes première* at the Cherry Lane Theater, New York
	New Music Society commissioned *Imaginary Landscape No. 4,* presented in Columbia University's McMillin Theater
	Composed first piece of tape music as score

	for a dance by Jean Erdman, *Imaginary Landscape No. 5*
(summer)	At Black Mountain College Prototype of happenings conceived by Cage with collaboration of Tudor, Richards, Olson, Rauschenberg, Cunningham Influenced there by Rauschenberg's all-black and all-white paintings
1952 (August)	First performance of *4′ 33″* at Maverick Concert Hall in Woodstock, New York
to 1954	Mainly on tour with the Cunningham Company at colleges and universities throughout the country
1954 (summer)	Moved with David Tudor, Mary Caroline Richards, David and Karen Weinrib to cooperative community in Rockland County established by Paul Williams and his wife Vera
1954	Concert tour with Tudor to Donaueschinger, Germany, Cologne, Paris, Brussels, Stockholm, Zurich, Milan, and London
1956 to 1958	Occasional classes at the New School for Social Research, New York, where students included George Brecht, Al Hansen, Dick Higgins, Scott Hyde, Allan Kaprow, and Jackson Mac Low
1958	At Town Hall, New York, in May, retrospective concert of his music covering the previous twenty-five years
(summer)	In Europe teaching a class in experimental music at Darmstadt, giving concerts and lectures Lecture at the Brussels World Fair: "Indeterminacy, New Aspect of Form in Instrumental and Electronic Music" Four months in Milan, working at tape studio attached to Milan radio; composed *Fontana Mix* Appeared on Italian TV quiz show "Lascia o

	Raddoppia" as mushroom expert and, in five appearances, presented *Amores, Water Walk, Sounds of Venice,* and won $6,000 by answering mushroom questions correctly
(winter)	Back in New York
1959 (spring)	Taught three courses at New School for Social Research
and	1) Mushroom identification
	2) Music of Virgil Thomson
1960	3) Experimental composition
1960–61	Fellow at the Center for Advanced Studies at Wesleyan University, Middletown, Connecticut, where he completed *Silence*
1961	Commissioned by the Montreal Festivals Society to write work for full orchestra, *Atlas Eclipticalis*
1962	Founded the New York Mycological Society with Lois Long, Esther Dam, Guy G. Nearing, and Ralph Ferrara
1962 (fall)	Six-week concert tour of Japan with David Tudor
1963	Directed first New York performance of Satie's *Vexations*
1964	Performance of *Atlas Eclipticalis* with *Winter Music* (electronic version) by the New York Philharmonic at Lincoln Center, New York
	World tour with Cunningham Dance Company
1965–68	President, Cunningham Dance Foundation Director, Foundation for Contemporary Performing Arts
1967	Composer in Residence, University of Cincinnati
	Published *A Year from Monday*, a compilation of his writings, mostly since 1961
1967–69	Associate, Center for Advanced Study, University of Illinois (presented *HPSCHD* with Lejaren Hiller)
1968	Elected Member, National Institute of Arts and Letters
	Received Thorne Music Grant ($10,000)

1969 Artist in Residence, University of California, Davis

Published *Notations* (with Alison Knowles), Something Else Press

Composed and executed *Not Wanting To Say Anything About Marcel* (with Calvin Sumsion) at Hollander's Workshop, New York

1970 Fellow at Center for Advanced Studies at Wesleyan University

Wrote *36 Acrostics re and not re Marcel Duchamp*

II 1927–39

In America, unlike most European cultures, there is no standard ladder to intellectual or artistic eminence, no single cultural establishment to which an ambitious young man can apprentice himself, no single audience that renders final judgments, no institutions that issue definite seals of success, no rewards or awards that are universally admired. . . . The only common outline for a propitious career seems to involve some relevant training or self-education, a lonely break with convention, a period of intense and exploratory work, a product that others can scrutinize, and then the surprise when total strangers hail it as excellent and persuasive. It is all but impossible to set out to contribute to the house of Western culture; but a man who does extraordinary work may learn, before he leaves, that a brick or two on top bears his name.—RICHARD KOSTELANETZ, *Master Minds* (1969)

Other People Think *John Cage*

This earliest of Cage's extended writings was presented in 1927 at the Hollywood Bowl, where Cage, representing Los Angeles High School, won the Southern California Oratorical Contest.

When Washington was proclaimed President of the United States, our country possessed most of the territory between the Atlantic and the Mississippi River. After the Mexican War, the Stars and Stripes were flown from ocean to ocean, from the Gulf of Mexico to the Great Lakes. Today the United States is a world power. In the New World, she calls Alaska, Porto Rico, and the Virgin Islands territories. She exerts a strong influence over Haiti, Nicaragua, Panama, and the Dominican Republic. She has circulated her dollar throughout the Latin American countries until she is spoken of as the "Giant of the North" and thought of as the "Ruler of the American Continent."

Many citizens of this powerful nation have come to believe that people south of the Rio Grande are by nature inferior to those north of that river. A great number of Latin Americans, however, are convinced of their superiority to Anglo-Saxons. Both beliefs are justified to a certain degree; but both are the results of a superficial knowledge of racial characteristics and an unfortunate lack of mutual appreciation and sympathy. Neither people has been able to catch a convincing glance of the other's worth. There is a Gulf of Misunderstanding between the Rulers and the Ruled of the American Continent. And little is done to span that gulf with bridges of harmony, although it is to the best interests of both peoples to do so.

In the past, many obstacles have hindered the advancement of civilization among the Latin Americans. The men that colonized South America, in contrast with the Pilgrims of New England, were pleasure-loving, avaricious, and adventurous. Under Spanish Dominion, they were never given the opportunity to develop self-government. Thus, they have found it difficult to maintain the sovereignty of their countries. Yet, in their beginning to recognize their problems, they prophesy progress.

Latin America is a land of the future. It is the potential producer of most of the food and raw products for all the world. Already each of the twenty Latin American countries is noted for a

By permission of John Cage.

product upon which the rest of the world is dependent. We rely on Brazil for our coffee, on Cuba for our sugar, and on Argentina for our wheat. These twenty countries also represent a market for the world's manufactures. Without doubt Latin America will experience a Golden Age in the near future. To cultivate friendly relations between North and South America will be a greater advantage mutually than it is at present or has ever been in the past.

It is the popular belief that we have promoted friendly relations with all Latin America. Our Foreign Policy has, in general, aimed to promote the general welfare of the southern people. Without our intervention in Ecuador, that country, because of its unsanitary conditions, would be spilling its poison over all the New World. With the practice of American Science, much of the dread of yellow fever in Central America has disappeared.

Because of Uncle Sam's military power, Venezuela has been protected from Germany, Cuba from Spain, Mexico from France; we have defended all weak countries from European domination. We are governing Santo Domingo because the natives tried but failed. We are educating the Negroes of Haiti so that they may learn how to handle their own affairs. The United States has rid many countries of the curse of revolution. Many of the smaller republics have progressed in civilization because of American Finance. Panama is Panama because of our interests in the Canal. All in all, our intervention in Latin America has been actuated by altruistic motives.

Why, then, is there any misunderstanding between the Latins and the Anglo-Saxons of this continent?

There are two sides to every question. For other people think otherwise.

Concerning the question of American Intervention in Latin America, many people are thinking otherwise. The foremost literary men of the Southern Countries, led by Manuel Ugarte, are instructing their readers how to think. The professors of the great South American Universities are teaching the students what to think. The statesmen, guided by Dr. Honorio Pueyrredon, are thinking and beginning to make their countries think.

This thought, that has penetrated the intellectual life of the Latin Republics so effectively, has been influenced by the actions of certain citizens of the United States. The great majority of these are capitalists who have zealously invested money in the Southern Republics and eagerly exploited them. They have not the hope of progress of others, but only the desire for their own material advancement. They are of the family of the utterly selfish. They have not only been financially successful; they have succeeded in gaining for themselves the contempt and the aversion of men. They belong to a crazed congregation of Gold-Worshippers. And it is difficult to convict them of wrong-doings, for they are extremely sly and hypocritical. These are our Ambassadors to Latin America. In the eyes of the Southern People, these men are the United States. These are the books in which Latin Americans read our history, the pictures which portray for them Anglo-Saxon ideals.

Six years ago, three American Banking Companies loaned 26 million dollars to the Republic of Bolivia. It was provided in the contract that 10 per cent of the principal should be paid annually in monthly installments, with the interest at 8 per cent. In the case of a default on the part of the Country, the Bankers will be given complete control of the Bolivian National Bank, certain Bolivian railroads, and the Revenues of the Republic. According to this contract of 1922, the Government of Bolivia is forbidden to borrow other money without the consent of the American Bankers. For the administration of these provisions and the supervision of Bolivian Finances, a permanent Fiscal Commission was formed. It consists of three members appointed by the President of Bolivia, two of whom are recommended by the Americans. As a result, the economic future of Bolivia is subject to the will of a handful of Bankers. This is, however, but one instance of the actions of American Capitalists. There are ties that have fastened the hearts of every Latin American Country inveterately with the counting-houses of Wall Street.

It was to protect the "Lives and Property" of just such money-grasping men as those in Bolivia that the United States Marines entered Nicaragua fifteen years ago. They are still there. Having taken charge of the politics of that country, they have been careful to keep a Conservative in the Presidency. The Admiral in charge, reporting to Washington, noticed that only one-fourth of the country was Conservative, and that all of his actions were done against the will of three-fourths of the Nicaraguans. A fear for the sovereignty of Nicaragua and other Latin American Nations was born. Other people began to think that no government could exist in Central America without the sanction of the United States.

Some have resolved the differences between the North and the South into the eternal race and religion problems. Other people think that a solution of these questions and the realization of Pan-American ideals are hopeless. Such is the result of our sponsoring American Capitalism.

Whether we deny the intelligence of those thinkers; whether we label this thought as the wild ravings of radical minds; whether we discredit some or all of it does not and cannot make any difference at all. For, withstanding everything, it is there, omnipresent, growing, and becoming, deeply rooted in the intellectual present and future of Latin America. Many have feared our interference in the past. Many will hate our intervention in the future. For the Youth of the South is being taught to think.

Is Latin America correct in calling our altruism masked imperialism? Should we continue to intervene in Latin America? What would the great men of our history do in this dilemma? Would not Lincoln champion the cause of the weak? But would not Roosevelt justify American Intervention?

What are we going to do? What ought we to do?

One of the greatest blessings that the United States could receive in the near future would be to have her industries halted, her business discontinued, her people speechless, a great pause in her world of affairs created, and finally to have everything stopped that runs, until everyone should hear the last wheel go around and the last echo fade away . . . then, in that moment of complete intermission, of undisturbed calm, would be the hour most conducive to the birth of a Pan-American Conscience. Then we should be capable of answering the question, "What ought we to do?" For we should be hushed and silent, and we should have the opportunity to learn that other people think.

It is our task to consider Latin American thought and respect it. It is the produce of the mind of man, and in that it is truly great. With it, we must compare and contrast our thought. When the two are together—Latin and Anglo-Saxon—we must separate the just from the unjust. Our actions in the past have been neither continually praiseworthy, nor have they been constantly worthy of blame. And Latin Americans have not always been infallible in their thinking and comprehension of the present.

Our Southern Neighbors must learn to accept our help in making themselves fit for self-government. We must learn that the day is coming when no one will need our aid. That day will be one of great responsibility for the United States. That day will witness one of the greatest tests that practical Democracy has ever experienced. For, if we should, at that time, continue to interfere in the affairs of any Latin American Nation, other people would be convinced that the United States is imperialistic. On the other hand, if we should not do so, we, and all of our actions in Latin America, would be hailed as altruistic.

Assuredly our posterity must not be slandered as the devotee of a Golden God. We must not follow in the ways of certain American Capitalists, for only when we cleanse our hands of gold-dust and share with the Latins of this continent an unselfish hand-clasp will the sun of Pan-Americanism illuminate the horizon.

Healed by the soothing rays of this sun, the Americans will prosper as never before. Economically, they will govern the world. Politically, they will prove that man can surpass misunderstanding. They will brilliantly prove that international life is not merely an ideal but a reality. Spiritually, the Americans will teach all mankind. They will not give lessons in self-applause, for it attracts destruction. They will tell men of the Science of Appreciating, Respecting, and Sympathizing with Others. Both Latin and Anglo-Saxon will have learned that Other People Think.

Our Distinguished Dropout *Richard Barnes*

This essay about Cage's recent activities as a reflection of his undergraduate aspirations originally appeared in Pomona Today *(July, 1966). The author is an associate professor of English at Pomona College, as well as a playwright, film-maker, and translator of drama.*

The interruptions in small caps are from John Cage's own writings and recorded interviews. They are, of course, quoted out of context, and it is no excuse for me that he should have done something of the sort in his article about Erik Satie. I simply put them in because it turned out to be the only way I could write this article. [R.B.]

By now John Cage is notorious, or famous. He's the composer who expects an audience to listen to a Waring blender in operation and then to the sounds produced in his own esophagus (picked up by contact microphones and enormously amplified) as he drinks the glass of vegetable juice he has just made in the Waring blender. They say he's the one American who has had much influence on the new music composed in Europe since the war.

WHEN A FLY BUZZES PAST ME NOW I HAVE, FROM AN ARTISTIC POINT OF VIEW, A FRIGHTFUL PROBLEM. BUT IT'S QUITE REASONABLE TO IMAGINE THAT WE WILL HAVE A LOUDSPEAKER THAT WILL BE ABLE TO FLY THROUGH SPACE.

His pieces have such an air of novelty that they often sound like mere stunts. Take the piano accompaniment to *The Wonderful*

Reprinted by permission.

Widow of Eighteen Springs (1942) in which the piano is completely closed; the "pianist" is told where to strike the wooden structure of the piano, how loudly, whether with finger or knuckle, and with which hand. A quite conventional percussion score, in fact. Why use a piano?

WE GOT TO TALKING ABOUT COOMARASWAMY'S STATEMENT THAT THE TRADITIONAL FUNCTION OF THE ARTIST IS TO IMITATE NATURE IN HER MANNER OF OPERATION. THIS LED ME TO THE OPINION THAT ART CHANGES BECAUSE SCIENCE CHANGES—THAT IS, CHANGES IN SCIENCE GIVE ARTISTS DIFFERENT UNDERSTANDINGS OF HOW NATURE WORKS.

Or take the notorious or famous "silent piece," *4′ 33″* (1952) (tacet, any instrument or combination of instruments), "a piece in three movements during which no sounds are intentionally produced," Peters catalog number 6777, price half a dollar. John Cage has often explained that there is always something to hear, even in an anechoic chamber, so long as you are alive, and if you have ears you can hear it.

THE SAND IN WHICH THE STONES IN A JAPANESE GARDEN LIE IS ALSO SOMETHING.

A piece in which no sounds are intentionally produced could hardly be less "expressive," in the ordinary sense. However, it has a point which is clear enough if you yourself have the experience. If you don't, it isn't. The same is true of any other music, or, for that matter, of any speech or poetry or writing. One thing about John Cage's development is that you have less and less chance to fall back on hearing what you are supposed to hear or what somebody else hears or says he hears. No wonder so many music critics and musicians feel underemployed when asked to deal with his recent works—though in their own way these works are always quite exacting.

I HAVE THEREFORE MADE A LECTURE IN THE COURSE OF WHICH, BY VARIOUS MEANS, MEANING IS NOT EASY TO COME BY EVEN THOUGH LUCIDITY HAS BEEN MY CONSTANT WILL-OF-THE-WISP.

I might as well try to explain what I think about the piano in *The Wonderful Widow of Eighteen Springs*. Doubtless John Cage would agree that it's theater. Since his earliest work he has been moving constantly towards the theater, first because of opportunity, when he found that dance groups wanted his music while orchestras and even string quartets didn't, and later because he came to think it important that we have eyes as well as ears. By now it seems clear that concerts always have been theater, in a sense, if we could only have used our eyes properly, and that the theatricality of certain conductors and soloists offended us not because it was theatrical but because the theatricality was too gross and was directed toward cheap effects.

IF I LIKED MUZAK, WHICH I ALSO DON'T LIKE, THE WORLD WOULD BE MORE OPEN TO ME. I INTEND TO WORK ON IT.

I doubt that John Cage would agree now, though he might have when he wrote the piece in 1942, that there is another reason why the percussive sounds are better produced by striking a piano. That is that whether we like it or not, we know it is a piano. In somewhat the same way I still think it important that the silent piece should have been written by John Cage who had studied with Henry Cowell and Arnold Schoenberg and had written, say, the twenty *Sonatas and Interludes;* whether we like it or not, we know it's by John Cage.

I USE, FREQUENTLY, VERY LOUD SOUNDS NOW . . . WE DO GIVE AND RECEIVE PAIN AND WE MIGHT AS WELL RECOGNIZE THE FACT.

All it is is hearing, and you do have to hear for yourself, but you ordinarily hear differently according to who it is you're listening with. Go to the same movie twice, once with your best friend and once with your grandmother. The same is true of other music which is one reason we still have courses in music appreciation.

THIS PLAY, HOWEVER, IS AN AFFIRMATION OF LIFE, NOT AN ATTEMPT TO BRING ORDER OUT OF CHAOS NOR TO SUGGEST IMPROVEMENTS ON CREATION, BUT SIMPLY A WAY OF WAKING UP TO THE VERY LIFE WE'RE LIVING WHICH IS SO EXCELLENT ONCE ONE GETS ONE'S MIND AND ONE'S DESIRES OUT OF ITS WAY AND LETS IT ACT OF ITS OWN ACCORD.

If eventually you come to realize what it means in the Vedas (and in some quite recent philosophers) about individual awarenesses being aspects of a single awareness, then presumably it won't matter whether it's by John Cage or not. The same is true of other music, which is one reason we still have John Cage.

THE WHOLE DESIRE FOR DEFINITIONS HAS TO DO WITH THE RENAISSANCE IN WHICH WE DEMANDED CLARITY AND GOT IT. NOW WE ARE NOT IN SUCH A PERIOD AND SUCH DEFINITIONS ARE NO LONGER OF USE TO US.

"Between Chuang Chou and a butterfly there must be *some* distinction! This is called the Transformation of Things."

SURELY THINGS HAPPENING AT DIFFERENT TIMES ARE ALSO RELATED.

I see in his POMONA COLLEGE PERSONNEL BLANK that John Cage's Occupational Outlook as he entered his freshman year was the *Ministry* and the next year *Writing*. You might say he did become some kind of preacher and writer after all. However, I see in his transcript that all he got was a B in his course in Religious Orientation the second semester of his last and sophomore year. Freshman Recreational Interests: *swimming, tennis, riding;* Sophomore: *sleeping and talking, stealing.*

FACTS ABOUT EDGARD VARÈSE'S LIFE AND WORK ARE DIFFICULT TO OBTAIN. HE CONSIDERS INTEREST IN THEM TO BE A FORM OF NECROPHILIA; HE PREFERS TO LEAVE NO TRACES.

Church: Membership *M. E.,* Preference *M. E.,* Father's Occupation *Electrical engineer and Inventor,* Mother's Occupation *Interested in Club work.* Summer Experience *(1928) Camping Trip during July; worked at beach during Aug.* Summer Experience *(1929) I merely proved that I possess neither character, will power, nor back bone.* This in a fairly sloppy-looking but quite legible hand that reminds me of his literary style which looks (as you see) so artless. The Registrar has added in red ink his scores on various tests, his second prize in the Jennings English Contest, and *June 1930. Does not plan to return. Going to travel in Europe.*

WHEN I FIRST WENT TO PARIS, I DID SO INSTEAD OF RETURNING TO POMONA COLLEGE FOR MY JUNIOR YEAR. AS I LOOKED AROUND, IT WAS GOTHIC ARCHITECTURE THAT IMPRESSED ME MOST. AND OF THAT ARCHITECTURE I PREFERRED THE FLAMBOYANT STYLE OF THE FIFTEENTH CENTURY. IN THIS STYLE MY INTEREST WAS ATTRACTED BY BALUSTRADES. THESE I STUDIED FOR SIX WEEKS IN THE BIBLIOTHEQUE MAZARIN [*sic*], GETTING TO THE LIBRARY WHEN THE DOORS WERE OPENED AND NOT LEAVING UNTIL THEY WERE CLOSED. PROFESSOR PIOJAN, WHOM I HAD KNOWN AT POMONA, ARRIVED IN PARIS AND ASKED ME WHAT I WAS DOING. (WE WERE STANDING IN ONE OF THE RAILWAY STATIONS THERE.) I TOLD HIM. HE GAVE ME LITERALLY A SWIFT KICK IN THE PANTS AND THEN SAID, "GO TOMORROW TO GOLDFINGER. I'LL ARRANGE FOR YOU TO WORK WITH HIM. HE'S A MODERN ARCHITECT." AFTER A MONTH OF WORKING WITH GOLDFINGER, MEASURING THE DIMENSIONS OF ROOMS WHICH HE WAS TO MODERNIZE, ANSWERING THE TELEPHONE, AND DRAWING GREEK COLUMNS, I OVERHEARD GOLDFINGER SAYING, "TO BE AN ARCHITECT, ONE MUST DEVOTE ONE'S LIFE SOLELY TO ARCHITECTURE." I THEN LEFT HIM, FOR, AS I EXPLAINED, THERE WERE OTHER THINGS THAT INTERESTED ME, MUSIC AND PAINTING FOR INSTANCE.

FIVE YEARS LATER, WHEN SCHOENBERG ASKED ME WHETHER I

WOULD DEVOTE MY LIFE TO MUSIC, I SAID, "OF COURSE." AFTER I HAD BEEN STUDYING MUSIC WITH HIM FOR TWO YEARS, SCHOENBERG SAID, "IN ORDER TO WRITE MUSIC, YOU MUST HAVE A FEELING FOR HARMONY." I EXPLAINED TO HIM THAT I HAD NO FEELING FOR HARMONY. HE THEN SAID THAT I WOULD ALWAYS ENCOUNTER AN OBSTACLE, THAT IT WOULD BE AS THOUGH I CAME TO A WALL THROUGH WHICH I COULD NOT PASS. I SAID, "IN THAT CASE I WILL DEVOTE MY LIFE TO BEATING MY HEAD AGAINST THAT WALL."

It is interesting that John Cage's father was an electrical engineer and inventor. After he came back from Europe John Cage worked for his father for a while checking out patents. I wonder if Schoenberg knew that when he said, "He's not a composer, he's an inventor—of genius."

IN THIS LATTER CASE, THE COMPOSER RESEMBLES THE MAKER OF A CAMERA WHO ALLOWS SOMEONE ELSE TO TAKE THE PICTURE.

But Herbert Brün, whose ideas about composition could hardly be farther from Cage's than they are, said, "With what he says and what he does, either he's a composer or he's an idiot. And—and—he's a composer." Pause. "His great big goofy smile." This after a lecture in Bridges Hall where Herbert Brün described his own way of calculating and achieving precise, verifiable musical effects.

ONE CHRISTMAS DAY, MOTHER SAID, "I'VE LISTENED TO YOUR RECORD SEVERAL TIMES. AFTER HEARING ALL THOSE STORIES ABOUT YOUR CHILDHOOD, I KEEP ASKING MYSELF, 'WHERE WAS IT THAT I FAILED?' "

That same year (1963 I think) John Cage and David Tudor gave a lecture-concert in Bridges Hall. The lecture was "Where Are We Going? And What Are We Doing?" which you can read in *Silence*. He reads or is silent into a microphone while his own voice reads or is silent from each of three tape recorders. Though he uses a stopwatch and a time score to make every performance pretty nearly identical to every other, no two people hear the same thing because you can't follow four voices at once and have to just listen to what interests you. As with the electronic pieces *Fontana Mix* and *Williams Mix* (when played with all four or eight separate tracks), the sounds themselves are fairly rigidly determined but indeterminacy enters into the actual perception. No doubt it does into the perception of any large orchestral or choral piece but it is not made so welcome.

HENRY COWELL REMARKED AT THE NEW SCHOOL BEFORE A CONCERT OF WORKS BY CHRISTIAN WOLFF, EARLE BROWN, MORTON FELDMAN, AND MYSELF, THAT HERE WERE FOUR COMPOSERS WHO WERE GET-

TING RID OF GLUE. THAT IS: WHERE PEOPLE HAD FELT THE NECESSITY TO STICK SOUNDS TOGETHER TO MAKE A CONTINUITY, WE FOUR FELT THE OPPOSITE NECESSITY TO GET RID OF THE GLUE SO THAT SOUNDS WOULD BE THEMSELVES.

Afterwards we all went over to Wig Lounge for an informal discussion and a snack of mushrooms. (Along with his other interests, John Cage is a mycologist.) The mushrooms we served were canned. He said that if the artist is supposed to seek beauty he will be more useful if he seeks it in what has seemed ugly.

LET US ADMIT, ONCE AND FOR ALL, THAT THE LINES WE DRAW ARE NOT STRAIGHT.

Earlier in the afternoon, while they were hooking up the electrical gear for the piano, somebody left a microphone on so that when a certain connection was made there was a blast of feedback that was, to me, just past the threshold of pain. John Cage and David Tudor clearly thought it was beautiful, a delightful surprise. Of course they quickly turned off the microphone.

CURIOUSLY ENOUGH, THE TWELVE-TONE SYSTEM HAS NO ZERO IN IT.

The Future of Music: Credo *John Cage*

Perhaps the single most influential of Cage's written texts, this was first delivered as a lecture in 1937 in Seattle, but not published until 1958 in the brochure accompanying George Avakian's recording of Cage's 25-Year Retrospective Concert.

I BELIEVE THAT THE USE OF NOISE

Wherever we are, what we hear is mostly noise. When we ignore it, it disturbs us. When we listen to it, we find it fascinating. The sound of a truck at 50 m.p.h. Static between the stations. Rain. We want to capture and control these sounds, to use them, not as sound effects, but as musical instruments. Every film studio has a library of "sound effects" recorded on film. With a film phonograph it is now possible to control the amplitude and frequency of any one of these sounds and to give to it rhythms within or beyond the reach of anyone's imagination. Given four film phonographs,

Copyright © 1958 by John Cage. Reprinted from *Silence,* by John Cage, by permission of Wesleyan University Press. Copyright Calder and Boyars Ltd. Reprinted by permission.

we can compose and perform a quartet for explosive motor, wind, heart beat, and landslide.

TO MAKE MUSIC

If this word, music, is sacred and reserved for eighteenth- and nineteenth-century instruments, we can substitute a more meaningful term: organization of sound.

WILL CONTINUE AND INCREASE UNTIL WE REACH A MUSIC PRODUCED THROUGH THE AID OF ELECTRICAL INSTRUMENTS

Most inventors of electrical musical instruments have attempted to imitate eighteenth- and nineteenth-century instruments, just as early automobile designers copied the carriage. The Novachord and the Solovox are examples of this desire to imitate the past rather than construct the future. When Theremin provided an instrument with genuinely new possibilities, Thereministes did their utmost to make the instrument sound like some old instrument, giving it a sickeningly sweet vibrato, and performing upon it, with difficulty, masterpieces from the past. Although the instrument is capable of a wide variety of sound qualities, obtained by the mere turning of a dial, Thereministes act as censors, giving the public those sounds they think the public will like. We are shielded from new sound experiences.

The special property of electrical instruments will be to provide complete control of the overtone structure of tones (as opposed to noises) and to make these tones available in any frequency, amplitude, and duration.

WHICH WILL MAKE AVAILABLE FOR MUSICAL PURPOSES ANY AND ALL SOUNDS THAT CAN BE HEARD. PHOTOELECTRIC, FILM, AND MECHANICAL MEDIUMS FOR THE SYNTHETIC PRODUCTION OF MUSIC

It is now possible for composers to make music directly, without the assistance of intermediary performers. Any design repeated often enough on a sound track is audible. 280 circles per second on a sound track will produce one sound, whereas a portrait of Beethoven repeated 50 times per second on a sound track will have not only a different pitch but a different sound quality.

WILL BE EXPLORED. WHEREAS, IN THE PAST, THE POINT OF DISAGREEMENT HAS BEEN BETWEEN DISSONANCE AND CONSONANCE, IT WILL BE, IN THE IMMEDIATE FUTURE,

BETWEEN NOISE AND SO-CALLED MUSICAL SOUNDS.

THE PRESENT METHODS OF WRITING MUSIC, PRINCIPALLY THOSE WHICH EMPLOY HARMONY AND ITS REFERENCE TO PARTICULAR STEPS IN THE FIELD OF SOUND, WILL BE INADEQUATE FOR THE COMPOSER WHO WILL BE FACED WITH THE ENTIRE FIELD OF SOUND.

The composer (organizer of sound) will not only be faced with the entire field of sound but also with the entire field of time. The "frame" or fraction of a second, following established film technique, will probably be the basic unit in the measurement of time. No rhythm will be beyond the composer's reach.

NEW METHODS WILL BE DISCOVERED, BEARING A DEFINITE RELATION TO SCHOENBERG'S TWELVE-TONE SYSTEM

Schoenberg's method assigns to each material, in a group of equal materials, its function with respect to the group. (Harmony assigned to each material, in a group of unequal materials, its function with respect to the fundamental or most important material in the group.) Schoenberg's method is analagous to modern society, in which the emphasis is on the group and the integration of the individual in the group.

AND PRESENT METHODS OF WRITING PERCUSSION MUSIC

Percussion music is a contemporary transition from keyboard-influenced music to the all-sound music of the future. Any sound is acceptable to the composer of percussion music; he explores the academically forbidden "nonmusical" field of sound insofar as is manually possible.

Methods of writing percussion music have as their goal the rhythmic structure of a composition. As soon as these methods are crystallized into one or several widely accepted methods, the means will exist for group improvisations of unwritten but culturally important music. This has already taken place in Oriental cultures and in hot jazz.

AND ANY OTHER METHODS WHICH ARE FREE FROM THE CONCEPT OF A FUNDAMENTAL TONE.

THE PRINCIPLE OF FORM WILL BE OUR ONLY CONSTANT CONNECTION WITH THE PAST. ALTHOUGH THE GREAT FORM OF THE FUTURE WILL NOT BE AS IT WAS IN THE PAST, AT ONE TIME THE FUGUE AND AT ANOTHER THE SONATA, IT WILL BE RELATED TO THESE AS THEY ARE TO EACH OTHER

Before this happens, centers of experimental music must be established. In these centers, the new materials, oscillators, generators, means for amplifying small sounds, film phonographs, etc., available for use. Composers at work using twentieth-century means for making music. Performances of results. Organization of sound for musical and extramusical purposes (theater, dance, film).

THROUGH THE PRINCIPLE OF ORGANIZATION OR MAN'S COMMON ABILITY TO THINK.

III 1940–49

When I first knew John Cage [in the early 1940's] he was stubborn, gifted, argumentative. As the gift took hold, he became more silent, preoccupied with himself and the growing of his thought. He entered the room like a *bodhisattva,* floating. After he had studied Japanese Zen philosophy and learned by it to master himself, he became, as he has remained, the man of the great smile, the outgoing laugh, willing to explain but not, in my recent experience, to argue, tolerant of misconception, self-forgetful, and considerate. Around him everyone laughs.—PETER YATES, *Twentieth Century Music* (1967)

Cage said that Schoenberg, when he emancipated the dissonance, should have gone farther and emancipated music from its notes. Therefore the *prepared piano* and other prepared media, the compositions for non-tonal sound-producers and noise, the piece for twelve radios, the arbitrarily combined noises of *Williams Mix,* and the many possible free fantasies by chance.—PETER YATES, "After Modern Music" (1963)

People Call It Noise—But He Calls It Music

Pence James

One of the earliest reviews of Cage's concerts, the following mixture of bemusement-outrage, puzzlement-interest was frequently echoed in subsequent newspaper criticism. This appeared in the Chicago Daily News *(March 19, 1942); the author was then a staff reporter.*

It wasn't mountain music. It wasn't red hot jazz. Nor was it boogie-woogie or swing. So what was it?

Intellectuals, including several members of the University of Chicago faculty, were trying to figure out the answer today. Last night they went to a symphonic concert in Mandel Hall. Charles Buckley's university orchestra played. Dr. Frederick Stock was guest conductor.

But, somewhere along the middle of the program, there was an invasion by a daring young man named John Cage and his "musicians," who play beer bottles, flower pots, cowbells, automobile brake drums, dinner bells, thundersheets, and in the words of Mr. Cage, "anything we can lay our hands on."

After a fairly sweet rendition by the symphony strings entitled *St. Paul's Suite for String Orchestra,* conductor Buckley retired and Mr. Cage and members of his "percussion group" set up for a number called *Canticle,* written by Lou Harrison of Oakland, Calif.

John's wife, Xenia, presided at the flower pots, Katherine Manning and Barbazon Lindsay took care of such things as wood blocks, cup gongs, rattles, and dragon mouths, and Marjorie Parkin had her hands full with a huge tamtam, or Chinese gong, a thundersheet, tambourine, and wind glass. Stuart Lloyd beat the drums.

Cage raised his baton, and the business was on. A savage sort of rhythm poured off the stage that had the audience squirming in its seats.

At first, because of the serious mien of the performers and the fearful novelty of the percussion orchestra, nobody smiled. Finally the audience began to enjoy itself, applauding enthusiastically, to be rewarded with a pleased-as-pie grin from Mr. Cage.

"It's better than Benny Goodman," said one man in the audience, who had previously announced that "Bach bores me."

Reprinted by permission of the Chicago Daily News.

For this piece, they used a beer bottle, dinner bell, iron pipe, cymbals, drums, wood blocks, the piano, and a garbage can.

In this number, Mr. Cage handled the piano. He began by fingering the keys, but then started beating them with the flat of his hand, and then with his elbows. Finally he seized a board that stretched the length of the keyboard and pressed it up and down so every note on the piano thundered. Then he caressed the strings under the open top.

The fox trot ended when Miss Manning broke the beer bottle and dropped the pieces into the garbage can.

When Mr. Cage was told later that a girl in the audience had characterized his music as "perfectly terrifying," he said: .

"We have a lot more terrifying numbers than these. She should hear us when we have the electricity on—buzzers and things like that."

Mr. Cage said he did not consider his percussion music an "end in itself, but we are trying to make all the field of audible sound available for music." He said this was his thirteenth concert. When he played his first percussion concert in 1938, there were only two pieces written for percussion groups. Now there are more than 100, he said, as he collected his gongs, flower pots, and brake drums.

Chavez and the Chicago Drouth *John Cage*

This is the first of several trenchant reviews and essays that Cage, performing as a tough-minded young critic, wrote for that essential professional magazine, Modern Music *(published 1924–47).*

Chavez was here. He conducted the Chicago Symphony Orchestra through three of his major works. The impression made was direct and vital. The rest of the music we have heard recently is weak and doesn't reach far enough to even touch.

I didn't hear Nicolai Berezowsky's *Concerto* for viola and orchestra. A criticism by Edward Barry mentions an "attractive sustained movement," the andante, and finds the "low musical comedy" of the second movement not "surpassingly deft." I did however hear Cadman's *Pennsylvania Symphony*. This has a variety of themes—of the forest or lurking Indian; of the pioneer, the river, the factory, the happy worker; and, finally The American

Copyright *Modern Music*. Reprinted by permission.

Theme. The only things missing were moving pictures. It is sad to think how seriously the work must have been written, and how little of this seriousness comes off.

The Illinois WPA Symphony Orchestra, which is to be commended for its many first performances of contemporary works, gave on this occasion two very dull *premières:* Radie Britain's *Drouth* and Leos Jánaček's *Lachian Dances*. The latter were written in the 1880's and might have been exciting then. Miss Britain's *Drouth,* like Cadman's *Symphony,* also needed an illustrative film, particularly for the plaintive cowboy song, which is heard toward the end of the composition, "expressing his loneliness and desolation as he sees the land blown away." The strings did most of the blowing and sighing. At one point a ratchet electrified the wind section and for a moment there were interesting jagged sounds. But these were written for a decorative-dramatic effect and not as an organic part of the composition. They were followed by moaning muted violins. Miss Britain is said, through this work, to exhibit her kinship with the great Middle West.

It is a relief to remember the Chavez performances: his arrangement of the Buxtehude *Chaconne*, his popular *Sinfonia India* and his *Concerto for Four Horns*. During the *Concerto*, a large part of the audience took fiendish delight in the trouble the horn players were having. The second movement, an adagio cantabile, was made mysterious by long sustained dissonances between the horns. The work was originally for horns alone. In 1937, seven years after its composition, it was turned into a concerto. Chavez says that not a note is changed, though some have been given to other instruments. The effect, however, in the second movement, is that the string parts are pasted on. Most of the time the orchestra sat and listened to the horns. Their quiet attention was very theatrical and made the whole situation seem intimate, magic, and private between Chavez and the horns. This second movement was the best of the three; the tempo was right for the horns. In the fast first and third movements, the expectations of the fiends were gratified. The last movement ends abruptly in a brilliant and affirmative character, but, unfortunately, the ending is not convincing. It belongs to Chavez but not to this particular work. It has the effect of a signature, not of a solution.

It is needless to say much about the well-known Buxtehude *Chaconne* and the *Sinfonia India*. The *Indian Symphony* could very easily become our Pan-American *Bolero*.

The composers mentioned here all find their material in the land and the people around them. The sources from which the music has been conceived account for some of the differences in the results. Miss Britain and Mr. Cadman have accepted certain literary and intellectual concepts of the American scene, which they have illustrated musically. The music is recognizably regional according to one's knowledge of the conditions that prompted it; it is not an expression in musical terms of a close contact with the country. When Chavez, on the other hand, quotes Indian melodies directly, as he does in the *Sinfonia India,* he has gone to a source that is essentially musical to begin with. It relies completely on musical elements that never call for literary explanations but speak in terms of rhythm and sound, to which everyone responds. Hearing this *Symphony* for the first time, one has the feeling of remembering it. It is the land we all walk on, made audible. (March-April, 1942)

For More New Sounds *John Cage*

For several years, a small but growing number of composers in America have been writing compositions for percussion instruments alone. Orchestras now exist, one in San Francisco, the other in Chicago, for the performance of these works. The instruments used are in many cases those found in the percussion section of the symphony orchestra, or in typical Oriental, Cuban, and hot jazz ensembles. Many objects not originally intended for musical purposes, such as automobile parts, pipe lengths, and sheets of metal have been used. In some cases, the word percussion has become a misnomer, the sound being produced through other means than hitting. Shells and whistles are blown; dials turned and buttons pushed; needles are lowered to records.

Elements of sound and rhythm have been used that may, with good results, be combined with the resources of the symphony orchestra. On the other hand, the similarity between the instruments of the percussion orchestra and the sound effects of the radio and film studios suggests the development of what might be called a radio or film orchestra. Such a development would be quite modest compared with some speculations put forward during the last twenty years by musicians and sound engineers alike.

In an article, which appeared in the *Journal of the Acoustical Society* in 1939, Dr. Vern O. Knudsen wrote the following:

Copyright *Modern Music.* Reprinted by permission.

> Certainly the acoustical engineer can devise instruments for percussional or frictional sounds which composers, musicians, and the large listening public will prefer to such "instruments" as a fireman's axe in a bucket. What appears to be needed is an instrument similar to that developed by Bell Telephone engineers for the artificial production of speech,—a type of "Voder" that not only can imitate or suggest the sounds of nature . . . but also can produce myriads of sounds heretofore unheard or even unimagined. Some of these new sounds fashioned from thermal noise could be made definitely musical by filters that select tonal bands forming a harmonic series; varied transitions from the tonal and harmonic to the atonal and inharmonic could be made continuously or by discrete steps.

In the same periodical in 1934, Dr. Harvey Fletcher mentioned the need to select apparatus so that the intensity of the tone produced, its frequency, and its overtone structure, could be varied throughout the audible range.

Many musicians, the writer included, have dreamed of compact technological boxes, inside which all audible sounds, including noise, would be ready to come forth at the command of the composer. Such boxes are still located somewhere in the future. At present the choice is either to wait and lament the fact that they aren't available now for experimental and musical purposes, or to continue to work with what "axes and buckets" can be found or made.

Recently the percussion group in Chicago had access to the sound effects collection of a Chicago radio station. An audio frequency oscillator was used in combination with electric buzzers, muted gongs, tin can xylophones, marimbula, a coil of wire, and recorded sounds. The coil of wire was connected through a phonograph pick-up arm to an amplifier and loudspeaker. This arrangement had been devised by a sound effects expert in order to represent various explosives and rumbling sounds of nature and war. The loudness and presence of high or low overtones was controlled by dial. It was possible to shift from the greatest loudness to complete silence and vice versa by pulling a switch. Frequency records and the recording of the whine of a generator were used on turntables, the speed of which could be varied, thus making sliding tones available. To produce the sound, a needle was lowered to the record, although this sometimes resulted in a blurred attack. A button arrangement was preferred, whereby it was possible to have the needle on the record before a required entrance, sound or silence being produced by the position of the button. Here again, the loudness of the sound could be controlled very exactly. One player can operate several turntables and perform a single line written for the sound of a landslide, that of rain, of compressed air, or any other recorded sounds. A small contact microphone, such as was used with the marimbula, transforms slight sounds into ones that have an imposing quality and character.

These instruments are by no means the ultimate ones dreamed of, but they are available and useful and constitute at least a step into the "hitherto unheard or even unimagined." It is possible, but with some difficulty, to transplant them from the radio studio to the concert hall. Loudspeakers, amplifiers, and turntables must be set up in the midst of a fantastic assemblage of wires and electrical connections. In using this material for musical purposes it would be easier and more natural to do so in the radio studios where the material has been developed. Organizations of sound effects, with their expressive rather than representational qualities in mind, can be made. Such compositions could be presented by themselves as "experimental radio music," or for the purpose of heightening dramatic effects in connection with a radio drama. Parallel possibilities exist in connection with the use of sounds recorded on film, film phonographs, and organizations of such material for the moving picture.

In writing for these sounds, as in writing for percussion instruments alone, the composer is dealing with material that does not fit into the orthodox scales and harmonies. It is therefore necessary to find some other organizing means than those in use for symphonic instruments. The sounds cannot be organized through reference to an underlying fundamental tone since such a tone does not exist. Each sound must be considered as essentially different from and independent of every other sound. A method analogous to the twelve-tone system may prove useful, but, in such a case, the "sound-row" would contain any number of elements. However, because of the nature of the materials involved, and because their duration characteristics can be easily controlled and related, it is more than likely that the unifying means will be rhythmic.

As more experimental orchestras are established (inside and outside radio and film studios) and as more composers enter this field, more of its problems will be solved. In proportion to the exchange of ideas and experience that will take place, we can expect the finding and invention of further instrumental resources, the development of an occidental theory of rhythm, and the establishing of another valid form of musical expression. (May-June, 1942)

South Winds in Chicago *John Cage*

We cannot complain about the Good Neighbor Policy and what it has done for spring programs in Chicago. The Illinois WPA Symphony offered two suites, Pedro Sanjuan's *Liturgia Negra* and Amadeo Roldan's *La Rebambaramba*, and a *Concerto for Violoncello and Orchestra* by Heitor Villa-Lobos. Hekel Tavares' *Concerto in Brazilian Forms for Piano and Orchestra* was played by the Chicago Symphony Orchestra.

Of all these works, the one by Tavares received the best performance and it was the least worthy. It was a superficial, uninteresting set of exhibition pieces. No part of the exaltation, grandeur, deep religious feeling, authentically American expression found in the program notes was reflected in the concerto itself. However, the idea of strengthening the cultural solidarity of the Americas got across, and the audience was very pleased, probably because there was nothing Brazilian about the work, and nothing unfamiliar, and the forms mentioned in the title were only informally present. Tavares, hailed as Brazil's Stephen Foster, earned the added distinction of being called Tschaikovskian.

The performance given the Villa-Lobos work was so uncertain and unconvincing that it was very difficult to get from it any idea or feeling about the music. It seemed to be a delicate, highly sensitive and carefully detailed piece. Climaxes which might have been powerful and expressive came upon the orchestra, taking it unawares. The soloist had a very difficult time and didn't conceal his anxiety. However, this occasion served to feed an appetite to hear more Villa-Lobos and in better performances.

The Sanjuan and Roldan suites presented Afro-Cuban materials, the Roldan far more successfully than the Sanjuan. It is impossible to overlook the fact that Roldan is no longer living. I would like to hear the music he might be writing now. *La Rebambaramba* is a clear and exciting score. Of its four movements, three have intoxicating dance qualities. The second movement is slow and seems like an animal that is sleeping beautifully and with strength. Six percussion players have integral parts in all the movements. Melodically simple and direct, rhythmically alive and rich, the work gave the orchestra a new sound character. José Echaniz, a guest, conducted the work and you could tell that he really meant it. Music and performances of this standard will turn our current flirtation into true love.

Copyright *Modern Music*. Reprinted by permission.

Of the first performances, one, Philip Warner's *Concerto for Piano and Orchestra,* played by the Illinois Symphony, was trivial and parlorish. The Chicago Symphony gave firsts of Heniot Levy's *Twenty-four Variations on an Original Theme* and David Van Vactor's *Gothic Impressions.* The Levy work was academic and sickly. Other works by other Chicago composers, but which have been heard before, included Felix Borowski's *Symphony Number 3 in G Major,* which gave rise to the adjective scherzophrenic, Leon Stein's *Chassidic Dances Numbers 1 and 3,* which were vigorous and refreshing, but not breath-taking. Albert Noelte's *Prologue to a Romantic Drama,* which kept struggling toward the same climax and falling away from it in the same way, until it arrived at a very unpleasant effectiveness.

We also heard Harl McDonald's *Overture (1941),* an empty, shallow work, and Ernst Toch's *Pinocchio, a Merry Overture.* It is too bad that Toch has not found some time to devote to experimental work, in which he has not only professed an interest, but to which, back in the twenties and in Germany, he made valuable contributions. I think we could get along without his popularities and music for films long enough to hear his *Fuge aus der Geographie,* written for speech nine times as fast as spoken, or something else he might produce now in that direction.

One of the most deeply moving experiences we have had this spring was that afforded by Piatigorsky and the Hindemith *Concerto for Violoncello and Orchestra.* It was magnificently played, Frederick Stock conducting. It is a concerto in which the soloist is not merely displaying virtuosity, but one in which the cello is an individual and the orchestra is the group and the musical relationships are also human relationships. This is particularly clear in the last movement in which the orchestra sets forth in martial character, the cello remaining distinct and apart, poetic and not marching, having, as it were, another point of view. The cello maintains this individual point of view with increasing intensity and up to the last possible moment. It is clear then that the choice is one between insanity and conformance. The latter course is followed and the cello becomes a subservient part of an overwhelming orchestra.

Chicago is fortunate in having a very sincere and not-to-be-discouraged New Music Group. Under the direction of its president, George Perle, the group has a strong twelve-tone bias. During the winter a concert was given, presenting Steuermann and twelve-tone piano music. More recently, in the course of an informal evening with a lecture, we heard a sonata for viola, flute and piano by Perle, a piano work by Ben Weber and a viola and flute piece by

Ernst Křenek. Of these pieces, the one by Perle was the most fluent, and this was due to the comparative lengthiness of his lines, the presence of clear repetitions, and the rhythms which were dull but constant. The Weber and Křenek pieces seemed fragmentary, busy, and nervous. Over all this work and its introversion, there seems to be a pall, and hearing it one can fancy himself at some sort of a shroud ritual. The New Music Group also presented Louis Krasner and Jacques de Menasce in a sonata program for violin and piano. A first performance was given of a work by de Menasce, and sonatas by Hindemith and Bartók were played. The *Sonata Number 1 for Violin and Piano* by Bartók was good to hear. In this work, ideas seem to be suggested but never grasped, every moment passes just as one begins to realize its presence. It makes for dreams and visions.

Harry Partch, who has been wandering around and between two continents for the last twenty years, always with only one idea in mind, has finally succeeded in Chicago in getting his Chromolodian constructed. This is an instrument that looks like an old-fashioned Harmonium, has the ordinary keyboard, but that produces Partch's overtone-inspired forty-three tone scale. Heretofore, Partch has performed his work using stringed instruments with special frets and a particular form of speech with exaggerated inflections and intonations. The Chromolodian gives a welcome definiteness to his work. (May-June, 1942)

Summer Music: The Parks *John Cage*

Large audiences enjoyed the music offered on the Mall in Central Park this summer. It is pleasant to report that the programs arranged for the twenty-seventh season of the Goldman Band and the second annual Festival of Folk and Contemporary Music presented by Associate Committee of the League of Composers (working with the Department of Parks and this time also the Common Council for American Unity) included some music written by composers of today, and that this music was well-received. However, judging both from the amiability of the audience and the interest in up-to-the-minuteness that characterizes both Edwin Franko Goldman and the League of Composers, there might have been more contemporary music played than there was. This failing was due perhaps chiefly to the exigencies of rehearsals, in some

Copyright *Modern Music*. Reprinted by permission.

instances of musicians newly together and for only the summer.

The League Festival began with two programs strictly limited to songs and dances of various European countries. The third night gave us American music: *Devotion* and *Cindy* by Harry Wilson, *The Mother's Vow* by Arthur Farwell, a *Psalm* by Normand Lockwood, *Prayer of the Slavic Children* by W. Golde, *Alleluia* by Randall Thompson, and *The Soul of America* by T. C. Whitmer (all sung by the Teachers College Chorus under the direction of Harry Wilson). There were also Negro spirituals, performed by the Hall Johnson Choir, and squares and rounds danced by the Don Chambers Group. The fourth and last program, played by the Juilliard Summer Orchestra under the direction of Peter Wilhouski, was mixed as to musical origin: a Haydn movement and several contradances by Beethoven preceded a performance of *Roots in the Earth* by Paul Bowles, *Melpomene*, an overture by G. W. Chadwick, Wayne Barlow's *Sarabande*, the *Country Dance* from a *Village Suite* by Douglas Moore, and an excerpt from Howard Hanson's *Romantic Symphony*.

Mr. Wilhouski often showed a clear sense of the grace and meaning in the music he played but he suffers alarmingly from what might be called "excerptitis." Though affected somewhat by this treatment, the Bowles work still managed to interest and excite me. Written for wind instruments and no strings but the double bass, a piano, and augmented percussion, the piece suggests that Bowles could very advantageously write for the band. The music is simple and clearly etched, beginnings and ends of phrases being undisturbed by thick effects. The audience thoroughly enjoyed the work, especially those parts that seemed to take humorously the Central American folk material from which the composition (originally a film accompaniment) stems.

Robert L. Sanders' *Symphony in B♭ for Concert Band* was performed early in the Goldman Band's season. This is an ambitious work in three movements. It is not always clear exactly what is going on, the music being contrived, for the most part, in an involute manner. If the ideas were more frequently presented straight, rather than pretentiously developed, they might give more pleasure. The work was conducted by the composer, without stint, bringing to mind the manner of Leonard Bernstein.

Henry Cowell's *Hymn and Fuguing Tune* was given its *première* by Mr. Goldman. The Cowell work is a straightforward piece with an effect of great sincerity. The Hymn, tantalizingly short, sings beautifully. I think the fine quality is achieved, in part, by remaining with the scale on which the music is based, instead of getting involved, as Mr. Sanders did, with the expressive interval.

The Band played Pasquale Mondrone's *Danza Campestra* and his *Pastel March*, which, at their first performance, pleased me so much that I made a point of hearing them a second time. Unfortunately, in spite of the charming tunes and simplicity of treatment that both pieces share, they seemed less pleasing than before. I did not at first realize the reason; for the first performance I was at the rear of the auditory space (near the ice-cream carts) and the music sounded like some merry-go-round in heaven; the second time I was on top of the music in the area reserved for the critics. The first hearing had emphasized the delicacy inherent in the music; the second, close hearing was simply too loud to be delicate. It was also too harsh; this was probably due not entirely to amplitude, but to the fact that the Goldman Band plays in a concrete shell rather than in a sympathetic, old-fashioned, wooden one. This loudness and harshness is not objectionable in the case of the standard band repertory (e.g., Goldman's *Hail Brooklyn*), for it mobilizes the attendant ears, and the sedentary character of both band and audience is, for the music's duration, disregarded. (November-December, 1944)

Expressive Percussion *Virgil Thomson*

Virgil Thomson was without doubt the most serious and influential American newspaper music critic during the 1940's and early 1950's, in addition to being a noted composer; and this review, published in the New York Herald Tribune *(January 22, 1945), was the first penetrating discussion of Cage's musical endeavor and its tradition.*

John Cage, whose recent compositions made up the program of a concert given yesterday afternoon at the New School for Social Research, is already famous as a specialist in the use of percussive sounds. Two years ago, the Museum of Modern Art presented pieces by him for a large group of players using flower pots, brake bands, electric buzzers, and similar objects not primarily musical but capable of producing a wide variety of interesting sounds all the same. The works offered yesterday included an even greater variety of sounds, all prepared by inserting bits of metal, wood, rubber, or leather at carefully studied points and distances between the strings of an ordinary pianoforte.

Copyright © by Virgil Thomson. Reprinted by permission.

The effect in general is slightly reminiscent, on first hearing, of Indonesian gamelan orchestras, though the interior structure of Mr. Cage's music is not Oriental at all. His work attaches itself, in fact, to two different traditions of Western modernism. One is the percussive experiments begun by [Filippo Tommaso] Marinetti's Futurist noisemakers and continued in the music of Edgard Varèse, Henry Cowell, and George Antheil, all of which, though made in full awareness of Oriental methods, is thoroughly Western in its expression. The other is, curiously enough, the atonal music of Arnold Schoenberg.

Mr. Cage has carried Schoenberg's harmonic maneuvers to their logical conclusion. He has produced atonal music not by causing the twelve tones of the chromatic scale to contradict one another consistently, but by eliminating, to start with, all sounds of precise pitch. He substitutes for the chromatic scale a gamut of pings, plucks, and delicate thuds that is both varied and expressive and that is different in each piece. By thus getting rid, at the beginning, of the constricting element in atonal writing—which is the necessity of taking care to avoid making classical harmony with a standardized palette of instrumental sounds and pitches that exists primarily for the purpose of producing such harmony—Mr. Cage has been free to develop the rhythmic element of composition, which is the weakest element in the Schoenbergian style, to a point of sophistication unmatched in the technique of any other living composer.

His continuity devices are chiefly those of the Schoenberg school. There are themes and sometimes melodies, even, though these are limited, when they have real pitch, to the range of a fourth, thus avoiding the tonal effect of dominant and tonic. All these appear in augmentation, diminution, inversion, fragmentation, and the various kinds of canon. That these procedures do not take over a piece and become its subject, or game, is due to Cage's genius as a musician. He writes music for expressive purposes; and the novelty of his timbres, the logic of his discourse, are used to intensify communication, not as ends in themselves. His work represents, in consequence, not only the most advanced methods now in use anywhere, but original expression of the very highest poetic quality. And this has been proved now through all the classical occasions—theater, ballet, song, orchestral composition, and chamber music.

One of the works was played yesterday by the composer, the other two by Arthur Gold and Robert Fizdale, duo pianists. The perfect execution of these young men, their rhythm, lightness, and absolute equality of scale, and the singing sounds they derived from their instruments, in spite of the fact that the strings were all damped in various ways, made one wish to hear them operate on music less special, as well. The concert was a delight from every point of view.

The Dreams and Dedications of George Antheil *John Cage*

In several of its important aspects, modern music of the twenties is now known only by hearsay. The Italian "Art of Noise" established by Luigi Russolo has totally disappeared; in memory it is mistakenly associated with Marinetti. The work done with speech orchestras, divisions of the half-tone, and electrical instruments is for the most part forgotten. Many composers exist today only as names. This is virtually true of Ives, Ruggles, and Varèse, although enough of their music has been heard during the past fifteen years to make its comparative absence from contemporary musical life lamentable. But in George Antheil's case, it is impossible to know whether the lack of his twenties music in the forties is a loss.

At one point (1937) one could spend the afternoon reading Ezra Pound's book, *Antheil and the Theory of Harmony*, and the evening going to the movies and hearing Antheil's score for *The Plainsman*. The following days were full of confusion. Was Antheil a musical genius or just another Hollywood hack? Those who knew Antheil, who had heard his earlier music, were unsatisfying in their assurances. "He was a good composer." "He was not a good composer." "He was a good composer." . . . Antheil's book, *Bad Boy of Music* (Doubleday, Doran and Co., 1945), is equally contradictory, although many things about it suggest that he was not a good composer.

It is a book in the tradition of *The Autobiography of Alice B. Toklas*, and about as entertaining as Bravig Imbs's *Confessions of Another Young Man*. Like the *Confessions,* it presents the author as just another young man devoid of nobility in a milieu of famous people. Its special quality is a gaudy cheapness that comes partly from the author's inconsistent activities—musician, lovelorn columnist, and so on—and partly from the many reasons he gives why the famous people, James Joyce, Igor Stravinsky, Hedy Lamarr, Gloria Vanderbilt, are famous.

Copyright *Modern Music.* Reprinted by permission.

Antheil the musician was very easily influenced. His first influence, probably the best, was from himself, from a dream he had in Trenton, N.J. This prompted him to go to Europe, to give up concertizing as a pianist, to concentrate on composing, and even provided him with certain musical motives, which were the stimuli for all his early work.

Trouble came with influences from outside, the first of these being Stravinsky and the business of neo-classicism. The poetry attaching itself to a composer who pursues music heard in a dream now began to fall away from Antheil. And this process of losing poetry, or what was really his personal life-necessity, even though the result of exterior influences, continued throughout his life.

He was persuaded to write operas with the pre-Hitler German opera-loving audiences in mind. This freed him from the Stravinsky attachment but carried him further from the dream. Upon arriving in New York, he was asked to write for the ballet. This was an influence back to Stravinsky, so, although he accepted it momentarily, he left the East and settled finally in Los Angeles, where he fell under the spell of Hollywood. He took some time to recognize Hollywood's commercialism as a bad influence, incompatible with serious composition. He partially exonerated himself by moving from a large house to a smaller one. The part of Hollywood that stays with him still is his interest in writing for the "great public." This confirms his present choice of models: late Beethoven, Mahler, Bruckner, and, as he himself says, "even Sibelius." There is no longer any remembrance of the dream; instead he dedicates the *Fourth Symphony* to "Hedy Lamarr and all the living heroes of all countries," the *Fifth* to "the young dead of this war, the young dead of all countries." Something quite empty is being inflated with a vast amount of volatile profundity.

One may wonder whether the emptiness and the cheap, gaudy quality shown in the book were not present, too, in Antheil's early work. Also whether the new forms and musical concepts admired by Pound, Satie, Cocteau, and others, were not merely façades for hollow nothingness. (January, 1946)

[*Sonatas and Interludes*] *John Cage*

This is the "Table of Preparations" for the *Sonatas and Interludes* (1946–48). Mutes of various materials are placed between the strings of the keys used, thus effecting transformations of the piano

Text reprinted by courtesy of George Avakian.

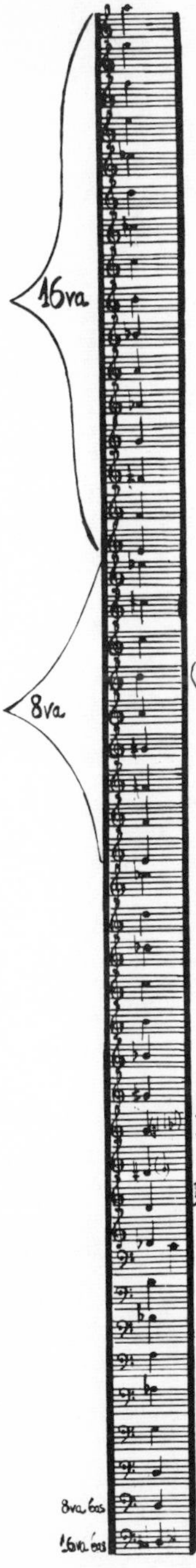

TONE	MATERIAL	STRINGS LEFT TO RIGHT	DISTANCE FROM DAMPER (INCHES)	MATERIAL	STRINGS LEFT TO RIGHT	DISTANCE FROM DAMPER (INCHES)	MATERIAL	STRINGS LEFT TO RIGHT	DISTANCE FROM DAMPER (INCHES)	TONE
16va				SCREW	2-3	1 1/4*				A
				MED. BOLT	2-3	1 3/8*				G
				SCREW	2-3	1 5/8*				F
				SCREW	2-3	1 13/16*				E
				SCREW	2-3	1 3/4*				E♭
				SM. BOLT	2-3	2*				D
				SCREW	2-3	1 11/16*				C♯
				FURNITURE BOLT	2-3	2 3/16*				C
				SCREW	2-3	2 1/2*				B
				SCREW	2-3	1 7/8*				B♭
				MED. BOLT	2-3	2 7/8*				A
				SCREW	2-3	2 1/4*				A♭
				SCREW	2-3	3 3/4*				G
				SCREW	2-3	2 15/16*				F♯
	SCREW	1-2	3/4*	FURN. BOLT + 2 NUTS	2-3	2 1/8*	SCREW + 2 NUTS	2-3	3 1/4*	F
				SCREW	2-3	1 13/16*				E
8va				FURNITURE BOLT	2-3	1 7/8				E♭
				SCREW	2-3	1 15/16				C♯
				SCREW	2-3	1 1/16				C
	(DAMPER TO BRIDGE = 4 7/16"; ADJUST ACCORDINGLY)			MED. BOLT	2-3	3 3/4				B
				SCREW	2-3	4 7/16				A
	RUBBER	1-2-3	4 1/2	FURNITURE BOLT	2-3	1 1/4				G♯
				SCREW	2-3	1 3/4				F♯
				SCREW	2-3	2 5/16				F
	RUBBER	1-2-3	5 3/4							E
	RUBBER	1-2-3	6 1/2	FURN. BOLT + NUT	2-3	6 7/8				E♭
				FURNITURE BOLT	2-3	2 9/16				D
	RUBBER	1-2-3	3 5/8							D♭
				BOLT	2-3	7 1/8				C
				BOLT	2-3	2				B
	SCREW	1-2	10	SCREW	2-3	1	RUBBER	1-2-3	8 1/4	B♭
	(PLASTIC (See G))	1-2-3	2 5/16				RUBBER	1-2-3	4 1/2	G♯
	PLASTIC (OVER 1 UNDER 2-3)	1-2-3	2 7/8				RUBBER	1-2-3	10 1/8	G
	(PLASTIC (See D))	1-2-3	4 1/4				RUBBER	1-2-3	5 7/16	D♯
	PLASTIC (OVER 1 - UNDER 2-3)	1-2-3	4 1/8				RUBBER	1-2-3	9 3/4	D
	BOLT	1-2	15 1/2	BOLT	2-3	11/16	RUBBER	1-2-3	14 1/8	D♭
	BOLT	1-2	14 1/2	BOLT	2-3	7/8	RUBBER	1-2-3	6 1/2	C
	BOLT	1-2	14 3/4	BOLT	2-3	9/16	RUBBER	1-2-3	14	B
	RUBBER	1-2-3	9 1/2	MED. BOLT	2-3	10 1/8				B♭
	SCREW	1-2	5 7/8	LG. BOLT	2-3	5 7/8	SCREW + NUTS	1-2	1	A
	BOLT	1-2	7 1/8	MED. BOLT	2-3	2 1/4	RUBBER	1-2-3	4 1/8	A♭
	LONG BOLT	1-2	8 3/4	LG BOLT	2-3	3 1/4				G
				BOLT	2-3	11/16				D
8va bas	SCREW + RUBBER	1-2	4 7/16							D
16va bas	ERASER (OVER D UNDER C♯ + E♭) AM. PENCIL CO. #346	1	6 3/4							D

*MEASURE FROM BRIDGE.

Page from score.

sounds with respect to all of their characteristics. The sizes of the bolts and screws, not given in this table, appear on the envelopes which contain the actual objects.

All the factors of the piano preparation, objects and their positions, were found experimentally. They represent a choice determined by taste rather than reasoned relations. In most cases, the preparation preceded a composition. In the course of writing, however, it was sometimes found desirable to introduce an additional mute.

The result is a gamut of sounds moving from lower to higher octaves without the correspondences of pitch characteristic of scales and modes. These sounds are of different timbres and of a decibel range comparable to that of the harpsichord. In effect, the prepared piano is a percussion ensemble under the control of a single player. Where mutes are placed only between the second and third strings, two different sounds are available, one produced with the soft pedal (which eliminates the effect of the first string), the other without it.

In practice, the preparation takes about three hours to make. It is left unchanged throughout the series of twenty pieces. In later works, e.g., *34′ 46.776″ for Two Pianists*, the performers change the preparations during the playing, removing some and introducing others.

Certain piano preparations bring about a combination of sounds though only a single key is played. This led to the gamuts of tones, intervals, and aggregates in the *String Quartet* and subsequent pieces.

[Memoir] *John Cage*

Cage contributed this memoir in the course of a symposium on "The Changing Audience for the Changing Arts," sponsored in 1966 by the Arts Councils of America and subsequently reprinted in The Arts: Planning for Change *(Associated Councils of the Arts, 1966).*

When, in the middle 1940's I was searching to find out why one would make a work of art in this society, I was thinking not in terms of theater, but specifically in terms of music. My search for a reason for making art came about because of this.

I had been taught in the schools that art was a question of com-

Reprinted by permission.

munication. I observed that all of the composers were writing differently. If art was communication, we were using different languages. We were, therefore, in a Tower of Babel situation where no one understood anyone else.

So I determined either to find another reason or give up the whole business. Lou Harrison and other composers joined with me in this quest. At the same moment, a musician came from India alarmed over the influence that Western music was having on Indian traditions. She studied in a concentrated fashion with a number of teachers of Western music over a six-month period. I was with her nearly every day.

Before she returned to India, I learned from her the traditional reason for making a piece of music in India: "to quiet the mind thus making it susceptible to divine influences."

Lou Harrison, meanwhile, was reading in an old English text, I think as old as the sixteenth century, and he found this reason given for writing a piece of music: "to quiet the mind thus making it susceptible to divine influences."

Now the question arises: What is a quiet mind? Then the second question arises: What are divine influences? One of the things that is happening to society now is that the East and the West no longer are separated. We are, as Fuller and McLuhan point out continually, living in a global village.

Formerly, we thought that the Orient had nothing to do with us; that we had no access to it. We know better now. We learned from Oriental thought that those divine influences are, in fact, the environment in which we are. A sober and quiet mind is one in which the ego does not obstruct the fluency of the things that come in through our senses and up through our dreams. Our business in living is to become fluent with the life we are living, and art can help this.

Defense of Satie *John Cage*

The following previously unpublished text was the sole long lecture that Cage delivered during the Black Mountain College Satie Festival, held in the summer of 1948. The audience there consisted largely of German refugees needing persuasion to "oblige them," as Cage later put it, "to listen to twenty-five concerts of Satie's music."

By permission of John Cage.

A most salient feature of contemporary art is the fact that each artist works as he sees fit, and not in accordance with widely agreed-upon procedures. Whether this state of affairs pleases or displeases us is not exactly clear from a consideration of modern clichés of thought.

On the one hand, we lament what we call the gulf between artist and society, between artist and artist, and we praise (very much like children who can only window shop for candy they cannot buy) the unanimity of opinion out of which arose a Gothic cathedral, an opera by Mozart, a Balinese combination of music and dance. We lament the absence among us of such generally convincing works, and we say it must be because we have no traditional ways of making things. We admire from a lonely distance that art which is not private in character but is characteristic of a group of people and the fact that they were in agreement.

On the other hand, we admire an artist for his originality and independence of thought, and we are displeased when he is too obviously imitative of another artist's work. In admiring originality, we feel quite at home. It is the one quality of art we feel fairly capable of obtaining. Therefore we say such things as: Everyone not only has but should have his own way of doing things. Art is an individual matter. We go so far as to give some credence to the opinion that a special kind of art arises from a special neurosis pattern of a particular artist. At this point we grow slightly pale and stagger out of our studios to knock at the door of some neighborhood psychoanalyst. Or—we stay at home, cherish our differences, and increase our sense of loneliness and dissatisfaction with contemporary art. In the field of music, we express this dissatisfaction variously: We say: The music is interesting, but I don't understand it. Somehow it is not "fulfilled." It doesn't have "the long line." We then go our separate paths: Some of us back to work to write music that few find any use for, and others to spend their lives with the music of another time, which, putting it bluntly and chronologically, does not belong to them.

Now I would like to ask and answer the questions: What kinds of things in art (music in particular) can be agreed upon? and What kinds of things can be not agreed upon? For I suspect that our admiring two opposite positions, that of the traditional artist and that of the individualist, indicates a basic need in us for this pair of opposites. We need, I imagine, an art that is paradoxical in that it reflects both unanimity of thought and originality of thought.

Music is a continuity of sound. In order that it may be distin-

1. John Cage prepares a piano. Preparation materials, inserted between the strings, customarily include rubber bands, wooden spoons, bits of paper and metal, and a variety of other objects. Both the keys and the strings of the piano are played.

2, 3. Teaching in Mendocino County, California, WPA Recreation Counselor's Camp, 1941. *Below:* With Xenia Cage (center, back to camera).

4. *Imaginary Landscape No. 3*, 1942. Page 1 of score. Copyright Henmar Press, Inc., New York.

5. *Quartet for Twelve Tom-Toms (She Is Asleep)*, 1943. Page 1 of score. Copyright Henmar Press, Inc., New York.

MUSEUM OF MODERN ART
11 West 53rd Street

Sunday Evening
February 7th, 1943
8:45 p.m.

A PROGRAM OF PERCUSSION MUSIC

Directed by

JOHN CAGE

Presented by

THE LEAGUE OF COMPOSERS

In association with

THE MUSEUM OF MODERN ART

Assisting Artist

RUTH STUBER JEANNE, *Marimba*

Ensemble

MARY ANTHONY
XENIA CAGE
DAVID CAMPBELL
JEAN CAMPBELL
ARTHUR CHRISTIE
MERCE CUNNINGHAM
RENATA GARVE
MOLLY HOWE
CECIL KITCAT
HELEN LANFER
EDWARD MCLEAN
JOAN PALMER

PROGRAM

Construction in Metal . . . . John Cage
thundersheets, orchestral bells, string piano, oxen bells cowbells, temple gongs, automobile brake drums, cymbals, anvils, gongs, tam tam

Counterdance in the Spring . . . . Lou Harrison
drums, dragon's mouths, gongs, cymbals, woodblocks, brakedrum

Ostinato Pianissimo . . . . Henry Cowell
(*first performance*)
string piano, rice bowls, marimba, Niger drum, hand drum, güiro, bongos, drums, button gongs

Canticle . . . . Lou Harrison
tambourine, woodblocks, bells, rattles, dragon's mouths, temple gongs, flower pots, cowbells, güiro, wind glass, triangle, cymbals, brake drum, tam tam, thundersheets, drum, gongs

Imaginary Landscape No. 3 . . . . John Cage
audio frequency oscillator, recorded sounds, tin cans, buzzer, gongs, marimbula, thunder sheet

INTERMISSION

Preludio a 11 . . . . Jose Ardévol
(*first performance*)
claves, güiro, maracas, triangle, anvil, cymbal, bongos, African drum, snare drum, bass drum, piano

Amores . . . . John Cage
(*first performance*)
string piano, drums, rattle, woodblocks

Ritmicas V & VI . . . . Amadeo Roldán
claves, cowbells, quijadas, güiro, maracas, bongos, drums, marimbula

Sound equipment furnished by the Sound Effects Department of the Columbia Broadcasting System. The co-ordination of the visual elements has been effected by SCHUYLER WATTS

Office of the LEAGUE OF COMPOSERS, 113 West 57th St.
ARTHUR JUDSON, Recital Management — Steinway Piano

6. Program of percussion music concert (Cage's New York début), Museum of Modern Art, February 7, 1943.

7

PERCUSSION ORCHESTRA SITS ON THE STAGE WAITING TO PLAY. AT FULL STRENGTH, ORCHESTRA INCLUDES ELEVEN PLAYERS, ALL OF WHOM DRESS FORMALLY FOR CONCERTS

PERCUSSION CONCERT

Band bangs things to make music

At the Museum of Modern Art in New York City a few Sundays ago, an orchestra of earnest, dressed-up musicians sat on the stage and began to hit things with sticks and hands. They whacked gongs, cymbals, gourds, bells, sheets of metal, ox bells, Chinese dishes, tin cans, auto brake drums, the jawbone of an ass and other objects. Sometimes instead of hitting, they rattled or rubbed. The audience, which was very high-brow, listened intently without seeming to be disturbed at the noisy results.

The occasion was a percussion concert, sponsored by the League of Composers and conducted by a patient, humorous, 30-year-old Californian named John Cage, who is the most active percussion musician in the U. S. Cage not only conducts percussion orchestras but also composes percussion music, as do other modern experimental composers. Percussion music goes back to man's primitive days when untutored savages took aesthetic delight in hitting crude drums or hollow logs. Cage believes that when people today get to understand and like his music, which is produced by banging one object with another, they will find new beauty in everyday modern life, which is full of noises made by objects banging against each other.

JAWBONE OF AN ASS IS WHACKED WITH FIST

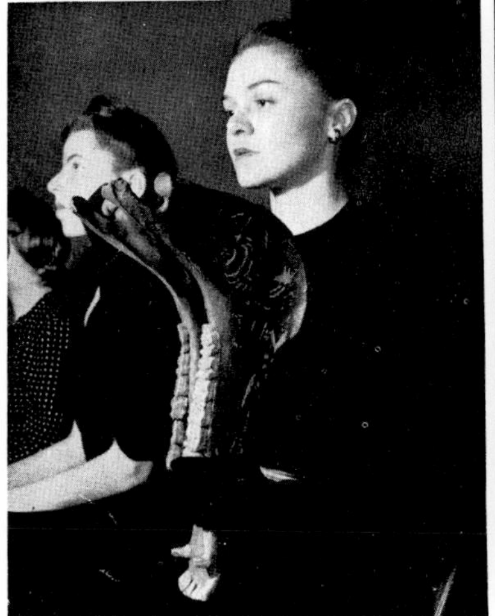

8

CAGE CONDUCTS MUSIC WRITTEN IN CONVENTIONAL NOTATION

9

THE MARIMBULA'S METAL TONGUES TWANG WHEN CLAPPED

10

7–16. Cage's New York début earned him this spread in *Life* magazine (March 15, 1943). Photographed by Eric Schaal, Zurich. © 1943 Time Inc. *(continued on next page)*

HALF-GALLON CANS CAN PLAY LIMITED SCALE

11

GRADUATED OXEN BELLS PRODUCE HIGH AND DAMPENED NOTES

12

CHINESE RICE BOWLS GIVE OUT A VERY PLEASANT TINKLING

13

14

Bongos are a pair of little Cuban drums tapped or rubbed with the fingers. Rubbing gives a kind of small roaring sound. Edge of bongo emits different note than center.

15

Automobile brake drum gives out clear bell-like sound. Best sounds come from brake drums of higher-priced autos. The instrument at left is gonglike Chinese tam-tam.

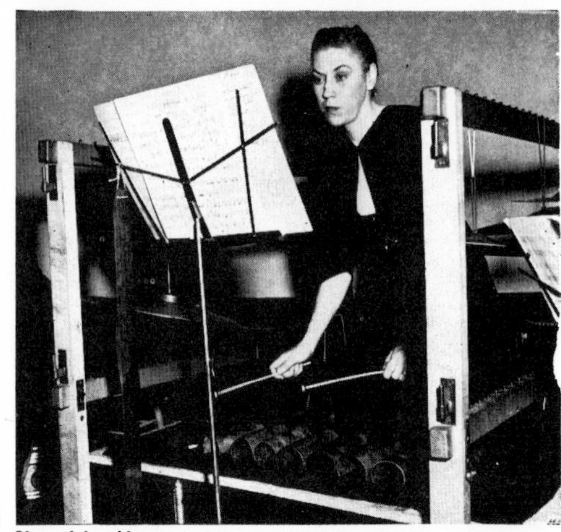

16

Pieces of shaped bronze sound like anvils. The different lengths give different notes. Player is Xenia Cage, the conductor's wife, who took up percussion after marriage.

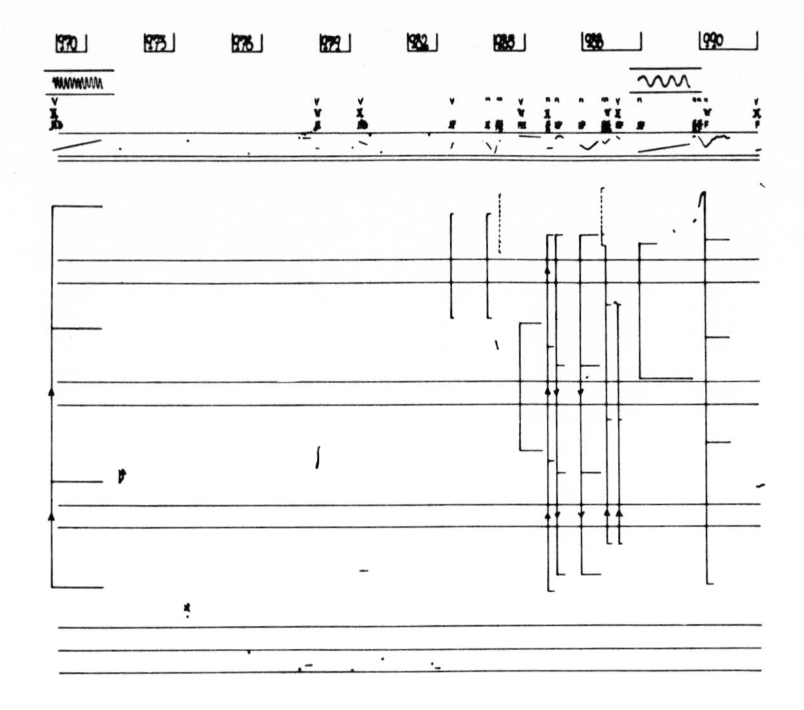

24. *26′1.1499″*, 1955. Pages 59 and 84 of score. Copyright Henmar Press, Inc., New York.

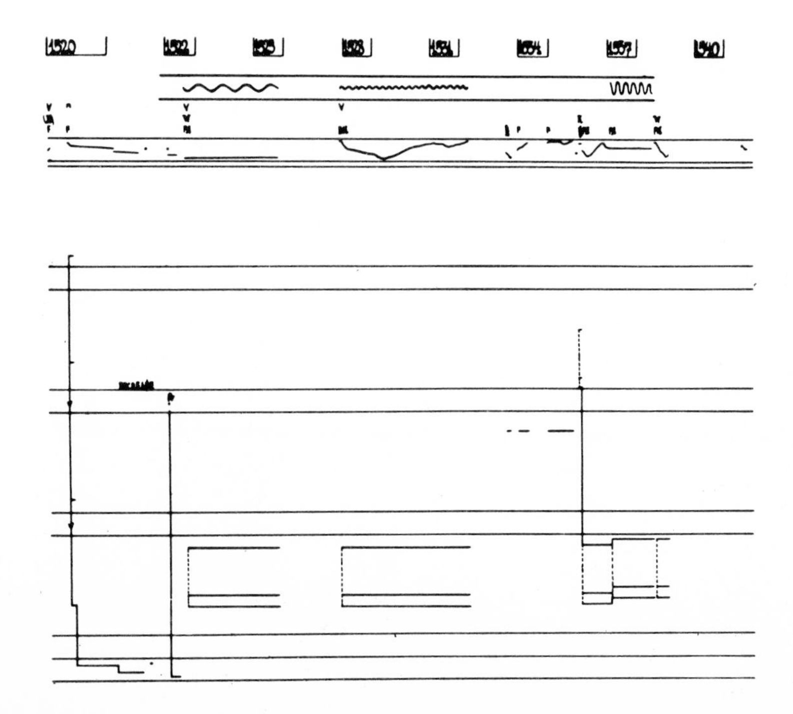

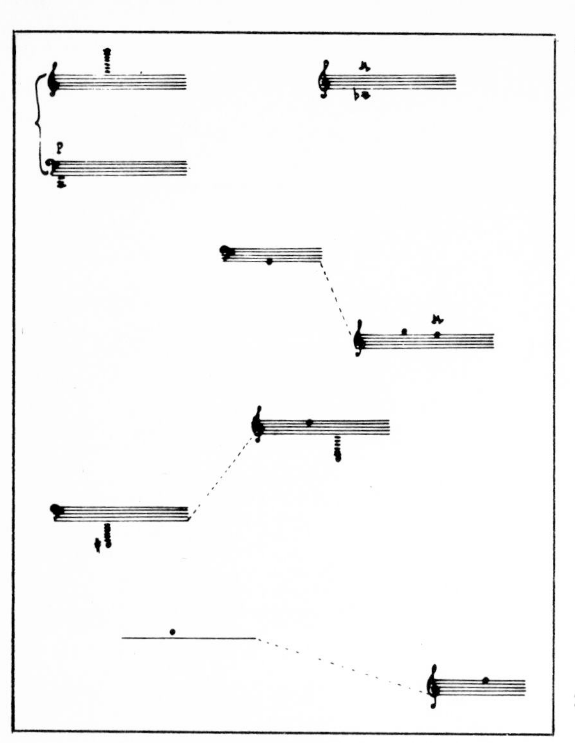

25. *Music for Piano 64*, 1955. Page from score. Copyright Henmar Press, Inc., New York.

26. *Winter Music*, 1957. One of twenty unnumbered pages. Copyright Henmar Press, Inc., New York.

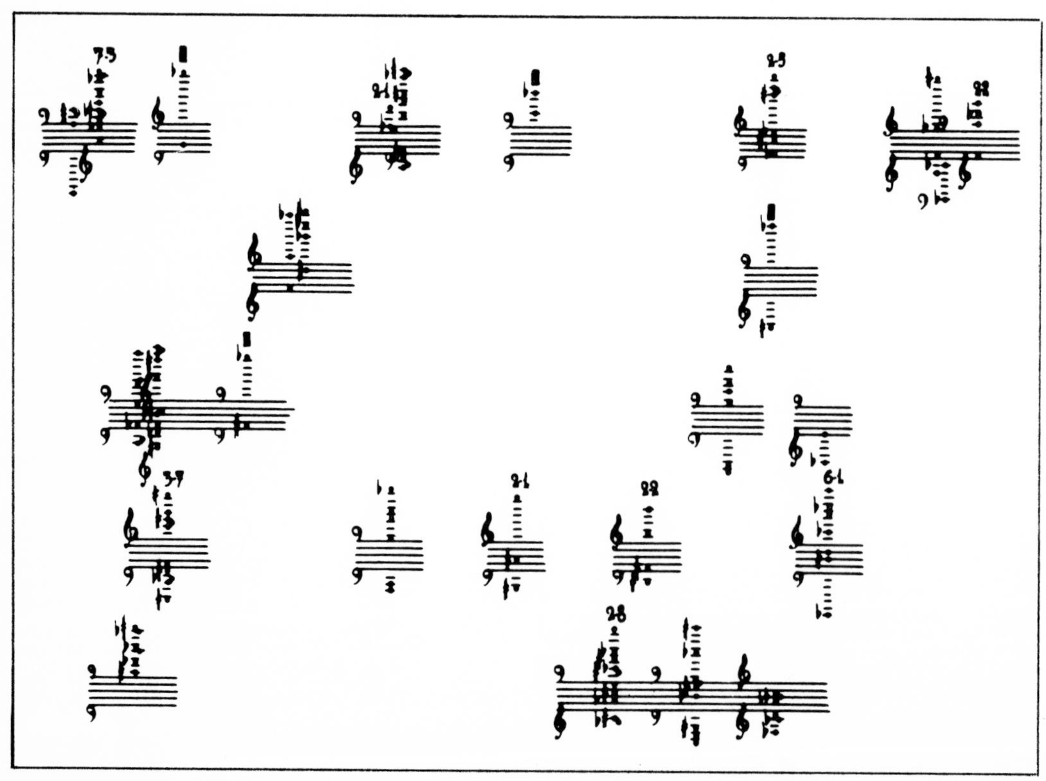

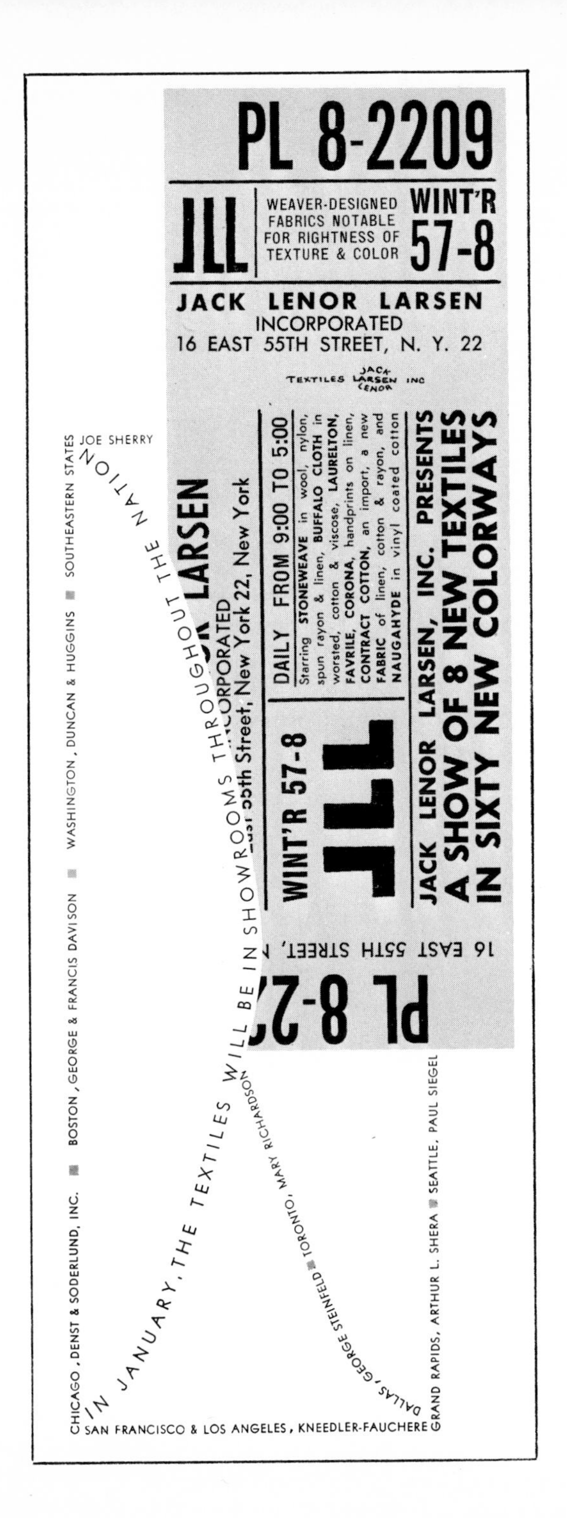

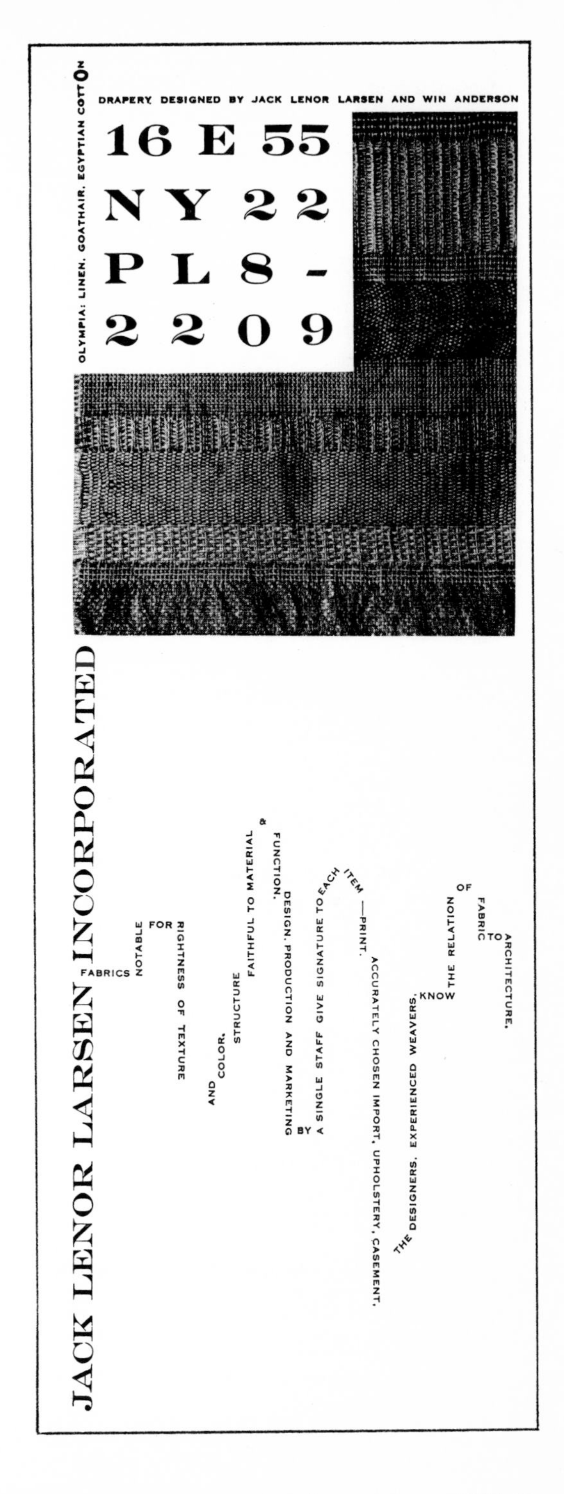

27, 28. Designs created by Cage while working for Jack Lenor Larsen, 1957–58.

PIANO

EACH PAGE IS ONE SYSTEM. FOR A SINGLE PIANIST TO BE PLAYED WITH OR WITHOUT ANY OR ALL PARTS WRITTEN FOR ORCHESTRAL INSTRUMENTS. THE WHOLE IS TO BE TAKEN AS A BODY OF MATERIAL PRESENTABLE AT ANY POINT BETWEEN MINIMUM (NOTHING PLAYED) AND MAXIMUM (EVERYTHING PLAYED), BOTH HORIZONTALLY AND VERTICALLY: A PROGRAM MADE WITHIN A DETERMINED LENGTH OF TIME (TO BE ALTERED BY A CONDUCTOR WHEN THERE IS ONE) MAY INVOLVE ANY READING, I.E., ANY SEQUENCE OF PARTS OR PARTS THEREOF.

A FOLLOWING THE PERIMETER, FROM ANY NOTE ON IT, PLAY IN OPPOSITE DIRECTIONS IN THE PROPORTION GIVEN. HERE AND ELSEWHERE, THE ABSENCE OF INDICATIONS OF ANY KIND MEANS FREEDOM FOR THE PERFORMER IN THAT REGARD.

B AN AGGREGATE MUST BE PLAYED AS A SINGLE ICTUS. WHERE THIS IS IMPOSSIBLE, THE UNPLAYABLE NOTES SHALL BE TAKEN AS HARMONICS PREPARED IN ADVANCE. HARMONICS MAY ALSO BE PRODUCED WHERE THEY ARE NOT SO REQUIRED. RESONANCES, BOTH OF AGGREGATES AND INDIVIDUAL NOTES OF THEM, MAY BE FREE IN LENGTH. OVERLAPPINGS, INTERPENETRATIONS, ARE ALSO FREE. THE SINGLE STAFF IS PROVIDED WITH 2 CLEF SIGNS. WHERE THESE DIFFER, AMBIGUITY OBTAINS IN THE PROPORTION INDICATED BY THE 2 NUMBERS ABOVE THE AGGREGATE, THE FIRST OF THESE APPLYING TO THE CLEF SIGN ABOVE THE STAFF. AN INKED IN RECTANGLE ABOVE A PAIR OF NOTES INDICATES A CHROMATIC CLUSTER.

C M = MUTE. P = PIZZ. ALL SINGLE TONES.

D LIKE B, BUT WITH VERTICAL ARPEGGIATION AND TIME TENDENCIES MAKING USE OF HARMONICS UNNECESSARY. THE ARPEGGIATION IS INDICATED BY DOUBLE ARROWS ACCOMPANIED BY A SERIES OF NUMBERS. THE SIGN ⇕ 1,1,1 MEANS 1 NOTE IN THE MIDDLE FOLLOWED BY 1 NOTE HIGHER, OR LOWER, FOLLOWED BY 1 NOTE LOWER IF THE 2ND WAS HIGHER, HIGHER IF THE SECOND WAS LOWER. ↓ 2,1 MEANS TWO NOTES OF WHICH AT LEAST 1 IS THE HIGHEST OF THE THREE FOLLOWED BY A THIRD LOWER NOTE. THE HORIZONTAL ARROWS REFER TO TIME AND THE TENDENCY OF THE TONES TO SOUND SOONER, LATER, OR AT THE POINT OF NOTATION.

E PLAY WITH HANDS INDICATED. WHERE CLEFS DIFFER, A NOTE IS EITHER BASS OR TREBLE. THE NOTES HAVING A SINGLE STEM ARE TO BE ARPEGGIATED (UP OR DOWN). PLAY NOTATIONS FROM LEFT TO RIGHT.

F NUMBERS ARE SECONDS OR OTHER TIME UNITS.

G OF NOTES WRITTEN PLAY NUMBER GIVEN IN ANY MANNER (KEYS, HARP) BEGINNING AND ENDING AS INDICATED BY ARROW. DYNAMIC INDICATIONS ACCOMPANY EACH CIRCLE ON THE CIRCUMFERENCE OF WHICH THE NOTES ARE PLACED. (SCALE ppp-fff)

H ANY ONE OF THESE, AS IN C, OR ANY NUMBER (INCLUDING ALL) IN SEQUENCE, MAINTAINING, IN THE LATTER CASE, THE CLEF SIGN OF THE ONE FIRST PLAYED.

I PIZZ. WHERE INDICATED. A SINGLE TONE, INTERVAL, OR A 3 NOTE AGGREGATE. REAPPEARANCES OF TONES TO BE PLAYED AS ORIGINALLY.

J NUMBERS ARE OF NOTES TO BE PLAYED BETWEEN LIMITS CONNECTED BY LINES. ARROWS INDICATE DIRECTION IN SPACE-TIME BACKWARDS AND FORWARDS. A STRAIGHT LINE ABOVE A NUMBER MEANS ASCENDING OR DESCENDING GAMUT. ∿ MEANS ASCENDING AND DESCENDING.

K DISREGARD TIME. PLAY ONLY ODD OR EVEN NUMBER OF TONES IN A PERFORMANCE, USING OTHERS OF A GIVEN 3, 4, 5 OR 6 SIDED FIGURE AS GRACES OR PUNCTUATIONS.

L PLAY FROM LEFT TO RIGHT WITH HANDS INDICATED. CLEF AMBIGUITY AS IN B. PERIMETERS WERE COMPOSING MEANS AND DO NOT HERE AFFECT TIME, AS THEY DO IN A.

M BEGIN AT LEFT, END AT RIGHT, CHANGING DIRECTION AT INTERSECTIONS IF DESIRED. MAY BE EXPRESSED AS ONE VOICE, A 'COUNTERPOINT', OR AS 3 OR 4 VOICES. PEDALS ONLY IN AREAS INDICATED, NOT OBLIGATORY. ⌊ PED. ⌊....⌋ U.C. ⌊ _ ⌋ SOSTENUTO.

N LIKE I, BUT WITH VARYING DYNAMICS. SOSTENUTO PEDAL GIVEN.

O AUDIBLE (AS CHORDS, LINES, ARPEGGIATIONS AS IND.) BUT FREE, ETC.) ONLY BETWEEN HORIZONTAL LINES. PEDALS AS IN M.

P ANY NOISES (INCLUDING AUXILIARY), DYNAMICS OF WHICH ARE NOTATED.

Q LIKE M, BUT IN TIME (ANY UNITS); GOING BACK INCURS NEED FOR INCREASED SPEED.

R RIGOROUSLY IN TIME. NOTES ABOVE STAFF: TREBLE; BELOW: BASS; ON: AMBIGUOUS. LINES WERE PART OF COMPOSING MEANS, THE INTERSECTIONS PRODUCING TONES OTHER THAN THE EXTREME PIANO KEYS.

S LIKE C, BUT WITH NOISES: ABOVE LINE = INSIDE PIANO CONSTRUCTION; BELOW = OUTSIDE PIANO CONSTRUCTION.

T INFLUENCES IN PITCH AND TIME NOTATED AS SHAPES WITH CENTER POINTS, TO BE AUDIBLE AS CLUSTERS, A SINGLE ONE CHANGING IN ITS COURSE. NUMBERS REFER TO LOUDNESS (1-64) (SOFT TO LOUD OR LOUD TO SOFT)

U CHOOSE ONE OF 3 MUTUALLY EXCLUSIVE AREAS, BOUNDED BY STRAIGHT LINES. PROCEED L. TO R. USING NUMBER OF TONES GIVEN WITHIN DOTTED PARTS.

V PERFORMANCE INDICATIONS ABOVE (READING DOWN) ARE DEGREE OF FORCE, MOST-LEAST; VERTICAL DISTANCE OF ATTACK, FAR-CLOSE; SPEED OF ATTACK, SLOW-FAST. ANY NOISES (BELOW LINE BETWEEN STAVES).

W LEGATO (TRIANGLES) AND STACCATO (ISOLATED NOTES).

X P's ARE PUNCTUATIONS (BEFORE, AT, DURING, OR END OF INTERVAL THEY ACCOMPANY. ∴ MEANS REPEAT SOMETHING (OR ALL, OR ANY AMT.) PLAYED BEFORE, BUT CHANGING AMPLITUDE. PEDALS ARE OPTIONAL.

Y 8 PITCH AREAS, CHROMATICALLY ADJACENT, AND HAVING NUMBER OF CHROMATIC TONES GIVEN (LARGE NUMBERS BELOW STAFF). WHEN NOTES ARE ON A LINE, THEY BELONG TO EITHER THE UPPER OR THE LOWER AREA. TIME IN SPACE SECONDS AS INDICATED. LOUDNESS GIVEN BY POSITION OF NOTE WITH RESPECT TO AREA VERTICALLY. HIGH IS fff. LOW IS ppp.

Z CLUSTERS ENDING AS SINGLE TONES. DYNAMICS AS IN T.

AA CLEF AT ALL TIMES AMBIGUOUS. 'STICKS' TO BE PLAYED FREELY (SINGLE TONES, INTERVALS, AGGREGATES, EVENTS, ETC. WITHIN PITCH LIMITS AND RELATIVE TIME LIMITS INDICATED BY THEIR EXTREMITIES (NOTES), USING GRACES AS 'ASSISTANCE'. GIVE EMPHASIS BY DYNAMICS, HARMONICS, REPETITION OR OTHER MEANS TO CIRCLED TONES AND MORE EXTREMELY TO THOSE CIRCLED TWICE OR 3 TIMES.

AB CLUSTERS AS IN Z. SOMETIMES BEGINNING AS SINGLE TONES (NUMBERS ARE DYNAMICS).

AC NOISES. OF THOSE NOTATED PLAY ONLY THAT NUMBER GIVEN. I = INTERIOR PIANO CONSTRUCTION. A = AUXILIARY NOISES. O = OUTER PIANO CONSTRUCTION. THE POSITION OF THE NOTE VERTICALLY GIVES ITS LOUDNESS (HIGH = fff) (LOW IS ppp).

AD SINGLE TONES, INTERVALS AND THREE NOTE AGGREGATES WITH AMBIGUOUS STAFF, LEGER LINES ABOVE, TREBLE, BELOW, BASS.

AE PITCH-TIME AREAS SILENT UNLESS ACCOMPANIED BY NUMBERS, MEANING NUMBER OF TONES (ANY) TO BE PLAYED.

AF EACH EVENT (LINE-CONNECTED NOTES) IS TO BE PLAYED BY ONE HAND ONLY. THE CLEF SIGNS ABOVE ARE FOR THE RIGHT HAND, BELOW FOR THE LEFT.

AG OMIT ANY 2 NOTES OF EACH AGGREGATE.

AH CLEFS FREE (TREBLE OR BASS). HANDS GIVEN. FOLLOW LINES IN DIRECTIONS GIVEN BY ARROWS.

AI PLAY 'WHEEL' OR 'AXLE' USING ONE(S) NOT PLAYED AS HARMONIC(S). PLAY FROM LEFT TO RIGHT.

AJ NUMBERS ARE PROPORTIONAL OF NOTES TO BE PLAYED IN DIRECTIONS GIVEN BY ARROWS CHANGING CLEF AT POINTS WHERE SIGNS APPEAR.

AK PLAY ANY 1 NOTE IN EACH 'UNIVERSE' ACCORDING TO TIME AND AMPLITUDE GIVEN.

AL ANY 8 TONE GAMUT. LARGE NUMBERS ARE PROPORTIONAL TIME BETWEEN SOUND EVENTS. ⌒ = LEGATO . = STACCATO.

AM SINGLE TONES AND INTERVALS EQUAL LENGTHS OF TIME BETWEEN MARKS ABOVE AND BELOW STAFF.

AN CLEFS REFER TO HANDS. FOLLOWING THE LINE FROM LEFT TO RIGHT PLAY ANY NUMBER OF NOTES WITH ONE HAND FOLLOWED BY A DIFFERENT NUMBER WITH LEFT (ETC., IF NUMBERS CHOSEN DO NOT USE ALL THE NOTES).

29, 30. *Concert for Piano and Orchestra*, 1958. Pages from score. Copyright 1960 by Henmar Press, Inc., New York.

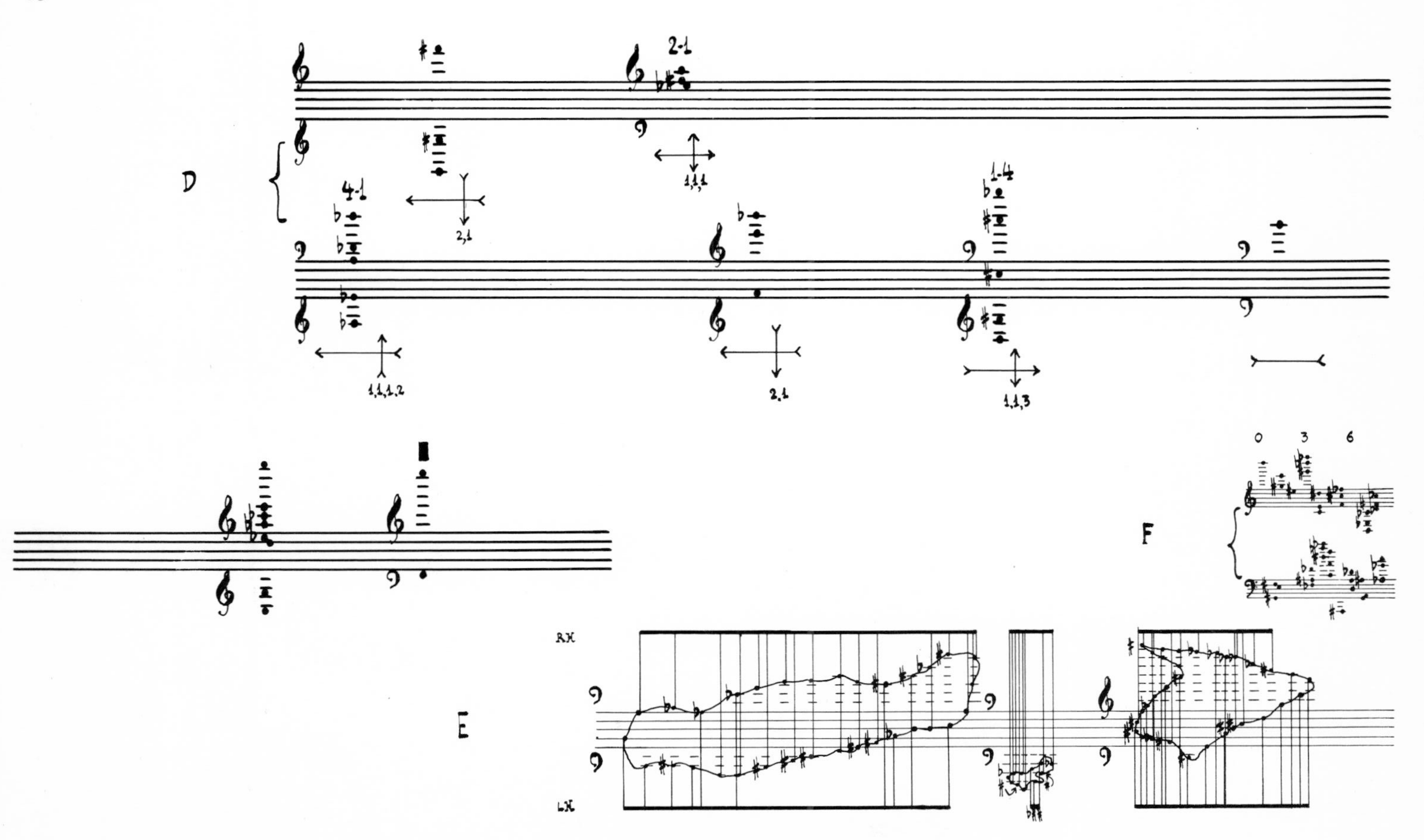
D
2-1
4-1
2,1
1,1,1
1-4
1,1,1,2
2,1
1,1,3
0 3 6
F
E
RH
LH

31. Merce Cunningham conducting *Concert for Piano and Orchestra,* 25-Year Retrospective Concert, Town Hall, New York, 1958.

32. Stage as set for 25-Year Retrospective Concert, Town Hall, New York, 1958. Photo George Moffett—Lensgroup.

guishable from nonbeing, it must have a structure; that is, it must have parts that are clearly separate but that interact in such a way as to make a whole. In order that this whole may have a quality of being alive, it must be given form. Form in music is the morphological line of the sound-continuity. To illustrate this differentiation between structure and form, which may seem at first only an arbitrary set of definitions, let me point out that many poets make use of a sonnet structure to make word-continuities; each sonnet, however, has its own life and death line, that is, its own form, which is characteristic of it. Or to give another illustration, we all have in common the fact of our structure as human beings, but the way in which we live, that is, the form of our life, is individual. The continuity of actions for each one of us is different.

Besides having structure and form, a piece of music must have method; that is, a continuity producing means. In poetry this is syntax; in life it is that observance of an orderly way of living that makes one to some extent dependable. On a primary level, method in life is simply sleeping, eating, and working at particular times rather than just at any. Method in life is being systematic.

A piece of music has not only structure, form, and method, but it has also material, its own sounds. In poetry, to continue the analogy, this is language. There are material differences of language between a Hopkins and a Shakespeare, even though they both wrote English. The material difference between French and English or other languages is obvious. In life, we have different physical differences and we wear different clothes.

Now, from my point of view, I would say that in life we would not be pleased if all of us dressed alike. Even a single individual enjoys dressing differently from one day to another. Likewise in poetry, differences of language are not only admirable but refreshing. We feel imposed upon by G.I. clothing, Baltimore housing, and we would not like poetry in standard English or Esperanto. In the area of material, we need and are enlivened by differentiation. I would say, therefore, we cannot and ought not agree on matters of material.

Proceeding, let us ask whether agreement is natural and desirable in the field of method. In poetry, there is known to be difference in syntax from one language to another; within a given language, less lack of agreement exists. However, the advent in our time of a Joyce, of a Stein, of a Cummings, of a Hopkins is possible only because of a variation in the normal syntax. In life, a Buckminster Fuller proposes a new method of living. Anthropologists reveal to us the fact that there are many ways of living, that agreement in this field is not supported by history. People live and have lived in different ways, and that is one of the interesting things about them.

We come now to the question of form, the life-line of a poem or an individual. This arises in both cases so obviously from feeling and that area known as the heart, speaking both vaguely, romantically, and physically, medically, that no illustrations need be given to make clear the necessity in the field of form for individuality rather than adherence to tradition. Copying as exactly as possible somebody else's life-line in all its emotional details is clearly not possible. The thought is maddening, but fortunately we need not think of it.

We are left with the question of structure, and here it is equally absurd to imagine a human being who does not have the structure of a human being, or a sonnet that does not have the relationship of parts that constitutes a sonnet. There may, of course, in life be dogs rather than human beings—that is, other structures—just as in poetry there may be odes rather than sonnets. There must, however, as a *sine qua non* in all fields of life and art, be some kind of structure—otherwise chaos. And the point here to be made is that it is in this aspect of being that it is desirable to have sameness and agreed-upon-ness. It is quite fine that there are human beings and that they all have a sameness of structure. Sameness in this field is reassuring. We call whatever diverges from sameness of structure monstrous.

In these terms, let us now examine contemporary music. We know, to begin with, that contemporary music is characterized by the fact that each composer works as an individual and nine times out of ten does not agree with any other one. What kinds of ideas have developed in twentieth-century music? Are there any that could and ought to be agreed upon?

New materials have been proposed: quarter tones by Alois Hába, forty-third tones by Harry Partch, electronic instruments by Edgard Varèse, screws, bolts, and bits of rubber by myself, dissonances by all and sundry. Our answer to all this is: fine, the more different costumes, the better. Variety is the spice of life. However, we need not take innovations of this kind too seriously, unless somebody tells us to.

New methods have been proposed: outstanding among these are continuity by means of continuous invention, by means of the twelve-tone-row, and by means of secundal intervallic control. As we accept differences in syntax from one language to another, or differing habits in people, so we can accept these differing methods of composing.

As for form, it is in its nature that there should be many varieties of it. We may recognize what may be called perhaps a new contemporary awareness of form: It is static, rather than progressive, in character. But this is a matter of individual feeling. What is unnatural about a great deal of contemporary music, neo-classicism in particular, is that it is not itself; it is not direct and instantaneously felt in form, but is derivative from whatever models of the past its particular composer chooses.

In the field of structure, the field of the definition of parts and their relation to a whole, there has been only one new idea since Beethoven. And that new idea can be perceived in the work of Anton Webern and Erik Satie. With Beethoven the parts of a composition were defined by means of harmony. With Satie and Webern they are defined by means of time lengths. The question of structure is so basic, and it is so important to be in agreement about it, that one must now ask: Was Beethoven right or are Webern and Satie right?

I answer immediately and unequivocally, Beethoven was in error, and his influence, which has been as extensive as it is lamentable, has been deadening to the art of music.

Now on what basis can I pronounce such a heresy?

It is very simple. If you consider that sound is characterized by its pitch, its loudness, its timbre, and its duration, and that silence, which is the opposite and, therefore, the necessary partner of sound, is characterized only by its duration, you will be drawn to the conclusion that of the four characteristics of the material of music, duration, that is, time length, is the most fundamental. Silence cannot be heard in terms of pitch or harmony: It is heard in terms of time length. It took a Satie and a Webern to rediscover this musical truth, which, by means of musicology, we learn was evident to some musicians in our Middle Ages, and to all musicians at all times (except those whom we are currently in the process of spoiling) in the Orient.

Beethoven represents the most intense lurching of the boat away from its natural even keel. The derivation of musical thought from his procedures has served not only to put us at the mercy of the waves, but to practically shipwreck the art on an island of decadence. Last night, in a discussion, I was willing to grant that there may be different physical evidences of structural principles. Today I will not be so pacific. There can be no right making of music that does not structure itself from the very roots of sound and silence—lengths of time. In India, rhythmic structure is called Tala. With us, unfortunately, it is called a new idea.

How did Webern and Satie come by it is our next question.

Tonality essential to the artificial harmonic structure of Beethoven disintegrated within fifty to seventy-five years, to bring into being the concept of atonality. This, by its denial of the meaning of harmony, required a new structural means or, let us say, the true structural means. Schoenberg provided no structural means, only a method—the twelve-tone system—the nonstructural character of which forces its composer and his followers continually to make negative steps: He has always to avoid those combinations of sound that would refer too banally to harmony and tonality. Satie and Webern went deeper and realized the exact nature of the problem of atonality, which is: How can music be given structure if not through its tonal relations? Their answer: by means of time lengths.

Today we hear two sets of pieces, one by Webern for cello and piano and one by Satie for violin and piano, both written in 1914, one in Vienna, the other in Paris. After hearing my argument that they exhibit the same structural principle, you will be surprised to find them so different in sound. The Webern pieces are extremely short, similar in extent to the chorales of Satie.

Brevity is a characteristic essential to the establishing of a principle. The seed has not the extent of the mature organism.

On this point, let me quote Paul Klee:

> It is a great difficulty and a great necessity to have to start with the smallest. I want to be as though new-born, knowing nothing, absolutely nothing, about Europe; ignoring poets and fashions, to be almost primitive. Then I want to do something very modest; to work out by myself a tiny formal motive, one that my pencil will be able to hold without technique. One favorable moment is enough. The little thing is easily and concisely set down. It's already done! It was a tiny, but real, affair, and someday, through the repetition of such small, but original, deeds, there will come one work upon which I can really build.

Beyond the brevity and unpretentiousness of expression that Webern and Satie have in common (just as Schoenberg and Stravinsky, the composers of our period ordinarily given the laurels I now wish to bestow elsewhere, have length and impressiveness in common), and, beyond their common structural means, there is little to connect them.

Webern's sounds are multicolored. His form is static and fragmentary. His method is one of continuous invention. Satie's sounds are, more often than not, relatively banal. His form, like Webern's, is static, but he is not unwilling to let it be extramusical in its implications. Just as Klee was willing to draw people and plants and animals, so into Satie's continuity come folk tunes, musical clichés, and absurdities of all kinds; he is not ashamed to welcome them in the house he builds: Its structure is strong. His method varies from one period to another, sometimes from one piece to another. And it was in search of method that he studied counterpoint, just as later on Webern adopted Schoenberg's twelve-tone syntax. There was no school that could have taught either of them what each already knew: the structure of music.

Before Beethoven wrote a composition, he planned its movement from one key to another—that is, he planned its harmonic structure. Before Satie wrote a piece, he planned the lengths of its phrases. This evening we hear first Satie's *Things Seen on the Right and on the Left.* It contains a Hypocritical Choral, A Fugue Which is Feeling its Way Along, and a Muscular Fantasy. The Choral has a structure of 5 successive 2-measure phrases. The fugue's rhythmic structure is as follows: a subject and answer of 8 measures each, an episode of 9 measures (1 more than 8), a reappearance of the subject (8 measures), an episode of 10 measures (1 more than 9, which was 1 more than 8), a third appearance of the subject (8 measures) an episode of 14 measures (which is 3 measures more than the expected 11) the subject again (8 measures) an episode of 3 measures (the number indicated by the difference between 14 and 11), a stretto at the measure, which makes this canonic appearance of the subject 9 rather than 8, and a coda of the 3 measures, which, now due to the stretto of 9, has the meaning of resolving in two ways the numerical relation between the numbers characteristic of the subject (8, now 9) and the numbers characteristic of the episodes: 9, 10, 11, 14, and 14-11 equaling 3 (1st: 3 is a simple part of 9; and 2nd: 9 [which 8 has become] is 9). The Muscular Fantasy has a structure that is a play on the numbers 4, 2, and 3 in the following way: three 4's are followed by one 2, four 4's are followed by two 3's; a humorous cadenza is followed by one 4 and one 1, and one 3, followed also by one 1, serves to end the piece.

To conclude: My answers to the questions asked at the beginning (What kinds of things can and ought to be agreed upon? and What kinds of things can and ought not to be agreed upon?) are: Structure can and ought to be agreed upon, and the underlying necessary structure of music is rhythmic. Form cannot and ought not be agreed upon: It is purely a matter of the heart. In the

Orient, it was always arrived at by means of improvisation within the law-giving rhythmic structure. Method and materials may or may not be agreed upon, and it is a matter of indifference whether they are or not.

The function of a piece of music and, in fact, the final meaning of music may now be suggested: it is to bring into co-being elements paradoxical by nature, to bring into one situation elements that can be and ought to be agreed upon—that is, Law elements—together with elements that cannot and ought not to be agreed upon—that is, Freedom elements—these two ornamented by other elements, which may lend support to one or the other of the two fundamental and opposed elements, the whole forming thereby an organic entity.

Music then is a problem parallel to that of the integration of the personality: which in terms of modern psychology is the co-being of the conscious and the unconscious mind, Law and Freedom, in a random world situation. Good music can act as a guide to good living. It is interesting to note that harmonic structure in music arises as Western materialism arises, disintegrates at the time that materialism comes to be questioned, and that the solution of rhythmic structure, traditional to the Orient, is arrived at with us just at the time that we profoundly sense our need for that other tradition of the Orient: peace of mind, self-knowledge.

[Cage's Studio-Home]

This morsel of gossip appeared in Junior Harper's Bazaar *(June, 1946); its point, in this context, is that a truly original imagination lets nothing escape its creativity.*

John Cage is a revolutionary young composer from California. He's been acclaimed for his percussion music and his compositions for "prepared" pianos—he specially arranges them by tempering their strings with all sorts of objects: nails, screws, rubber bands, paper clips, clothespins. Results: curiously archaic music, like ghost harpsichords playing or mice dancing upon piano keys. Forced from his Manhattan studio because the house in which it was located was to be converted, John Cage decided that he would have to find a new studio even better than the old. It would have to be inexpensive, large, light, in Manhattan, and a suitable place in

Copyright *Harper's Bazaar*. Reprinted by permission.

which to live and work. He combed the city, but, of course, he found nothing. Finally he decided to investigate Manhattan's residentially anonymous lower East River shore. Chic Sutton Place had not so long ago been a slum; perhaps there would be something convertible farther down the river. He found that something—a large, dark, obviously impossible loft. It had no kitchen and no bathroom. Although one of the most dramatic vistas in New York stretched out in front of the building, there was no way of looking at it from the loft. Today John Cage has a river view framed by two large windows; he cut them through a blank wall. He has a kitchenette; the entrance to his studio is through this compact little comestible workshop. He has a bathroom, and he has a large studio. Its walls are painted white and there are no decorations—the river scenes dwarf any attempts at hanging pictures. There is a brown-beige studio couch, but no chairs. Cage doesn't like chairs, and his guests like to sit on the straw matting that covers the whole studio floor. There is, of course, a grand piano, replete with working materials essential to Cage's musical compositions. The general effect, despite the absence of decoration and furniture, is one of utter livability. Cage's rent is infinitesimal; his studio is wonderful for work, musicals, and parties (no one complains of the noise), and he has launched a trend in living: Artists, musicians, and writers are beginning to invade slum and industrial districts bordering on the lower East River.

IV 1950–54

So I say, looking back over this record, that John Cage would appear to be the most influential living composer today—whatever opinion you or I may hold about his music. Instead of fighting Cage and laughing loudly at every fresh newspaper's description of his latest escapade, wouldn't it be more sensible to treat him as an aesthetic philosopher—at least, one of the most decisive intelligences of our creative century, a mind so unconventional that before long its very unconvention may *be* the convention?—PETER YATES, "After Modern Music" (1963)

Satie Controversy *John Cage, with a reply by Abraham Skulsky*

These letters on the French composer Erik Satie first appeared in two separate issues of Musical America *(December 15, 1950; April 1, 1951). Cage's later essay on Satie was included in* Silence.

To the Editor:

Over and over again in Satie criticism, the complaint is filed that humor was used as a mask behind which to hide an inability to write music. (Equally outrageously, one might imagine that St. Francis sermonized to birds because of an inability to convey his ideas to other animate beings.) Your last issue of *Musical America* contains an example: The article on Erik Satie by Abraham Skulsky. It seems not to have occurred to Mr. Skulsky, nor to Rollo Myers in his recent book, *Erik Satie*, that Satie may not have been forced but may, on the contrary, have been free to laugh.

When one takes oneself, one's gains and losses, one's popularity and disfavor seriously, it is quite impossible to laugh (except forcedly, or at someone). Satie, however, was disinterested, and was thus able to laugh or weep as he chose. He knew in his loneliness and in his courage where his center was: in himself and in his nature of loving music. There is no great difference between hearing "Consider the lilies of the field, how they toil not, neither do they spin" and a piece by Erik Satie.

Forced, nervous laughter takes place when someone is trying to impress somebody for purposes of getting somewhere. Satie, free of such interest, entitled his first pieces commissioned by a publisher *Three Flabby Preludes for a Dog*. It being fairly clear who is referred to by the word "dog," giving that title was evidently a social act militant in nature, not nonsensical, as Mr. Skulsky would have it.

Mr. Skulsky records that all of Satie's music is humorous, excepting the *Gymnopédies*, the *Sarabandes*, and *Socrate*. This is simply not true. Think, for instance, of the *Nocturnes*, the *Quatre Mélodies*, the *Danses Gothiques*, and other posthumous works, and of *Sylvie* (which, contrary to Mr. Myers's information, has not disappeared, and contrary to Mr. Skulsky's judgment *re* the

Copyright *Musical America*. Reprinted by permission.

Gymnopédies is the first work of the composer to bear the stamp of his originality). In fact, if one tries to think of a funny piece by Satie, it's really tough: *Les Corses*, perhaps the *Embryons Desséchés*, and certainly *La Belle Excentrique*. When Satie used words (cf. T. S. Eliot's "I gotta use words when I talk to you"), his expression was often humorous, always brilliantly imaginative, When he wrote music, he was unexceptionally the art's most serious servant. He performed his tasks simply and unpretentiously. He wrote, more often than not, short pieces, as did Scarlatti and Couperin and, as will, let's hope, etc. . . . (Cf. Paul Klee, who said something about wanting to ignore Europe and about needing to make things small like seeds.)

It appears we have reached the second complaint filed by critics against Satie: He wrote no big works, with the exception of *Socrate*. The length of a work, however, is no measure of its quality or beauty, most of post-Renaissance art-propaganda to the contrary. If we glance momentarily at R. H. Blythe's book on *Haiku* (the Japanese poetic structure of five, seven, and five syllables), we read (p. 272): "Haiku thus makes the greatest demand upon our internal poverty. Shakespeare (cf. Beethoven) pours out his universal soul, and we are abased before his omniscience and overflowing power. Haiku require of us that our soul should find its own infinity within the limits of some finite thing." My mind runs now to Satie's *Vexations*, a short piece to be played 840 times in a row. A performance of this piece would be a measure—accurate as a mirror—of one's "poverty of spirit," without which, incidentally, one loses the kingdom of heaven.

More and more it seems to me that relegating Satie to the position of having been very influential but in his own work finally unimportant is refusing to accept the challenge he so bravely gave us.

Reply by Abraham Skulsky

John Cage's remarks on my article about Satie are typical of the difference of opinion that often prevails between a composer and a critic when both seek to judge the same work or composer. When a composer is related to another composer in character and aesthetic, the judged composer becomes a centrifuge of enthusiasm for the judging composer; the latter tends to regard the works of the former as musically valid in themselves, without reference to surroundings, time, or social significance. The judging composer is quite right in taking this attitude, for his concentration on those aspects of the judged composer's work that affect him, gives him creative impetus toward the achievement of his own ideals.

On the other hand, a critic—especially when he is considering a composer of the past—must take into account various factors of historical development. He must try to find out whether the subject of his judgment was a man of his time, with a normal place in society as it then existed, or whether he was ahead of his time, writing works that were valid only for some later generation.

Nevertheless, I have the impression that John Cage's viewpoint and mine are not as far apart as they may seem to be. We do not appreciate Satie with the same degree of enthusiasm, but we both appreciate him. Mr. Cage, however, attributes to me certain statements for which I look in vain in my article. Where, for instance, did I assert that Satie's laughter was forced, or that he was unable to write music? The expression "laughter as self-defense," which I used, may perfectly well mean free laughter, or even innate and unconscious laughter. As for the charge I am supposed to have made that Satie was unable to compose, what I wrote was that he was unable to attain his ideals—which is quite a different matter. Certainly none of Satie's works reveal compositional shortcomings. But they do suggest the possibility of achievements of bigger scope, which Satie seems to have been unable to undertake. This inability, I think, explains the fact that he went back to study at the age of forty.

I still believe that most of Satie's music is humorous. A piece of music is destined for the audience, which reads the title and creates an association between the title and the music. The audience can hardly be expected to discern serious hidden meanings in such titles as *Flabby Preludes for a Dog* or *Pieces in the Shape of a Pear*. It cannot take seriously such indications as those in *Le Fils des Étoiles*—"Without too much trembling," "Very good," "Fall until weakening," "Ignore your own presence," etc.

As Mr. Cage puts it, Satie was free to laugh, no matter how. This is, I believe, one of the main reasons for the controversy about his music. He loved music and felt himself entirely free. Writing for himself, he became immured in an ivory tower. He not only ignored conventions, publishers, and critics—which did not matter much—he also ignored any real or imagined audience.

Satie influenced many composers, and for this influence I said that he was important. To Debussy and Ravel, Milhaud and Poulenc, Sauguet, Virgil Thomson, and John Cage, he is a great composer. In my view, however, a composer cannot be called great when only a few composers and specialists hold so exalted a view of his merits. The composer's message must reach beyond those who are in the same business.

This Satie's music has not yet done. He was ahead of his time, and 25 years after his death he is still ahead of his time. He gave us significant examples, great hints of new aesthetics; but others developed them and brought them to life. The chief defect of Satie's music is not the smallness of each work, but the smallness of his whole output. This output, influential with three generations of composers, still has not reached today's serious audience through its wall of wit and humor: And until it does reach its audience, I cannot concede that it contains the elements that justify calling its composer great.

More Satie *John Cage*

To the Editor:

Mr. Skulsky's letter in reply to mine (re Satie) was not appetizing; I have delayed answering it until I regained stomach. That having happened, on with the second course in this feast! May we continue until Satie-ated.

Mr. Skulsky's letter resounds with ideas and attitudes that have nothing whatsoever to do with art: e.g. (I quote): "surroundings, time, social significance"; "achievement of his own ideals"; "various factors of historical development"; "normal place in society"; "audience"; "the composer's message (!) (exclamation point mine) must reach beyond those who are in the same business" (nuts) (the nuts are mine too); "ahead of his time"; "great hints of new aesthetics"; "others developed them and brought them to life" (What? Who? Where?) (monosyllabic questions are mine); "the smallness of his output" (Mr. Skulsky is thinking—that is, of course, the source of his difficulty—of Satie as some kind of a small unsuccessful business man who had a few bright ideas about manufacturing music, but who never managed to get going into "really good" production—actually Satie wrote about twenty-eight hours of music; leaving out *Vexations*, which lasts for twelve hours and ten minutes, he wrote circa fourteen hours of music which is nothing to sneeze at (Webern would not have sneezed; Varèse doesn't; but Mr. Skulsky, who has a cold when it comes to Satie, "cannot concede that it [Satie's work] contains the elements that justify calling its composer great." And so he says, "Writing for himself, he [Satie] became immured in an ivory tower."

Now, for Mr. Skulsky's information (and incidentally *Musical America*'s, too), let it be said that art is not a business; *if* it is, it is "swinishness" (I quote Antonin Artaud) and nothing more. *Art is a way of life.* It is for all the world like taking a bus, picking flowers, making love, sweeping the floor, getting bitten by a monkey, reading a book, etc., ad infinitum (business may also provide a way of life, but in that case, it has nothing to do with profit and loss).

The old pond,
A frog jumps in,
Plop!

(BASHO)

When life is lived, there is nothing in it but the present, the "now-moment" (I quote Meister Eckhart); it is thus impossible to speak of being ahead of one's time or of historical development. When life is lived, each one is "the most honored of all creatures" (I quote the Buddha), living in "the best of all possible worlds" (I quote Voltaire), and when this is done there is "no silliness" (I quote my former wife, Xenia Cage). Art when it is art as Satie lived it and made it is not separate from life (nor is dishwashing when it is done in this spirit).

If, however, art *is* a competitive business as Mr. Skulsky intimates, then on with the ivory, and up with the towers, and the quicker the better!

Satie, however, never lived in an ivory tower, nor does any artist of his quality ever need to: for there is nothing in life from which he separates himself. Satie was as at home in a night club as in a church. An ivory tower is "heaven" (I quote X. C. again), but an artist (if sides are taken) is necessarily on the side of hell (I quote William Blake).

An artist as artist has as his "highest responsibility" (I quote W. H. Blythe) "the hiding of beauty" (compare Skulsky's "great hints of new aesthetics") and as man the "knowing of himself" (I quote Socrates) which brings us back "past riverrun" (I quote James Joyce) to Satie's *Socrate* and the shocking fact that we haven't heard it yet in NYC 1951. The publishers, "the dogs" (I quote Satie), have not even made its score available for our ocular pleasure. I hope publishers and performers hurry, for I myself am bored with Satie. The music I love now (besides what I myself am currently writing) is that being written by Pierre Boulez, by Morton Feldman, and by Christian Wolff, and these attachments (passionate) are not, as Abraham Skulsky would have it, related to the "achievement of my ideals," for I have none. There is not a moment in life as far as any one of us is concerned that is not "ideal" and in a state of successful and utter "achievement." To think otherwise would be to be in hell rather than in league with it, which latter state turns the tables bringing about "The (eternal) Marriage." Dear Skulsky, rejoice! for at any moment, you may see the light. You will then love Satie wholeheartedly.

P. S. I read the above to a friend over the phone. She said, it's all right until you come to that part about Boulez, Feldman, and Wolff. I said, what's wrong then? She said, it invalidates everything you've said because it's like a brick. I said, I'll think it over. I did and saw that the letter is full of bricks. Bricks have the function of hitting blocks, but, glory be! they sometimes knock them off. Among the truths that Satie expressed in words was "Show me a new idea—I'll give up everything I've ever done and start all over again." Since Feldman, Boulez, and Wolff are doing precisely that (presenting new ideas), Satie would be the first to agree that an article about him in 1951 would of necessity broadcast the names Feldman, Wolff, and Boulez.

Current Chronicle *Henry Cowell*

Cage remained closest to Cowell of all his teachers; and the elder composer wrote the first extended essay on his wayward pupil's work. Still the most incisive and detailed study of Cage's early music, this originally appeared in The Musical Quarterly *(January, 1952)*.

When I first met John Cage about 1932, he was writing strange little piano pieces with an unusual sense of the sound interest created by odd tonal combinations. Then, as now, the music showed little desire to move about actively; it rather depended on very slight and subtle changes for its elaboration. Influences to which he subjected himself in the mid-1930's enlarged and enriched, without changing, this orientation. He studied dissonant counterpoint and composition with me for a season in California, and, when he went to New York to prepare with Adolph Weiss for lessons with Schoenberg, he continued intensive explorations of his

Copyright *The Musical Quarterly*. Reprinted by permission.

own into rhythmic form and percussion music, and the musical systems of other peoples, particularly in the Orient, in my classes at the New School. Later, he studied with Schoenberg, who felt that Cage was more interested in his philosophy than in acquiring his techniques. Since then, Cage has written a great deal for the dance, and he has organized percussion orchestras to play music especially composed by himself and other people. Some of his more recent music uses conventional instrumentation for string quartet and for small orchestra. Concerts of his music are a regular feature of the season in New York and, for the past several years, in Paris also, where his music has been extravagantly admired.

To John Cage, a brief series of sounds, or even a single combination of them, has come to seem complete in itself, and to constitute an audible "event." But he does not use the conventional organization of music, in which such events are related through planned rhythmic, melodic, and harmonic succession to produce what we are accustomed to consider an organic musical development. Instead, since Cage conceives each musical "event" to be an entity in itself that does not require completion, he simply places them one after another and sees them as being related through their coexistence in space, where they are set in a planned order of time. Each "event" is an aggregate of materials of sound that cohere, making a tiny world of their own, much as physical elements find themselves joined together in a meteorite. A work of Cage's, therefore, might well be likened to a shower of meteors of sound.

Cage's pieces for what he calls the "prepared piano" offer an array of tightly organized little sounds of many colors. They are played on an ordinary grand piano whose strings have been muted at various specified points with bits of wood, rubber, metal, or glass. These mutes produce a variety of timbres, whose pitch and tone quality are entirely altered from those of the unmuted strings. Each piece may have its own recipe for the arrangement of the altered sounds, a kind of tone-row of timbres. They suggest the sound of the gamelan or the jalatarang, with some delicate buzzes, clacks, hums, and sometimes an unaltered tone as well. The player is guided by a piano score that is read and played entirely conventionally but produces, of course, sounds entirely different from those suggested to the eye, in accordance with the mechanical preparation for the particular piece.

In spite of his idea of the separateness of musical "events," Cage has always had an intense interest in rhythmic structure, in absolute time values, and in the dynamics of sound and silence. His wide palette of minuscule timbres, used in what may be thought of as melodic succession, is made rhythmical by the recurrence of such successions. This is the most noticeable aspect of Cage's music on first hearing. What is less obvious is that for many years his works' larger rhythmical forms have been based on one or another set division of absolute time, such as a unit of sixty seconds. For example, a five-minute work may be divided into five sections of one minute each, and each of these one-minute sections may then be divided into five phrases of twelve seconds each. The tempo may be varied by the performer in accordance with any scheme of his own, just so the large units of the work take exactly the specified number of seconds, no more and no less. This basis for establishing form can be found in Cage's prepared piano music, in the piece for twelve radios, and in much of his other music as well.

Enough amused curiosity to overflow McMillan Theater at Columbia University was aroused when the first performance of John Cage's *Imaginary Landscape,* a composition for twelve radios, took place last spring. This was not a broadcast of Cage's music played at and transmitted from one, or from twelve, radio stations. Twelve radios were, instead, to be treated like musical instruments and played in concert. How does one turn a radio into a musical instrument? This was not entirely clear in advance, so avant-garde New York appeared in person to find out.

On the stage were the twelve radios, with two players at each, and the composer-conductor—twenty-five people in all. The score calls for one performer to manipulate the dial that selects the various stations desired by the composer to be heard in the course of the work, and another performer for the dial that regulates the dynamics. The composer's directions for tuning the various stations in and out use notes and rests; the wave length for each station is indicated in kilocycles. Therefore if the piece is played in New York City, one set of stations will be drawn upon; if in Denver, another set of stations, the ones using the same wavelengths in that locality, will be heard. The player who regulates the dynamics follows indications in the score that correspond to numbers along the dial from zero up, producing a dynamic range from the barest whisper to a full *fortissimo.* Like the choice of wavelengths, the dynamics have definite rhythmic indications.

This is a music in which some elements customarily imprecise, such as dynamics and rubato, and everything on which form depends, are indicated with the greatest exactness. Melodic lines, harmonies, and instrumentation, which we have come to expect the composer to interest himself in controlling precisely, are on the other hand entirely determined by the accident of radio station programming.

At the actual performance of *Imaginary Landscape*, the hour was later than anticipated before the work's turn came on the program, so that the "instruments" were unable to capture programs diversified enough to present a really interesting specific result. Members of the performing group said that some of the rehearsals captured much more exciting ingredients for the montage, and expressed regret that a recording of one or two of the practice sessions was not played at the concert instead. Cage's own attitude about this was one of comparative indifference, since he believes the concept to be more interesting than the result of any single performance. One aspect of the work's failure to communicate must be laid frankly at the composer's door: His ever-present interest in the most delicately minute distinctions and gradations led him to admit too many low amplitude dynamics, through setting their range too low to begin with, so that many parts could not be heard at all as far away as the audience.

The dynamics of silence, a relativity of silence as well as of sound, expressed by rests and extreme *pianissimi*, is a major concern in most of Cage's music. This feeling for the rhythmical pregnancy of silence seems an ultimate sophistication. In primitive music, beats must always be actually sounded; as music becomes more elaborately cultivated there are more and more places in which the beat, once established, may be taken for granted. Sometimes in the improvisatory jam sessions of jazz players, there will be, by agreement, at fixed intervals in the music, a sudden two-measure silence, after which everyone comes in full tilt with gusto. Obviously the exact duration of two measures and their division into beats must be forcefully present in the minds of the performers during that silence. Cage enjoys presenting longer and more complex silences in the course of his works. Sometimes he leads one toward absolute silence by increasingly greater degrees of softness, until one can hardly tell whether one is really hearing anything or not.

As this article was being written, George Antheil called my attention to the score of his *Ballet Mécanique*, which has a section in which silent measures of 8/8 appear periodically. This was written in 1924, and its generative ideas derived from long sessions spent with George Herzog in Berlin, listening to recordings of the music of India, China, and more primitive cultures. Around this time Antheil developed an interest in the time-space concept and music in absolute time; Ezra Pound's book on Antheil gives an account of these theories.*

In Cage's recent (fall, 1951) *Music of Changes*, for piano solo, he uses this instrument without special "preparation" for the first time in many years. He does not abandon his predilection for extraordinary sound, for at almost no point does the piano sound as one expects. Rather he seems now to be interested in discovering how nearly like a prepared piano he can make an unprepared piano sound, by means of special tone combinations, timbres, and dynamics. An original feature is that highly controlled changes of tempo are used to establish the rhythmic structure. One starts at a given metronome mark (quarter note = 69), then accelerates for 3 measures to quarter = 176, then retards for 5 measures to quarter = 100 for 13½ measures, then retards 5 measures to quarter = 58, and so on. The form is thus presented in terms of a sliding scale of tempos rather than by an arrangement of fixed numbers of measures to constitute phrases, sentences, and sections. Note durations, often complex, are measured horizontally with 2½ centimeters to equal a dotted quarter note. Measurements are made from one note stem to another. Precisely noted dynamic extremes (*pppp* and *ffff* are sometimes next to each other in eighth notes) help to make *Music of Changes* an unprecedented experience in sound.

If these pieces by a single composer were the only ones of the sort to appear now, interest in them might be more casual. They are, however, examples of a new approach to composition that has drawn a number of adherents, all of them younger men who are friends or students of Cage; several of them have had works performed in New York recently. The compositions of Christian Wolff, Morton Feldman, Pierre Boulez, and John Cage vary widely in style, but a common philosophy unites them: a concentration upon unfamiliar relationships of space and time, and sound and silence, rather than on new melodies and chords, and a conviction that all musical relationships, whether arrived at by chance or by design, have potential value and are worth examination. They all believe there should be more room in music for improvisatory factors, for the elements of casual choice and chance.

In their hands, however, chance is called upon to operate sys-

* *George Antheil and the Theory of Harmony*, Paris, 1925. See also Antheil's discussions of time-space and absolute time in music in *De Stijl* (Rotterdam, 1924–25), *Transition* (Paris, 1925), and the *Little Review* (1925).

tematically. Cage has often used the *I Ching,** an old Chinese method of throwing coins or marked sticks for chance numbers, like our use of dice. Cage's method of employing the *I Ching* to ensure that his compositions are "free of individual taste and memory in their order of events" is based on a complicated system of charts. These govern "superpositions" (the number of events happening at once during a given structural space), tempos, durations, sounds, and dynamics; and all the charts are derived from tosses of the coins.

The concrete operation to produce the *Imaginary Landscape* for twelve radios proceeded more or less as follows: "The first tossing related to superposition and tempo of a certain tuning, and the second tossing related to structure; the third tossing to duration (whether sound or silence), and, finally, dynamics." The actual tossings brought a form represented by 8 plus 4 plus 15, repeated 25 times. Dynamics ranging from *ppppp* to *sffffz* are selected by further tossings, and applied to the station-selecting (wave-length tuning) dial of the radio (upper numbers in Ex. 1) and the dial-controlling dynamic amplitudes (lower numbers in Ex. 1). Because the figures obtained in this way do not always correspond to the center of the band for any given station, the station might happen to be heard rather vaguely, from the peripheral point along the dial that was established by the tossing. Similarly, the amplitude numbers are sometimes too low for audibility. Cage, however, insists on consistency in allowing the operation of chance, and sticks faithfully to its decisions. Thus chance determines whether things remain static or change, what type of change is to occur, whether there is an event or a silence, whether a given radio will play or not, whether the dynamics will vary or remain constant: and, if they change, which of the dynamics will apply. And chance, operating in another way, is also responsible, of course, for what will be heard on the twelve radios. No one can say in advance what tunes, rhythms, chords, timbres, or other simultaneous elements of the heterophony will be contributed to any given performance. All one can be sure of is that they will never be twice alike.

The station selection and dynamic structure, once tossed for, are, of course, retained; and this constitutes the composition, if composition it be.

Various combinations of chance and choice, pre-established or improvised, are not without respectable musical precedent, in the

* See *I Ching, Book of Changes,* translated from the Chinese by Cary Baynes, New York: Bollingen Series XIX, Pantheon Books, 1950.

Ex. 1

tala and raga systems of India, and possibly, on a less serious plane, in the music of Mozart. Mozart is said to have composed a set of country dances in which dice are to be thrown to determine the order in which the measures are to appear. Ex. 2a shows Mozart's chart, and Ex. 2b the directions for using it. However, Mozart eliminated many of the hazards accepted by Cage, for he composed and set down all the measures that might be called for by the dice; a typical collection of opening measures for the first cast, a typical set of second measures for the second cast, and so on. Otto Luening has an early work in which there is a plan for partly controlled improvisation; Charles Ives wants performers to

Ex. 2a

Zahlentafel.
Table de Chiffres.

	A	B	C	D	E	F	G	H
2	70	14	164	122	25	153	18	167
3	10	64	100	12	149	30	161	11
4	33	1	160	163	77	156	168	172
5	36	114	8	35	111	39	137	44
6	105	150	57	71	117	52	132	130
7	165	152	112	15	147	27	73	102
8	7	81	131	37	21	125	49	115
9	142	106	40	69	43	140	23	89
10	99	68	86	139	120	92	143	83
11	85	45	90	158	82	123	78	58
12	145	97	6	121	56	67	63	16

Ex. 2b

INSTRUCTION

To compose, without the least knowledge of Music, Country-dances, by throwing a certain Number with two Dice.

1.) The Letters A--H, placed at the head of the 8 Columns of the Number-Tables show the 8. times of each part of the Country-Dance, Viz. A, the first, B, the second, C, the third, &c: and the Numbers in the Column under the Letters show the Number of the time in the Notes.

2.) The Numbers form 2. to 12, show the sum of the Number than can be thrown.

3.) For instance, in throwing for the first time of the first part of the Dance, with two Dice, the Number 6, one looks next to that Number in the Column A, for the 105th. time in the Notes. This time is written down, and makes the beginning of the Dance. — For the second time, for instance, the Number 8, being thrown, turn to the same table Column B, and the Number 81. shall be found. This time is put next to the first, & one continues, in this manner till the eight times shall be thrown, when likewise the first part of the Dance shall be finish'd. — The sign of repetition is further placed & the second part begun.

feel free to make certain kinds of changes in his music, under some circumstances.

Ex. 3 shows the opening of Morton Feldman's *Intersection* No. 3, for strings, woodwinds, and solo cello. It is written on coordinate paper, the squares taken horizontally representing a time-unit of M.M. = 72.

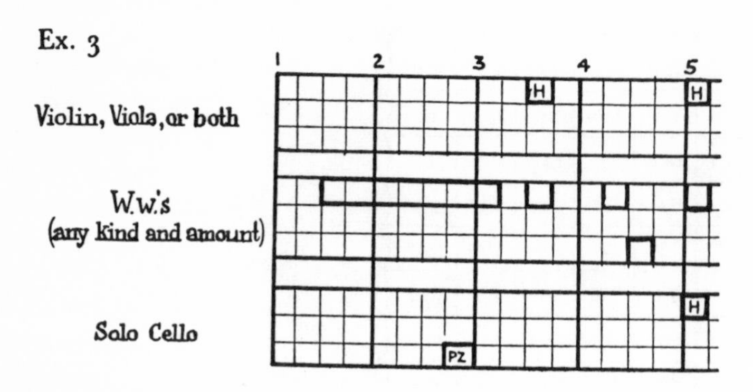

Vertically, each of the three squares represents a general pitch level: low, medium, and high. Each instrument comes in when its part has a blocked-in square; it may enter at any time during the period represented by the square, but, once it has entered, the tone or tones must remain until the blocked-in square ends. Sometimes the composer indicates by an H that he wishes a harmonic, or by Pz that a pizzicato tone would be appreciated. But the actual pitches and their duration are entirely left to the players in all other respects. So a conservative group will employ familiar types of sound, and some "modernists" might employ the less familiar. This is a plan for the control of improvisation and the music will of course never sound twice alike. Its success depends upon what the players contribute.

I should like to follow the above strictly lay account with Mr. Feldman's own statement about his set of pieces:

> My *Projections and Intersections* is a weight either reminiscent or discovered. Weight for me does not have its source in the realm of dynamics or tensions, but rather resulting from a visual-aural response to sound as an image gone inward creating a general synthesis. Weight involves the finding of a pulse which allows for a natural fluidity. Discovered weight implies discovered balance. Discovered balance implies discovered movement from this pulse. The notation is presented graphically where each box is a clock-time duration. What is desired in the execution is a pure nonvibrating tone.

Ex. 4 shows the first four measures of a trio for flute, clarinet, and violin by Christian Wolff. Only three different tones are used. No two measures are alike; the changes are rung on the possible combinations of three tones on three instruments, in various rhythms. Listening becomes a reaction to the intricacies of these variations. An interest in exploring all the possibilities of certain musical materials handled within strict limits is characteristic of the thinking of this entire group of composers.

It will be observed that Wolff's concept of variability in the order of measures is especially close to that of the coin tossers.

Pierre Boulez, a young Frenchman whose *Second Sonata* was played in New York at a League of Composers concert not long ago, and John Cage met in Paris, exchanged ideas, and have since spent much time together. Cage says: "Boulez influenced me with his concept of mobility; my influence on him is that he accepts my idea of aggregates." An aggregate in Cage's sense is the relationship of miscellaneous and apparently disparate objects established by their juxtaposition in space, as furniture and other objects in a room are related by their simultaneous presence there. Similarly, different sorts of musical media may be conceived as constituting an aggregate, and so used as a unit of building material for the creation of musical forms.

Boulez deals with what he calls the drama of the contrast between the thematic (tone relations derived in a rather distant fashion from the twelve-tone-row) and the athematic (rhythmic essence). A basic rhythmic unit he calls a cellule; this consists of some related time values (a quarter note plus an eighth note, for instance). Each of these time elements may be "developed" by subdivision, the quarter note then becoming 2 eighths, or a triplet, or 4 sixteenths, and so on. Boulez's rhythmic process has been described by a nonbeliever as "dividing two rhythmic units into as many small notes as possible, tossing the notes into the air, then

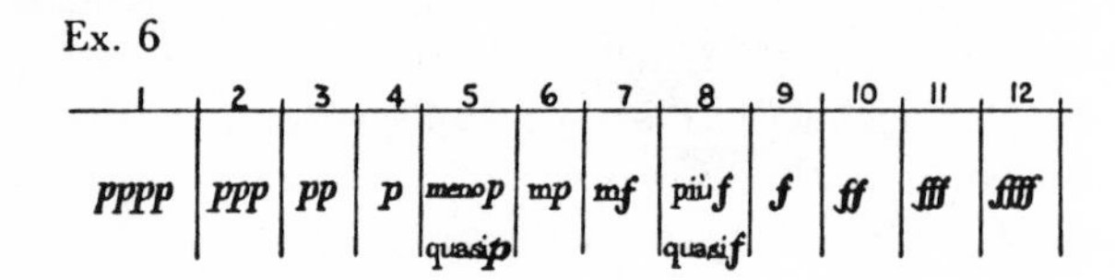

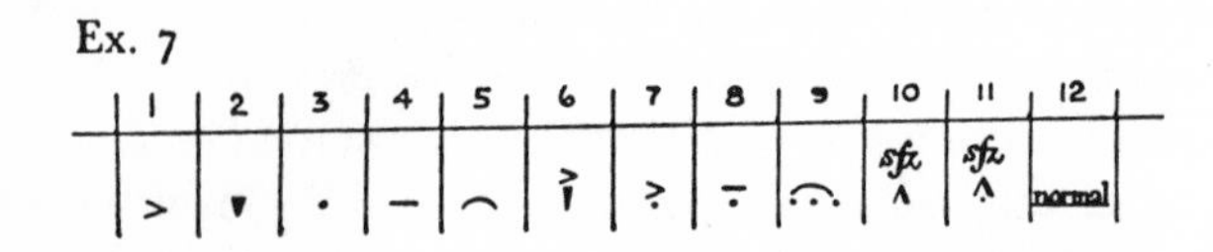

Ex. 8

1 2 3 4 5 6 7 8 9 10 11 12

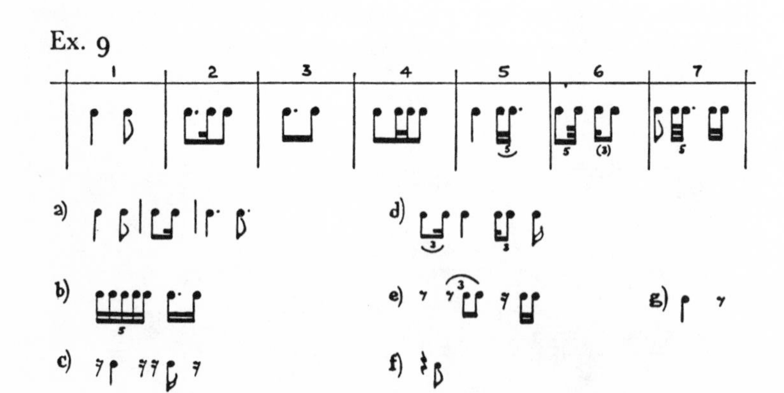

taking them the way they light, and calling it a composition." On the other hand, recent Paris performances of music by Boulez have had sufficient impact to generate comment circulated in this country by the big press services.

Boulez's main investigations have been into extensions of the twelve-tone-row idea. By changing the row numbers according to his plan, he may obtain a complete transposition (Ex. 5); and, for formal unity, he applies his row to dynamics (Ex. 6), stresses (Ex. 7), duration (Ex. 8), and rhythmic figures (cellules) (Ex. 9).

John Cage speaks for all these young men when he voices enthusiasm over freeing musical continuity from "individual taste and memory," and from "the literature and traditions of the art." It is in the accomplishment of perfection along these severely logical, if hitherto uncharted, unaccustomed paths that Cage and his friends employ their creative fervor, even in the case of the more subjective Feldman. Shocking as it may seem to their elders, it is certainly true that, for these young men, no fact or set of factual aggregates is incapable of giving aesthetic pleasure under some circumstances.

However, it is evident that much more remains to be done in this direction, for in spite of his best efforts to the contrary, Cage has not succeeded in eliminating his highly refined and individual taste from the music derived from the *I Ching*. Unfortunately, from the point of view of this group of composers, no order of tossings can give anything more than a variety of arrangements of elements subjectively chosen to operate upon.

Since it can be shown that Cage and his friends have come together at one time in one room, the group may be considered an aggregate. So we may toss to decide whether the group is to change or to remain the same, and toss again to decide whether the aesthetic pleasure to be derived from the work of its members is to play the role of silence or of an event in sound.

And if one must decide whether genuine value is, or is not, to be found in this music, a last throw of the coins of *I Ching* will have to determine that for us, too.

Inferential Art *Richard Kostelanetz*

This excerpt, which opens an essay on "Inferential Art" originally written in 1967 but not published until 1969 (and then reprinted in the author's Metamorphosis in the Arts

© 1969 Richard Kostelanetz. Reprinted by permission.

[1971]), discusses the significance of Cage's most outraging composition, 4′ 33″, performed in its initial form only thrice —in Woodstock, New York, in 1952 (see illustrated program); at Carl Fischer Hall, in New York City in 1954; and in Cologne, Germany, in 1956; each time with David Tudor at the piano. Cage recently admitted that he first conceived of the piece in the late 1940's but hesitated to present it then. The paradox familiar to modern art is that a work first regarded as a joke, particularly by critics, now earns the respect of unashamedly serious aesthetic criticism.

Among the more profound intentions of contemporary vanguard art is the continual questioning of traditional definitions, procedures, and values—in music and poetry, painting and sculpture, as well as even "Art" itself. In a radical metamorphosis, this traditionally critical task has been assimilated by a particular kind of creative work, which, though negligible in itself, manages to imply (and, thus, have inferred from it) a challenge to conventional rationales. Art of this kind usually presents an appearance that might at first seem prosaic, if not stupid—a piece of concert music without any sound, a field of painted canvas with absolutely no contrasting marks, a dance without any movement, and so forth; yet precisely in a disarming pretense of idiocy is a mask for deeper speculative concerns that may not be immediately, or even intrinsically, evident. Of course, all art embodies implications, but only certain rare works successfully express far more inference than artistry. In inferential art, as I shall call it, the work's aesthetic implications, which are usually deduced by reasoning, are many times more significant than its ontological interest or achieved craftsmanship; therefore, only through our recognition of these implications does idiocy reveal unusual and perhaps profound intelligence.

A work of inferential art often offers no path into its meanings; but, once an outside source, either the artist or a fellow spectator, informs us of its implied theme (or, more rarely, we deduce it ourselves), we not only recognize the inference but appreciate other things besides. That is, in addition to serving a polemical function in an aesthetic argument, these works usually possess the capability of initiating sensory perceptions where the spectator initially discerned chaos or nothing at all; and some of them, once understood, induce an experience that includes, but transcends, aesthetic apprehensions as it is traditionally conceived. Inferential art, by definition, implies the creation of an object or perceptual experience to demonstrate, or generate, the particular idea; for meanings alone belong to pure philosophy or criticism. The problem in appreciating inferential art is generally not that we are ignorant—none of the works described here require particularly complex or educated modes of perception—but, rather, that we are too thoroughly imbued with ideas about what art should be to grasp such works immediately. Once we learn to appreciate an example of inferential art, it, in turn, continues to educate us.

In modern music, the idea of using a musical composition as a substitute manifesto extends back at least to the Italian-born German composer Ferruccio Busoni, who, early in the twentieth century, created several works primarily about the use of semitones and the development of wholly original scales; and perhaps because these works were designed to be little more than experiments, Busoni's polemic had small subsequent influence, and these pieces have since disappeared from the modern repertoire. (Johann Sebastian Bach's *Well-Tempered Clavier*, supposedly written in haste to demonstrate the efficacy of a new system of keyboard tuning, has, in contrast, survived.) The later experiments of Busoni's pupil the French-born American composer Edgard Varèse similarly integrated polemical designs into a musical work; for his *Ionisation* (1930) implied the question of whether nonmusical sound sources could be legitimate "instruments" in serious composition. At the time, this implication probably seemed more important than the sounds produced; however, the answer to the implied question was so affirmative that this piece, along with others, entered the modern canon and, along with others, initiated a readjustment in musical consciousness. "Noise," or nonpitched sounds, has since become a staple of the musical idiom—something most ears have learned to accept, if not appreciate.

In recent American music, the most consequential example of inferential art has been John Cage's *4′ 33″* (1952), in which David Tudor comes to the piano and just sits for four minutes and thirty-three seconds, silently deploying his arms three times in ways that suggest the work might have three distinct movements. Admittedly, a distinguished-looking gentleman before an unplayed piano provides limited aural interest; but, by importing this nonmusical image into a concert situation in which musical sounds are expected, Cage's piece implies that the "music" consists of all the accidental noises in the room, whether humanly produced or not. Therefore, whereas a spectator originally observed that the piece contained no music at all, once he grasps the implications of *4′ 33″*, he can infer that literally everything he hears within that frame of four minutes and thirty-three seconds belongs to the piece. Among the anomalies of inferential art is that a single hearing or a glance can provide someone with a description of the piece—the absence of declarative content—that is perfectly accurate and yet superficial; for such a summary hardly explains, or even confronts, the real meaning of the work.

Moreover, the theme inferred from Cage's piece implies three further corollaries. The first holds that, in all performed pieces, what is written as a silent passage is actually filled with extraneous sound (noise), because pure silence is physically impossible; therefore, every piece of music we hear contains sound both intentional and non-intentional—not only what was written in the score, but also what was inadvertently produced in the auditorium (or even at home) during the piece's duration. From this follows the rather obvious idea that no musical piece can twice give us exactly the same aural experience. The third major corollary of *4′ 33″* is that accidental noise and humanly produced music have equal status within a listening experience; thus, just as it is difficult to discern whether one arrangement of non-intentional music is "better" than another, so it is perhaps equally unrealistic to use similarly evaluative terms with intentional sounds.

In addition to generating these aesthetic inferences, Cage's non-intentional piece intends to make us revise our sensory receptivity, in order that we may continually appreciate all the "music" that is constantly present in our environment. "My favorite piece," Cage once said, "is the one we hear all the time if we are quiet." Thus, although *4′ 33″* may at first strike many people as a joke—and outside of its original concert-hall context it would indeed be frivolous—immediate impressions here only deceive an innocent spectator into missing its extraordinary richness. Among the profound purposes we can infer from *4′ 33″* is a redefinition of musical art and the enhancement of our everyday aural lives.

In nonsense there is often great sense, modern art tells us over and over again; for human intelligence invariably imposes significance upon absurdity. It was Harold Rosenberg who shrewdly discerned that the central difference between the original comic-strip figure and the same image in pop art was that the latter "was painted for a museum with an eye to art history." Or, as the literary critic Hugh Kenner quipped in *The Stoic Comedians* (1967), "Nor is it easy to decide whether a man who has made a banknote is a government employee, a counterfeiter, or a pop artist, unless we have evidence of how he meant his work to be regarded." These comments point up the crucial difference between Cage's silent piece and, say, one by me—why we can infer such meanings in his negations, and why serious people will inconvenience themselves to experience his rather than mine. And were I to stage four-and-one-half minutes of no-sound in 1969, everyone *au courant* would justifiably accuse me of plagiarizing "Cage's piece."

[*Williams Mix*] *John Cage*

This note sketches Cage's compositional processes in one of the first electronic pieces composed in this country, Williams Mix *(1952).*

This is the fifth page of the *Williams Mix*. It is a full-size drawing of 8 tracks of ¼-inch magnetic tape running at 15 inches per second. It is intended as a pattern for the cutting and splicing of tape-recorded sounds. These sounds are catalogued as A (city sounds), B (country sounds), C (electronic sounds), D (manually produced sounds, including the literature of music), E (wind-produced sounds, including songs) and F (small sounds requiring amplification to be heard with the others).

They are further catalogued in terms of pitch, timbre, and loudness: When one of these has been controlled or is known, a "c" designates this; absence of control or unpredictability is designated by a "v." Thus, Dvvv (first system, track 1) is a manually produced sound, the pitch, timbre, and loudness of which have not been controlled. Underlining of the capital letter indicates that the tape has rhythmic pattern characteristics (produced by rerecording a loop of tape). Electronically mixed sounds have double designations, e.g., BvcvCcvv (first system, track 2).

The categories overlap. For example, the sound of laughter might be catalogued A, B, or E. Nevertheless, the system served to establish a library. Any other set of sounds, answering the same designations, could be used to make another *Williams Mix*.

The composing means employed chance operations derived from the *I Ching* (Chinese *Book of Changes*). These means, as they pertain to two earlier works, *Music of Changes* for piano solo and *Imaginary Landscape No. IV* for twelve radios, are described in detail in *trans/formation* (Vol. 1 No. 3). Briefly, three coins tossed six times give one or two numbers from 1 to 64. Separate charts were made having 64 elements, one to determine the rhyth-

Text reprinted by courtesy of George Avakian.

mic structure (11 times 46 divided 5, 6, 16, 3, 11, 5), another to determine factors that shortened or lengthened the structural parts, 16 for sounds and silences, 16 for durations, 16 for attack and decay of sounds. Another chart determined how many of the 16 were active within a given structural division. There being only 8 tracks, 8 active at one time brought about maximum density, 16 maximum fragmentation.

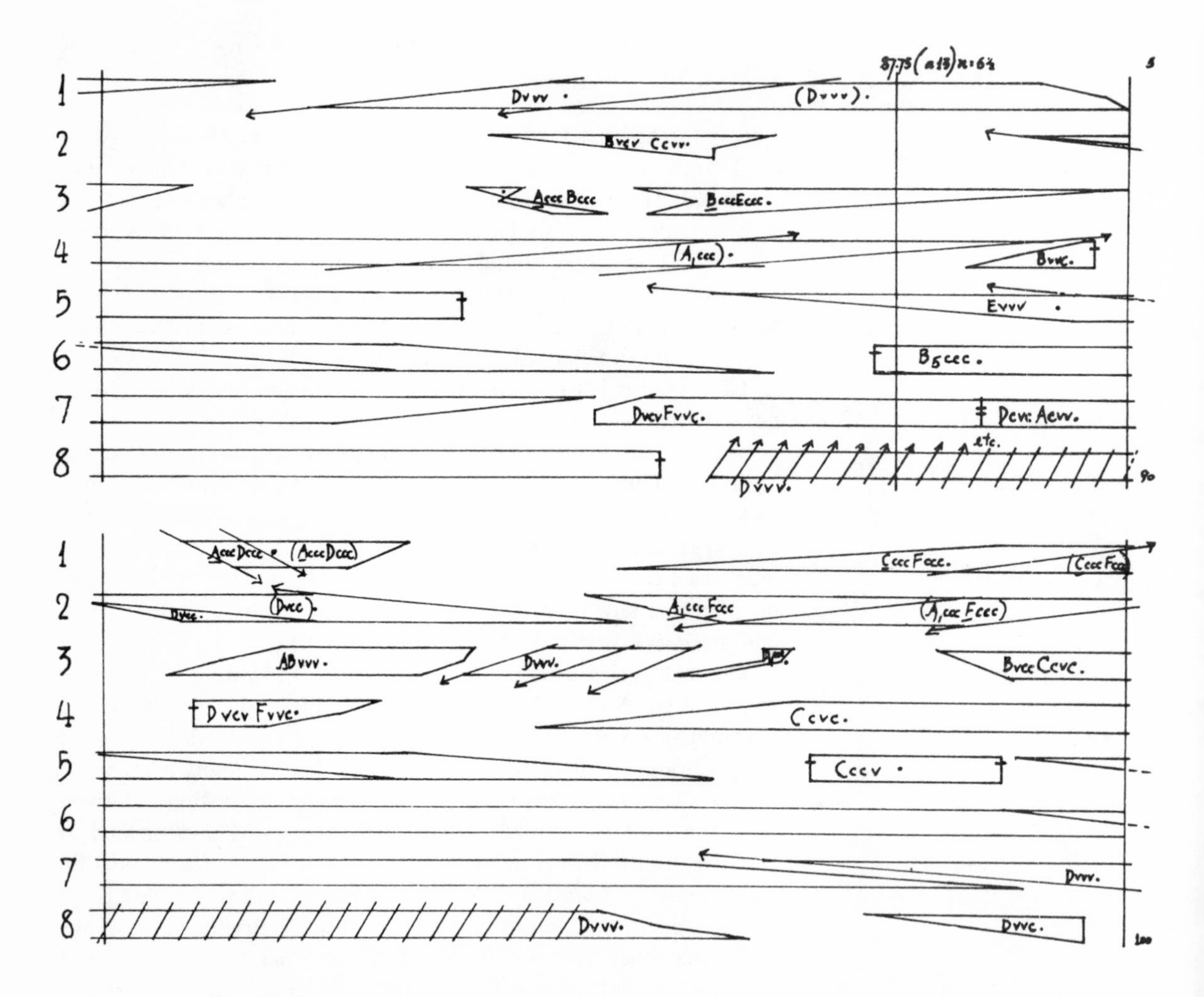

Diagram of *Williams Mix.*

Copyright 1960 by Henmar Press, Inc., New York.

At the beginning of each of the 11 structural units, it was determined which of the 16 charts (the even- or the odd-numbered) were mobile and which immobile. If a chart was mobile, an element in it, once used, disappeared, giving rise to a new one; if immobile and used, remained to be used again. The replenishing of the mobile charts was from a deck of appropriate cards (giving a sound, a duration, or a pattern of attack or decay, each obtained by permutation of possibilities but not previously employed in the charts). These cards had been shuffled in a way conventional to the Tarot.

The vertical bar in the first system indicates the beginning of the third structural part. The following information is given above it; its position in inches from the beginning (5.85 seconds); the number of charts to be used; and the factor (n) which multiplied by 16 (the third number of the rhythmic structure) established the length in inches of the third section.

[Robert Rauschenberg] *John Cage*

To those puzzled by its exhibition of Robert Rauschenberg's notorious White Paintings late in 1953, the Stable Gallery extended the following statement, written by Cage, who returned to the subject of his friend's art in another essay written several years later and published in Silence.

To whom
No subject
No image
No taste
No object
No beauty
No message
No talent
No technique (no why)
No idea
No intention
No art
No feeling
No black
No white (no *and*)

From Emily Genauer's column. Reprinted with her permission.

After careful consideration, I have come to the conclusion that there is nothing in these paintings that could not be changed, that they can be seen in any light and are not destroyed by the action of shadows.

JOHN CAGE

Hallelujah! the blind can see again; the water's fine.

V 1955–59

To trace the genealogy of pop art, one must recreate the atmosphere in which it came into being. That atmosphere was generated mainly by the composer John Cage, whose essays and lectures have been instrumental in forming the sensibility of some of the most important young composers, choreographers, painters, and sculptors at work today. Cage's aesthetic, derived in equal parts from Dada and Zen, in many respects served to open a situation that had closed down, much in the manner that Surrealism helped open the door to Abstract Expressionism.—BARBARA ROSE, *American Art Since 1900* (1968)

On Film *John Cage*

The following text was written for the Creative Film Foundation in New York City, and delivered as remarks at a meeting on April 6, 1956. It appears here in print for the first time.

I am interested in any art not as a closed-in thing by itself but as a going-out one to interpenetrate with all other things, even if they are arts too. All of these things, each one of them seen as of first importance; no one of them as more important than another. In theater, as Artaud points out, it is death to place literature in the only central position; and so I do not agree that "film is a visual form." The images don't interest me any more than the sound. Nor am I interested in the artistic arrangement of sound to go with or against the images. All that comes about in a successful such situation is a composite of two, not an imitation (which is the artist's traditional responsibility) of nature in her manner of operation as, in our time, her operation is revealed. The life situation from a natural, rather than anthropomorphic, view is more complex than art or putting arts together tastefully. The ancient Chinese knew this, and, in speaking of art, the *I Ching* remarks that the really important problems require greater earnestness.

The sound materials available now through magnetic tape are virtually unlimited. Anything can be done, if you can manage to put your hands on the machines and to get a corps of workers together and keep them alive while they are working. With magnetic tape, the possibility exists to use the literature of music as material (cutting it up, transforming it, etc.); this is the best thing that could have happened to it. Ordinary film music is ignored by the average person because he assumes that it is (film is) a visual form. He is therefore not entirely alive under film bombardment, but if the building he is in begins to burn down, he will wake up and use his liveliness to save himself.

In other words, I am not interested in emotional response, but rather in bringing about a situation in which life on the part of everyone concerned is an obvious necessity. A few examples:

In Seville around 1929 or 1930, I stayed on longer than I had planned in order to see a film, Homer's *Iliad*, a performance having been announced a week off. Loitering around, I was one day on a street corner and found myself surrounded by three radio loud-speakers, each playing a different program, and the traffic

By permission of John Cage.

and pedestrians visible and audible all at the same time. When the day for Homer came along, I went to the "theatre," which was an outdoor café: The picture screen was placed in the center of two such cafés, and I suppose that the image was seen straight from one side, reversed from the other, though the arrangement is marvelously suggestive of new possibilities. The program had been changed. Homer was never performed. The manager was surprised that I was concerned to see it.

Just a few years ago, I was on my way to Boston with friends. We stopped to get some lunch. The situation was a bar and a glass-walled dining room, overlooking a small lake with diving apparatus in its center. There were people swimming (I could see them); there was a juke box playing (I could hear it). I was eating lunch and conversing. It all went together.

What helps in the complex situation I am describing more than anything else—more, that is, than structure, form, content, method, devices, imagination, what have you—is the identification of activity with inactivity. That is to say: If I am not acting, acting is going on anyway. A haiku says this (describing the situation of a farmer taking a nap): By going to sleep, I pound the rice.

Therefore, the most important thing to do in film now is to find a way for it to include invisibility, just as music already enjoys inaudibility (silence).

[Letter to Paul Henry Lang] *John Cage*

The following letter, dated May 22, 1956, was addressed to the principal music critic of the New York Herald Tribune, *where it did not appear. This represents its first publication.*

Dear Paul Henry Lang:

Following the report of your recent newspaper reading and its suite of opinions, friends telephoned me, two reading over the wire your last Sunday article, *Music by Hardware.* You err in ascribing to me a work for ten radios (the *Imaginary Landscape No. 4* is for 12; *Radio Music,* to be performed May 30th at the Carl Fischer Concert Hall, is for eight); you will permit me, following the convention "even-Steven," a few mistakes regarding your remarks. Error is an excellent thing: mine, which shall be

By permission of John Cage.

unintentional, may induce you to an "adventure in ideas"; yours will probably bring about a new composition by me for the number of radios you mention.

Will you consider such a work of mine, not yet composed, a "stunt?" You may be, with this word, pointing out the quality of virtuosity, which I admire, and have for the past twenty-three years always admired, for it adds skill to devotion, indicating the passage of time in faithfulness to the latter. But my supposition is probably incorrect, for you declare my works, even those that seem patently conventional to me (e.g., my works, 1938–50, for the prepared piano), "preposterous as art." Clearly, we must not be seeing eye to eye.

For example, you are pleased that the machine has made possible the hitherto unequaled "dissemination" of culture we nowadays everywhere observe. It is precisely this function of the machine that, filling me with concern, makes it necessary for me, annually at Teachers College, Columbia University, to give a lecture "On How to Become Uncultured." The question is serious, for people must decide whether their homes are going to be those of curators or the homes of artists, hangers-on-to-what-has-happened, or makers-of-what-is-and-is-becoming.

I gather that you find me concerned with shocking the man in the street. However, my work is almost characterized by being insufficiently exciting. I do not know whether you attended the first and only performance of the *Imaginary Landscape* for twelve radios. You will remember, if you did, that McMillin was jammed. Everyone stayed, though the hour became late, for my work was programmed at the end, circa 11:30. I had advised against this, for I knew the piece was quiet and tranquil, by no means a rousing finale. The majority of the audience expected an uproarious joke, which "never came off." A fellow composer, in fact, apologized for me in print, theorizing that the lateness of the hour had brought about an excessive thinness of texture.

But I have never gratuitously done anything for shock, though what I have found necessary to do I have carried out, occasionally and only after struggles of conscience, even if it involved actions apparently outside the "boundaries of art."

For "art" and "music," when anthropocentric (involved in self-expression), seem trivial and lacking in urgency to me. We live in a world where there are things as well as people. Trees, stones, water, everything is expressive. I see this situation in which I impermanently live as a complex interpenetration of centers moving out in all directions without impasse. This is in accord with contemporary awarenesses of the operations of nature. I attempt to let sounds be themselves in a space of time. There are those, and you are no doubt one of them, who find this attempt on my part pointless. I do not object to being engaged in a purposeless activity. Like Debussy on a spring day I would prefer walking in the country's fields and woods to going to a concert. Nevertheless, I do go to town now and then and I do pass through Times Square, with which for many years I was unable to make my peace. With the help, however, of some American paintings, Bob Rauschenberg's particularly, I can pass through Times Square without disgust. And, similarly, having written radio music has enabled me to accept, not only the sounds I there encounter, but the television, radio, and Muzak ones, which nearly constantly and everywhere offer themselves. Formerly, for me, they were a source of irritation. Now, they are just as lively as ever, but I have changed. I am more and more realizing, that is to say, that I have ears and can hear. My work is intended as a demonstration of this; you might call it an affirmation of life. Life goes on very well without me, and that will explain to you my silent piece, *4′ 33″*, which you may also have found unacceptable.

Machines are here to stay, or for the time being. They can tend toward our stupefaction or our enlivenment. To me, the choice seems obvious and, once taken, cries out for action.

[The New School] *John Cage*

Cage wrote this statement in the early 1960's at the request of Clara Meyer, formerly a dean of the New School for Social Research. She was then preparing a monograph on the school's earlier activities.

My first connection with the New School was in the early 1930's when I came from California to study with Henry Cowell. The unconventional work he gave me to do—in modern harmony and rhythm—was unobtainable elsewhere. Furthermore, he presented regular informal concerts that brought about a parade of modern composers, their music and ideas, that was more to my liking than anything offered by the League of Composers or the International Society for Contemporary Music.

Later, in the 1940's, I was living in New York City. When

By permission of John Cage.

someone wished to study with me, I taught privately. Now and then Henry Cowell asked me to substitute for him at the New School when he had some conflicting engagement.

In the 1950's, I moved to the country, making matters difficult for those living in the city who wished to work with me. Since my musical thought was changing and at the same time exciting, on the part of others, greater interest than it had previously, I felt the responsibility to teach, which I understood simply as a responsibility to make myself available. It never entered my mind to teach in any other place in New York City than the New School. Nor is it likely that any other school would have accepted me, since my work and ideas are controversial.

Money was never a question. When I studied with Henry Cowell, it was as a "scholarship" student. I helped him as a secretary of sorts. When I myself was teaching, it was at my own expense: What I received from the school was less than what it cost me to get there.

The classes in "Composition of Experimental Music" were small: from three to a maximum of twelve students. There were some who returned year after year. Others appeared for a single session and disappeared. I began each series of classes by meeting the students, attempting to find out what they had done in the field of music, and letting them know what I myself was doing at the time. The catalogue had promised a survey of contemporary music, but this was given only incidentally and in reference to the work of the students themselves or to my own work. For, after the first two classes, generally, the sessions were given over to the performance and discussion of student works. There was often not enough time to play everything that had been prepared, and we would have to leave the room in order that the next class could come in.

Many did excellent work. Toshi Ichiyanagi and Jackson Mac Low have perhaps since been the most successful. Ichiyanagi's work is now dominant in the Japanese musical avant-garde. Mac Low's *The Marrying Maiden* had a long run at The Living Theatre. Richard Higgins, Al Hansen, George Brecht, and Allan Kaprow, along with others who did not attend the classes, established a theatrical form now well-known as a "Happening," which does not depend on plot conventions for its taking place. The composing means involve chance operations and composition that is indeterminate of its performance.

Occasionally I asked other composers to take the class in my place. They were Morton Feldman, Earle Brown, and Richard

Maxfield. Richard Maxfield later joined the faculty of the New School to teach orchestration and electronic music.

During the years I worked at the New School, I was helped by the absence of academic rigor there. There were no standards that I had to measure up to. No one criticized or suggested the alteration of my methods. I was as free as a teacher could be. I was thus able, when opportunity offered, to learn something myself from the students.

[Two Short Poems] *John Cage's Class*

The following text represents a collective effort, written in the summer of 1958 at the New School.

i

the sun
seen
scrub
wood
something
pah
some sesame seeds

ii

doughs
cat
often
electrocution
elucidate
what?
car

[On Cage's Classes] *Al Hansen and Dick Higgins*

Both Al Hansen and Dick Higgins have written of those classes—the former in his book A Primer of Happenings and Time/Space Art *(Something Else Press, 1965) and Higgins in a letter to this book's editor (1970). Hansen is an artist living in New York; and Higgins, now on the staff of the California Institute of the Arts, is a poet, composer, critic, and publisher.*

Al Hansen:*

I got to the first session late. When I entered, Cage explained that everyone had just finished telling who they were and where they were from and why they were there, and so why didn't I tell about myself before class began. I said my name was Al Hansen and I was interested in experimental music composition.

He asked me what my experience was in music composition, and I said that I had had no experience in music composition. And he said, "Yes, but you must have studied things like rhythm?"

"No," I said.

"Harmony?"

"No."

"Counterpoint?"

"No."

"Yes, but you play a musical instrument, don't you, like the guitar?"

He was quite sure that someone who was going to take his course must have studied some kind of music somewhere before, but no matter how many different hooks he could think of, I didn't fit on any of them. As he began to run out of things, he became more and more delighted and his face began to hang open in the smile that I've come to love so much, and the other members of the class seemed to enjoy it too.

Finally, he said, "But why are you here?" It was then that I explained that I had read in Eisenstein that all the art forms meet in the film frame and if I was going to make experimental films I wanted to know more about music and the most experimental composers. This seemed to pacify him beautifully. Everyone else seemed to think that was a good idea, too.

Actually, by the time I had finished the course, I realized that all art forms do not meet in the film frame, but in the eyeball. In the head of the observer, for better or worse. Therefore, in the happening—which I developed as a way of overlapping and interpenetrating art forms in the hope of finding a new one, without at first realizing that the happening was the form itself—I realized my solution. This would be my party platform and the thing I would stand on. This would be the wall I would beat my head against faithfully.

Some of the other members of Cage's class were Allan Kaprow, Dick Higgins, George Brecht, Florence Tarlow, and photographer Scott Hyde. We tended to bring our friends in as visitors: film-

* Copyright © 1965 Something Else Press, Inc., New York. Reprinted by permission.

maker Harvey Gross, George Segal, Jim Dine, and Larry Poons. I first met most of the well-known contemporary artists in this class. To a great extent, and probably to John Cage's disgust, the class became a little version of Black Mountain College. (It is on the basis of that season, with both Dick Higgins and myself in full glory, that Cage is said to have vowed that he would never again accept students whose last name began with an "H.")

June–July, 1958

DICK HIGGINS: *

Cage came into the classroom carrying a paper bag. He said to Steve Addiss, who has since turned into a State Department folk singer, "You really should try these mushrooms. Wild ones have much more taste than the domestic ones, and these boletes are really marvelous."

Cage speaks in a slightly nasal, resonant way that is so startlingly marvelous that Alan Hovhaness once wanted to compose a piece especially for Cage's voice.

In the first class, he spoke about notation—"So much space equals so much time." He wrote both words on the blackboard. "Sort of makes you feel you're thinking in the right century, doesn't it."

He showed the class about the various properties of sound and how they could be altered. And stuck a pink pearl eraser in the piano strings. It made a dull, bell-like sound. "Nice," he said as the sound died out.

Problems were given to the class—what to do with guitars and paper clips (Al Kouzel, the animator, did that one), how to make an array of numbers controlling durations, etc. Everybody in the class came up with a different solution, though Scott Hyde (the photographer) and Al Hansen had quite similar results. Hansen's solution, later that year, turned into the basis for *Alice Denham in 48 Seconds*, one of his main pieces.

Cage also showed how he had solved some problems himself, but told the class he would be quite angry if they copied any of these. Then, to reassure people, he said not to worry, he wasn't very frightening when he was angry.

The usual format of our sessions would be that, before the class began, Cage and George Brecht would get into a conversation, usually about "spiritual virtuosity," instead of the virtuosity of technique, physique, etc. This would continue as the people ar-

* Reprinted by permission.

rived, then gradually expand, until the subject matter became hard to follow. There was a very pretty Israeli girl—sometimes brunette, sometimes blonde—who liked Steve Addiss, who had been assigned to "monitor" the class for student attendance, and who kept writing very primitive Bartók-sounding things. She would begin to peck at the piano, then Cage would get annoyed—very gently so—and would ask the class, "Well, who besides Dick Higgins brought any pieces." I usually had some, so usually I waited to let others who were less prolific have a chance. The piece would be played, and then its philosophy would be discussed. The technique of the piece was seldom mentioned, except that inconsistencies and incongruities would be noted. My pieces were hard to deal with in the class, though, because they tended to be more complicated than the other peoples'.

Once or twice Cage read a theoretical article . . . the short theoretical statements from *trans/formation 2*, and a (then) unpublished article by Christian Wolff on the relations of time and sound. Some of us, particularly Hansen and myself, couldn't for the life of us imagine why Cage was interested in those things. They seemed so abstract, compared with the very concrete observations that Cage favored in connection with the pieces played in class, and so terribly old-fashioned in their implications. Mostly they read like legal contracts.

Once Cage invited Jackson Mac Low to read some of his new "chance poems" to the class—*Peaks and Lamas*, I think, and some passages from *The Marrying Maiden*. Most of the people in the class seemed to feel that the poems were not pushed far enough, that even the sources should have been randomized. But the poems were haunting, and, in the 1960's, MacLow really emerged as the main experimental poet of his generation.

That August Cage was scheduled to leave for Darmstadt, to take over Boulez's class, since Boulez had other commitments. So the last two sessions were turned over to Morton Feldman and Richard Maxfield. Feldman showed what might have happened if Cage had used an academic format. He just stood in front of the class, talked down to us, played passages from Chopin and said how beautifully the harmonies followed the emotional line of the melody (it was a very banal prelude that he chose to use as an example), and told us how important "taste" was for musical composition. Even if he were right, we felt, he was totally unconvincing. Maxfield was also formal; but he gave objective information, about sine waves, square waves, saw-tooth waves, ring modulators (then unknown), sum- and difference tones. He filled us with things to think about, then capped it off by playing pieces of electronic music of all sorts.

But the best thing that happened to us in Cage's class was the sense he gave that "anything goes," at least potentially. Only George Brecht seemed to share Cage's fascination with the various theories of impersonality, anonymity and the life of pieces outside of their perceivers, makers, or anyone else. For the rest of us, the main thing was the realization of the possibilities, which made it easier to use smaller scales and a greater gamut of possibilities than our previous experience would have led us to expect.

Ultimately, of course, this contributed to the developing of happenings.

Morris Graves *John Cage*

Cage's essay on his painter-friend Morris Graves was first published in the catalogue for a summer, 1957, exhibition of Pacific Northwest painters and sculptors at the Museum of Art in Ogunquit, Maine.

Just as Morris Graves lives in the country, not in the city, so his work stands apart from the most recent concerns of American art and the New York School in particular. His paintings, in this connection, are not paintings. They are invitations. The surfaces, by their beauties, attract, but the colors, lines, and textures do not provide an absorbing aesthetic play. They are representative of a fox, a bird, the top of a tree, a bronze, and the representations are placed with urgency in the space's center. They are invitations Home, that Home which is never left but ordinarily ignored. Ordinary living conspires to keep the earth busily separate from heaven, but now and then experience transcends business, revealing in clock-time the timeless time.

Such transcendent experience is continually and everywhere offered, but it is most easily noticed where man has done least, as in unfrequented parts of nature, and when, as on a vacation from his purposes and thoughts, he is empty enough to contain it. Morris Graves wrote in 1952:

> The Sumi ink drawings are the result of a continuing discovery during a few hours of experience on a lost lake shore last summer, which held, juxtaposed superbly, a need and its fulfillment, which

Reprinted by permission.

during the experience had the intensity of a revelation. While it occurred, I knew something anew about where and how the best in my life transpires.

The Loon and Duck paintings are an attempt to convey that eternal morning and eternal evening stillness that falls over nature near a reedy forest lake. The alert and evasive water birds, drawn with a few sparse lines in watered ink, for me hint that untroubled solemn stillness.

Graves does more than hint that stillness. He flavors it with three of the emotions traditionally known in India as permanent: the erotic, the wondrous, and fear. With him the erotic is in its highest aspect of devotion. He so gives himself to his subject that, as he draws, the bird or animal appears, and he, Graves, disappears to reappear in it.

But his drawing is also an "attempt to convey," for the artist does not keep his experience to himself alone. He loves his fellowmen and fears that they may overlook the opportunity for revelation their living on earth affords, occupying themselves as they do with measurements, plans, and abstractions. Geometry in some of Graves's work exists as an obscuring web or an eccentric distraction from the centered image. The meaning is that man, the measurer, must go through and beyond himself to experience reality, else he will remain separate from his true nature. For a man of Graves's awareness, these days are fearsome and black indeed. He works to bring others to information that is "bright as lightning and serene as moonlight." In 1947, he wrote:

> To the one whose searching is not similar to ours—or those who do not feel the awful frustrations of being caught in our individual and collective projection of our civilization's extremity—to those who believe that our extroverted civilization is constructively "progressing"—those who, seeing and tasting the *fruits* and new buds of self-destructive "progress," are still calling it good, to them the ideas in the paintings are still preposterous, hence not worth consideration.

"The fruits and new buds," atomic bombs among them, are seen by the artist as unnatural, evil, and fearsome. He then adds to his invitation a message written in symbols, some with traditional meanings, others he has discovered (*Ku with Moons*, *Bird with Minnow*). His work becomes, in such cases, a warning, and he appears not only as prophet of bliss but like a Jeremiah.

In some of his drawings, birds, though at the center, are not at rest, but in a posture of separation and tension. The surrounding space, however, is made mysterious, inviting, and full of wonder, quiet and still. Or, the wondrous looks straight into the eyes of the observer out of the eyes of a bird, hypnotically drawing him into the unknown and unmeasurable.

In some recent work he suggests the art of his neighbors, the Northwest Indians. These Indians have long known what Graves knows: The transcendent experience that is given to him who identifies himself with the "outside," dissolving the ego in the equation, among others, bird-man.

For such a person, this world itself is the goal, this moment eternal. We live at the tranquil center surrounded by gifts. That is the meaning of those works by Morris Graves, not included in this exhibition, which have nothing extraordinary about their subjects. They are the fruits and flowers that come from ordinary orchards and gardens.

To the self-destructive inventions of civilization they are the replies of nature.

Art Review: Cage, Composer, Shows Calligraphy of Note *Dore Ashton*

This review appeared in The New York Times *(May 6, 1958). Dore Ashton, then an art critic for* The Times, *has since written several books on modern art.*

A reliably unorthodox composer, John Cage, is exhibiting a group of unorthodox manuscripts at the Stable Gallery, 924 Seventh Avenue. Since Cage's notations have been invented by Cage, these compositions exist as items in a world of their own. They are set down in a complex system of numbers, notes, letters, and geometrical formations, and each page has a calligraphic beauty quite apart from its function as a musical composition.

Cage works in India ink with fine pens. In some pages, there are cataracts of notes, linked together with parabolas; in others, just one or two notes and a carefully designed letter. One composition suggests the string of a harp wailing a plangent monody as it is strangely caressed. In all of the manuscripts, there is a delicate sense of design at work that transcends the purely technical matter of setting down music.

© 1958 by The New York Times Company. Reprinted by permission.

[On Earlier Pieces] *John Cage*

These notes on selected earlier compositions first appeared in the brochure accompanying the recording of the 25-Year Retrospective Concert (1958).

1934

The *Six Short Inventions* (written in Carmel, California), are the final part of a trio entitled *Solo with Obligato Accompaniment of 2 Voices in Canon.* It was the last of a series of chromatic pieces begun in 1933, which dealt with the problem of keeping repetitions of the twenty-five individual tones within a two-octave span as far apart as possible. Although each of the three voices employs the same range, none introduces a repetition until all twenty-five tones have appeared. Row technique is not used. Nevertheless, these pieces led Henry Cowell to suggest my studying with Arnold Schoenberg and Adolph Weiss. The scoring is recent (1958), the original pieces being without instrumentation.

Construction in Metal was written about five years later in Seattle. Since Arnold Schoenberg had impressed upon me the structural function of tonality, I felt the need of finding some structural means adequate to composing for percussion. This led me eventually to a basic reexamination of the physical nature of sound. Sounds, including noises, it seemed to me, had four characteristics (pitch, loudness, timbre, and duration), while silence had only one (duration). I therefore devised a rhythmic structure based on the duration, not of notes, but of spaces of time. The whole has as many parts as each unit has small parts, and these, large and small, are in the same proportion. Used for the first time in the *Construction*, this principle appears in nearly all my work (symmetrically or asymmetrically) until 1952. It is analogous to Indian Tala (rhythmic method), but it has the Western characteristic of a beginning and an ending.

In this work, the rhythmic structure is 4-3-2-3-4, 16 times 16 measures of 4/4. The first four 16's are in exposition of individual bodies of material characterized by differences of rhythmic pattern and instrumentation. The remainder is development (without re-exposition), to which is added a 12-measure coda. The instruments used are orchestral bells, 5 thundersheets, piano muted by metal cylinders manipulated on the strings by an assistant to the pianist (the pianist also sweeps the bass strings with a tympani

Reprinted by courtesy of George Avakian.

stick), a 12-gong gamelan, 8 cowbells, 3 Japanese temple gongs, 4 automobile brake drums, 8 anvils, 4 Turkish and 4 Chinese cymbals, 4 muted gongs, water gong, suspended gong, and tamtam.

1939

The *Imaginary Landscape No. 1* was written to be subsequently broadcast or heard as a recording. It is in effect a piece of proto-*musique concrète,* though naturally, since at that date there was no tape, the instruments were records of constant and variable frequencies (then available chiefly for audio research), cymbal, and string piano (Henry Cowell's manually muted grand piano). The original performance took place in two separate studios, the sounds being picked up by two microphones and mixed in the control booth. It has been used as dance accompaniment by Bonnie Bird (*Imaginary Landscape*) and by Marian Van Tuyl (*Horror Dream*).

1942

The Wonderful Widow of Eighteen Springs was commissioned by the late mezzo, Janet Fairbank. The text, adapted from page 556 of James Joyce's *Finnegans Wake,* is as follows:

> Night by silentsailing night Isobel wildwood's eyes and primarose hair, quietly, all the woods so wild, in mauves of moss and daphnedews, how all so still she lay, neath of the whitethorn, child of tree, like some losthappy leaf, like blowing flower stilled, as fain would she anon, for soon again 'twill be, win me, woo me, wed me, ah weary me! deeply, now evencalm lay sleeping; Night, Isobel, sister Isobel, Saintette Isabelle, Madame Isa Veuve La Belle.

The accompaniment was produced by striking differently resounding parts of the completely closed grand piano with fingers or knuckles.

1943

The hypnotic-muted effect of the *Quartet for 12 Tom Toms* depends on two factors—on playing center and edge with the fingers, less frequently with wire brush or tympani stick, and on the rhythmic length of the structure, the parts of which are expressed sometimes by sound and sometimes by silence.

The *Duet,* also 1943, is a vocalise. The piano preparation is very simple: Four pieces of rubber between the strings of four high piano keys. Until 1943, I had used the prepared piano chiefly for dance and theatrical occasions, having first changed the sound of the instrument in 1938 when the Negro dancer, Syvilla Fort, asked me to write for her *Bacchanale*.

1946–48

The *Sonatas and Interludes,* dedicated to the pianist, Maro Ajemian, were written when I began living at the East River, and first became seriously aware of Oriental philosophy. After reading the work of Ananda K. Coomaraswamy, I decided to attempt the expression in music of the "permanent emotions" of Indian tradition: the heroic, the erotic, the wondrous, the mirthful, sorrow, fear, anger, the odious, and their common tendency toward tranquility. These pieces were the first product of that effort (the ballet, *The Seasons*, commissioned by Lincoln Kirstein, was a further expression of still another Indian philosophical concept).

Here the sonata used is the two-part form with repetitions. The interludes are composed without structural repetitions. Only the first half of the entire series of twenty is performed at this concert.

1952–54

Music for Carillon was suggested by Oliver Daniel and dedicated to Mary Caroline Richards. The process of composition was fairly complex. On first studying the sound of a carillon, I realized that the duration of a given bell's resonance could not be strictly delimited. For the first time, I decided not to specify duration. Whole notes appear in a space, which takes the place of a time indication. The notes were determined first as points on paper found by placing template stencils at structural centers. These were then conventionally notated for church carillon (three octaves). It is here heard in transcription for the two-octave Schulmerich electronic instrument. . . .

Since the pioneer work of Pierre Schaeffer at the Radio Diffusion of Paris in 1948, the making of tape music has become international. (The different approaches of the various world centers —Paris, Cologne, Milan, New York—are excellently set forth in an article by Roger Maren in *The Reporter*, issue of Oct. 6, 1955, pages 38–42.) As I see it, tape has brought about, in a very tangible way, a profound alteration of musical action, the consequences of which are not limited alone to tape but will affect all music, no matter how traditional the instrumentation. Radical changes in the uses of sound have already been adumbrated by much music of this century, particularly the works of Anton Webern, Alois Hába, Charles Ives, Igor Stravinsky, Olivier Messiaen, and Edgard Varèse. It is now practical to produce sounds in any combination or sequence, an aesthetic possibility recognized even much earlier in the century by Claude Debussy.

The *Williams Mix* was composed, though not produced, in 1952. It follows my *Imaginary Landscape, No. 5*, written and performed in January of that year. This latter work, so far as I can ascertain, was the first piece of music for magnetic tape made in this country.

The chief technical contribution of my work with tape is in the method of splicing, that is, of cutting the material in a way that affects the attack and decay of sounds recorded. By this method, I have attempted to mitigate the purely mechanical effect of electronic vibration in order to heighten the unique element of individual sounds, releasing their delicacy, strength, and special characteristics, and also to introduce at times complete transformation of the original materials to create new ones.

The score is written for tape traveling at 15 inches per second. Each page lasts 1⅓ seconds, and the whole score (192 pages) lasts a fraction over 4¼ minutes. The materials employed fall into six categories, which are described elsewhere in this book. Some 500 to 600 sounds were recorded by Louis and Bebe Barron; the eight tapes were assembled over a nine-month period by Earle Brown, David Tudor, and myself. *Williams Mix* was first performed at the Festival of Contemporary Arts, University of Illinois, Urbana, 1953, and subsequently at Donaueschinger Musiktage, 1954, the Diaghilev Exposition, London, 1954, and in San Francisco, Marine Memorial Theater, 1955. This is the New York *première*.

1957–58

The *Concert for Piano and Orchestra* is dedicated to Elaine de Kooning. It is without a master score, but each part is written in detail, both specific directives and specific freedoms being given to each player, including the conductor. My intention in this piece was to hold together extreme disparities, much as one finds them held together in the natural world, as, for instance, in a forest or on a city street.

The conductor, by his gestures, represents a chronometer of variable speed. Harmonious fusion of sound is not an objective. For audible and visual clarity, the players are separated in space as far as is convenient in a concert hall. The pianist's part is a "book" containing eighty-four different kinds of composition, some, varieties of the same species, others, altogether different. The pianist is free to play any elements of his choice, wholly or in part and in any sequence. The orchestral accompaniment may involve any number of players on more or fewer instruments, and a given performance may be extended or shorter in length. Indeed, I regard this work as one "in progress," which I intend never to consider as in a final state, although I find each performance definitive.

The Concert *(1957–58) was performed a few weeks later with different instrumentation—piano, voice, and only four instruments; and, for that occasion, Cage collaged the following text and program note. The anti-manifesto at the bottom of the page was originally prepared for Julian Beck and Judith Malina, directors of the Living Theatre, for use in their program booklet for a season at the Cherry Lane Theatre, New York.*

The text for the *Concert for Piano, Voice, and 4 Instruments* is as follows: U, LI, 10, IJ, mud-luscious, IU, E-H, Glory′, W, Shem, In Feld und Wald″, sur le feu avec du beurre°, erfreuen sich″, the cold ashes@, water@, A, fickle, freckled (who knows how?)′, A, a Naga, or a Nagi, or a Yaksha, or Yakshi, or an Asura, or an Asuri, or a Garuda, or a Garudi, or a Kinnara, or a Kinnari, or a Mahoraga, or a Mahoragi, or a Gandharva, or a Gandharvi, or a Bhuta, or a Bhuti, or a Kumbhanda, or a Kumbhandi, or a Pisara, or a Pisaci, or an Austaraka, or an Austaraki, or an Apasmara, or an Aupasmari, or a Rakehasa, or a Rakshasi, or a Daka, or a Dakini, or an Aujohara, or an Aujohari, or a Kataputana, or a Kataputani, or an Amanushya, or an Amanushyi**, Why@, far and wee , unhemmed as it is uneven!, hoppy on akkant of his joyicity, Die Voglein schweigen im Walde%, letting go as I do@, OE, (W) D, Er steht‴, UB, intricate imperfect various, U, LNL, Tell me, tell me, tell me, elm!

written in response)
to a request for) instantaneous and unpredictable
a manifesto, 1952)

nothing is accomplished by writing a piece of music) our ears are
" " " " hearing " " " ") now
" " " " playing " " " ") in excellent condition

′ Gerard Manley Hopkins; ″ Friedrich Schnack; ° L. Dufour; @ Huang-Po Doctrine of Universal Mind; ** Lankavatara Sutra; % Johann Wolfgang von Goethe; ‴ Anon.

VI 1960–65

Our intention is to affirm this life, not to bring order out of a chaos or to suggest improvements in creation, but simply to wake up to the very life we're living, which is so excellent once one gets one's mind and one's desires out of its way and lets it act of its own accord.—JOHN CAGE, *Silence* (1961)

I never imagine anything until I experience it.—JOHN CAGE, in conversation (1969)

Form Is a Language *John Cage*

A symposium entitled "Form Is a Language," sponsored by Art News *in 1960, prompted this statement on musical notation.*

Current graphism in musical notation was implicit in my manuscripts (1951–52), where space on a page horizontally represented time. Later, space vertically represented frequency events. The common denominator of many camps of the musical avant-garde is the assumption that each aspect of sound is not available only at discrete points (scales, modes, series), but rather at any points in a total field. A diehard must act in the face of this the moment he enters the electronic studio to make music on tape or with a synthesizer. Conventional notation, for as many reasons as sound has aspects, is insufficient. Graphism, useful, is not the only way. (Human beings are gifted explorers.) Composition becomes distinct from performance. One cannot determine exactly what effect the notation causes—thus, indeterminacy. The observer-listener is able to stop saying I do not understand, since no point-to-point linear communication has been attempted. He is at his own center (impermanent) of total space-time. How are his ears and eyes? Serious questions. The complex of existence exceeds mentation's compass. Emptiness of purpose does not imply contempt for society, rather assumes that each person whether he knows it or not is noble, is able to experience gifts with generosity, that society is best anarchic.

© *Art News,* April, 1960. Reprinted by permission.

Ladies of the Monday Club and Gentlemen of the Faculty *John Cage*

This previously unpublished lecture was originally given in 1960 at Wesleyan University, where Cage has been a Fellow of the Center for Advanced Studies.

The center of the Center for Advanced Studies lies somewhere in the air-conditioning system. This air-conditioning system is essentially dehydrating. To avoid drying up, the Fellows are obliged

By permission of John Cage.

to drink a good deal. There is therefore a water fountain on each floor. There are two floors. In the skit that follows, the upper floor is suggested by high stools with Fellows sitting on them. These Fellows are the actual Fellows of the Center, but in real life, naturally, they don't sit on high stools. The one Fellow who was to be present this evening who is on the ground floor is Sir Leslie Munro. He sits in an easy chair. That means he's on the ground floor. However, he is not here; he is not in the easy chair. He was obliged to stay in New York at the last minute, this evening. I have, therefore, put my Indian Calendar in his place. That symbolizes Sir Leslie's interest in world affairs.

Coming back to drinking: If the Fellows didn't drink, they'd dry up. But, if they dried up, they wouldn't blow away because the windows won't open. Of course, some of the Fellows have doors, and these doors open on a balcony that runs along the outside of the building. None of the Fellows use this balcony. When any one of the Fellows visits another, he does so internally, using the hallway. Though the Fellows who have doors on to the balcony have no real need for drinking, they drink anyway: water, tea, and coffee. Unlike the other Fellows, Sir Leslie, Sir Ronald, and I can't open our windows, and though Sir Ronald and Sir Leslie have doors, they have been instructed not to use them, for if they do, the doors will not be weather-proof: They will leak. Therefore, Sir Leslie, Sir Ronald, and I are, so to speak, in the same boat. As a consequence, we go farther than water, tea, and coffee and, toward five o'clock, begin drinking ale and whisky. When this is done in my rooms, it has an effect on all the Fellows, because I keep my door open, in order to keep from feeling closed in.

Besides the Fellows, there are a number of people without whom the Center could not function. They are: the Pearls (who are, as Sig Neumann said when he introduced me to them, indeed pearls), Tanya Senff, the secretary, and Kay Briggs who spends her time at the Honors College. In the absence of Sig Neumann, who, it turns out, is not absent at all, it is Kay Briggs who brings us our mail and our flowers. When we have outgoing mail, it is Mrs. Senff who takes it out. The Pearls do everything else for us, and their daughter Cathy lets Mr. Pearl know when Mrs. Pearl wants to find him. For there are many rooms in the Center for Advanced Studies. You can get lost there. You can also hide. For this reason, we used to play hide and seek of an evening. But that was in the good old days.

One of the things we used to do and still do is answer the telephone. From nine to five, when it rings, Mrs. Senff answers it first. Then she leaves her desk, runs to the appropriate room on the right floor, finds out whether the Fellow is in, lets him know there's a call for him, and then runs back to the desk followed by the Fellow and resumes typing when the Fellow begins his conversation. It's all very complicated; and there doesn't seem to be any reason to simplify it. It gives the Fellows exercise, and it keeps Mrs. Senff hopping. After five, just when I've begun drinking seriously, I answer the telephone.

Strictly speaking, the Center for Advanced Studies has no one center. It has as many centers as it has Fellows. The number of these is constantly changing, and I would be willing to bet there are Fellows I don't even know. In fact, I would win this bet, because I don't know Dr. Hansen. I've phoned him, but he doesn't answer. Like Walter Clark, he works at home, approaching the nominal Center only for the purpose of picking up his mail. This home-working situation is suggested by placing the sign, which takes the place of Dr. Hansen, at the back of the audience. Mr. Clark is sitting on a high stool also at the back of the audience. This high stool is partly to make him more visible, and partly to suggest that, even though he works at home, he does so upstairs.

Academically speaking, the Center for Advanced Studies is way off base, nowhere near the center of the Wesleyan campus. Its front door, appropriately enough, is on Pearl Street. Unfortunately, there is something wrong with this street. Therefore, the gates, and the garden, and the front door are all left unused. Everybody comes in the back door. As you approach the back door of the Center, you hear the efficient roar of the air-conditioning. This lets you know that it is either too hot or too cold inside. Every room has a thermostat, but the thermostats were installed only for musical reasons. When they are turned up, you hear the delightful sound of water flowing through pipes in the ceiling; but this sound has no effect whatsoever on the room temperature. The Fellows therefore are prepared to either put something else on or take something off as the case may be. If, as has happened, the whole heating and air-conditioning system collapses, then all the Fellows who are not on vacation or for some other reason absent simply come together in a group and use the event as an excuse for a tea party.

I do not want to conclude this lecture even though it is merely introductory. I want to go on indefinitely. However, I do not want to speak for the Fellows. I want them to speak for themselves, and all at once. This they will do from their published works or from those that are not yet published. Even if you can't hear what they're saying because they're all talking at once, you'll at least get an idea of my attitude toward musical composition.

Let me take this opportunity to thank President Butterfield, the Wesleyan faculty, the board of trustees, and above all, the Monday Club, for having made me not only a Fellow of the Center for Advanced Studies, but also the first Fellow to actually live in the Center itself, even though it might be proven not to have a Center. In a sense, I may be thought of as a guinea pig; and my being here at Wesleyan may be thought of as an experiment. The experiment was apparently considered not a total flop. I have been asked to stay on, probably, for further and more subtle observations. Two knights, Sir Ronald and Sir Leslie, on the basis of my having remained in good health, have moved into the apartments downstairs. There was, until today, no vacancy upstairs. A sign should be put up outside, on Washington Street, giving this information, thus implementing the cogent term, Sig's Motel.

List No. 2 *John Cage*

As a Fellow of Wesleyan's Center for Advanced Studies in 1960–61, Cage was asked to compile a list of ten books having the greatest influence on his thought.

Gertrude Stein — Any title

Having responded to Eliot, Pound, Cummings, Joyce, *Transition,* etc. ("the twenties"), here choose Stein on principle: ladies first.

Alfredo Casella — *The Cadence*

This convinced that Western music had disintegrated.

Luigi Russolo — *The Art of Noise*

Put with this *New Musical Resources,* by Henry Cowell, and the early book by Carlos Chavez and you get (circa 1935) a sense of music renaissance, the possibility of invention.

Sri Ramakrishna — *Gospel*

A gift from India, which took the place of psychoanalysis.

Ananda K. Coomaraswamy — *The Transformation of Nature in Art*

No separation between East and West. Constancy of tradition

By permission of John Cage.

no matter when-where. Makes answering the ? why write music 20th-century koan.

Huang-Po *Doctrine of Universal Mind*
(In the original 75¢ form)
"Nothing is accomplished by writing, performing, hearing a piece of music (instantaneous-unpredictable): our ears are now in excellent condition." Couldn't have written this otherwise.

Kwang-tse *Writings*
Humor and chaos. *I Ching* gave useful means.

Eckhart, Meister *Meister Eckhart*
(The early two-volume translation) Again West is East: no separation.

Buckminster Fuller Any Book
Still unread; but he, personally, gave view of history, practicality, necessity.

C. H. Kauffman *The Agaricaceae of Michigan*
Led to the observation of nature.

"Live" Electronic Music *Richard Teitelbaum*

This note to the Columbia recording of Variations II *(MS 7051) was written by Richard Teitelbaum, an American composer and critic who has recently been living and working in Rome, where he also collaborates with the MEV (Musica Elettronica Viva) group.*

> I believe that the use of noise to make music will continue and increase until we reach a music produced through the aid of electrical instruments, which will make available for musical purposes any and all sounds that can be heard.

This statement was made by John Cage as long ago as 1937. Yet, with a few "prehistoric" exceptions, it was not until the development of magnetic recording tape around 1950 that the fulfillment of this prophecy began to be truly realized. The establishment of tape studios in Paris, Cologne, Milan, New York, and elsewhere enabled composers to create finished works directly on tape, utilizing both electronically generated signals and live sounds recorded through microphones. In both cases, the sounds could be

Copyright Columbia Records. Reprinted by permission.

further proceeded by electronic modifications or tape manipulations.

With the aid of such new musical resources, composers have pursued two increasingly divergent interests, the first leading toward invention and discovery of "any and all sounds that can be heard," the second toward precise control over musical materials beyond the limits of the human performer. To facilitate such control, particularly over rhythmic problems, sophisticated programming devices, such as the RCA Music Synthesizers, the Moog Synthesizers, and high-speed digital computers have been employed. Enabling the composer to specify precise values of frequency, amplitude, duration, and succession of all sound events, such devices produce a completed tape composition requiring little or no editing. Milton Babbitt's *Ensembles for Synthesizer* is an eminent example of works in this genre.

To composers whose demands had already exceeded the capabilities of most instrumentalists, the elimination of the performer was most welcome, assuring a perfect "performânce" every time. To others, more interested in questions of process and change, chance and indeterminacy, plus the actions and interactions of human performers, the medium of fixed-tape music seemed increasingly "deadly." Thus, in the late 1950's, a number of musicians began experimenting with "live" electronic performances. Foremost among these were David Tudor and John Cage (whose live electronic works actually extend back to *Imaginary Landscape No. 1* of 1939).

For more than thirty years, it has been Cage's consistent concern to expand our consciousness and enhance our appreciation of the sounds—intended or accidental—that are always around us. To these ends, he has composed works for conventional and unconventional instruments alike, believing all sounds to be acceptable musical materials. In *Imaginary Landscape No. 1* (1939), he used variable-speed phono turntables; objects "to be found in a living room" comprise the instrumentation of *Living Room Music* (1940); tin cans and audio frequency oscillators are employed in *Imaginary Landscape No. 3* (1942); twelve "live" radios make up the entire instrumentation of *Imaginary Landscape No. 4* (1951). In 1952, Cage "opened the doors of music to the sounds which happen to be in the environment" with his famous *4′ 33″*, "a piece in three movements, during all three of which no sounds are intentionally produced."

Cage's interest in sound, and his wish to allow sounds to "be themselves," has led his work away from "ideas of order to ideas of no order." Thus, moving from the method of "considered improvisation" in *Sonatas and Interludes* (1946–48), Cage has increasingly applied chance operations to the determination of frequency, amplitude, timbre, and duration in his music. In recent years, he has sought to create situations or processes that maximize the possibility of the unexpected by composing works "indeterminate with respect to performance. . . . I try to keep my curiosity and awareness with regard to what's happening open, and I try to arrange my composing means so that I won't have any knowledge of what might happen. And that, by the way, is what you might call the technical difference between indeterminacy and chance operations. In the case of chance operations, one knows more or less the elements of the universe with which one is dealing, whereas in indeterminacy, I like to think . . . that I'm outside the circle of a known universe and dealing with things I literally don't know anything about."

Variations II (1961) is a composition indeterminate of its performance, for any number of players, any sound-producing means. The score consists of six transparent plastic sheets having single straight lines, five having points. These sheets are to be superimposed, and perpendiculars then dropped from each point to each line. Measurements of these lengths are then used to determine values for each of the six "parameters": frequency, amplitude, timbre, duration, point of occurrence, and structure of event.

In preparing the composition for performance, David Tudor's realization of the score evolved from his initial decision concerning the instrumentation. Having previously used amplification in several performances of Cage piano pieces, Tudor decided to make a version of *Variations II for Amplified Piano* in which the total configuration would be regarded as the instrument. Therefore, any sound generated in the system (such as audio feedback) would be accepted and utilized in the performance. In working out the score, it became evident that the nature of the instrument was not compatible with specifying discrete values for each parameter. Therefore, after experimenting with a continuous scale of complexity, Tudor discarded the intervening values in favor of a concept of two basic states or conditions, simple or complex. For instance, if a timbre was specified as simple, it might be one with few harmonics; if an amplitude was complex, it might be changing in a rapid, aperiodic manner. The interpretation of each parameter with respect to the two states is limited only by its interaction with the other parameters, and by the performer's imagination. The nature of each event is determined by the state of each of the parameters, the duration of each event is as long as is required for the performer to carry out his task of interpreting all six. Thus, a composition that entails a process for its completion is given a performance that is itself a process.

Since the late 1950's, in such works as *Cartridge Music*, "for amplified small sounds," Cage and Tudor have explored the nature of electronic amplification and its magnifying effect on sounds and on our perceptions of them. In this performance of *Variations II*, each of four channels uses a contact microphone attached to the piano and a phono cartridge to play on the strings. In addition, contact mikes and cartridges are attached to a wide variety of materials (plastics, toothpicks, pipe cleaners), which are stroked, scraped, and struck on the strings. The variety and complexity of sounds that David Tudor draws forth from the piano with this odd array of everyday objects is astounding.

Freed from the conventional restraints of system, style, or the control of the rational faculty, this music participates (in Cage's words) in "disorganization and a state of mind, which, in Zen, is called *no-mindedness.*" The listener, similarly liberated, is offered an experience that is hallucinatory, spaced out, and very beautiful.

Atlas Eclipticalis with *Winter Music* (Electronic Version)—John Cage

Edward Downes

The following note, written by Edward Downes, appeared in a program of the New York Philharmonic in 1964. The two pieces, combined into a single performance, were respectively written in 1961–62 and 1957.

Atlas Eclipticalis and *Winter Music* were originally two separate compositions, and either work may be performed alone or in combination with the other.

Winter Music may be performed by from one to twenty pianists using all or part of the twenty pages of the score to provide a program of agreed upon length. The composing of the score involved "both chance operations and observation of imperfections in the paper on which the music was written."

The score of *Atlas Eclipticalis* may be performed in whole or in

Reprinted by permission of the New York Philharmonic.

33. John Cage, conducting at 25-Year Retrospective Concert, Town Hall, New York, 1958. Photo Remy Charlip.

34. With Karlheinz Stockhausen, about 1958.

35. *Fontana Mix*, 1958. Copyright Henmar Press, Inc., New York.

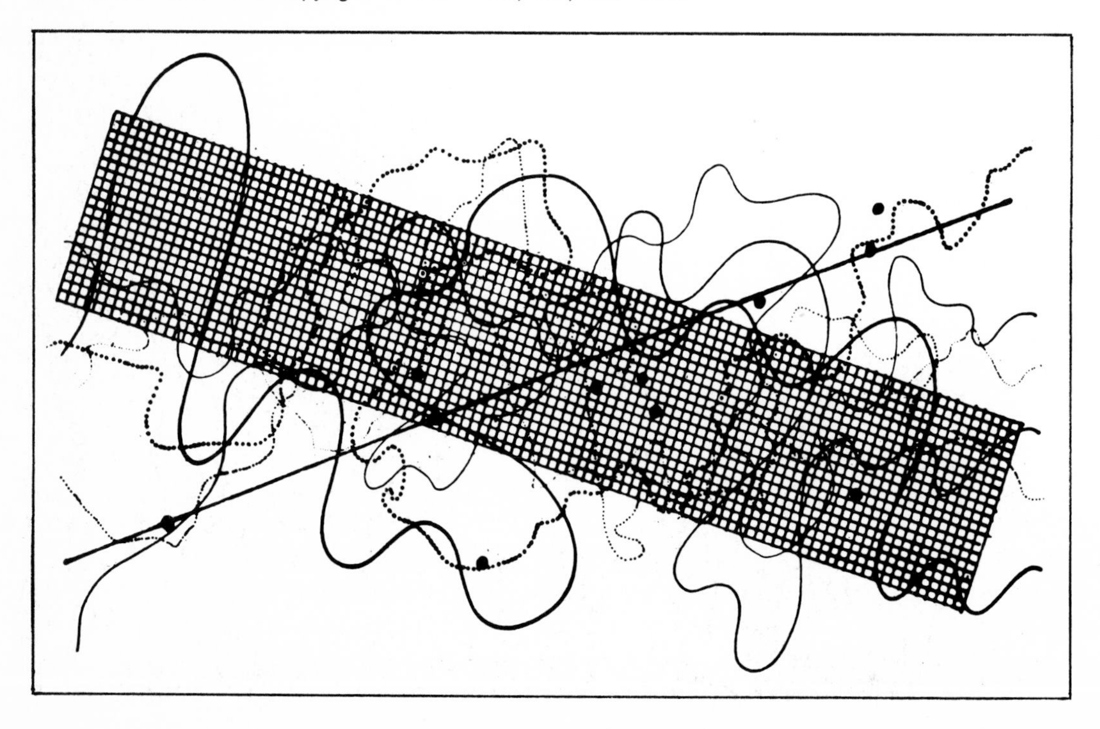

36. *Variations I and Variations I, Extra Materials*, 1958. Copyright Henmar Press, Inc., New York.

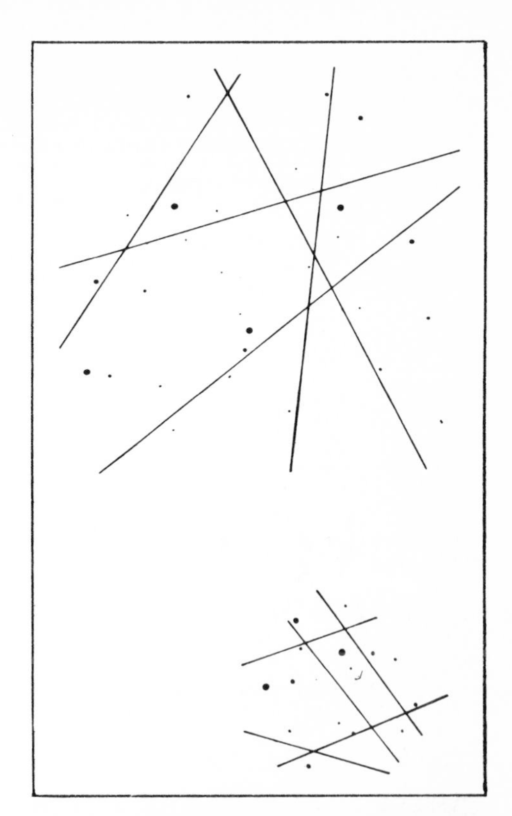

37. On Peggy Guggenheim's roof, Venice, 1958.

38. With several modern composers, Brussels World's Fair, 1958. Included here, in addition to Cage, supine, are (front row, left to right) Mauricio Kagel, Earle Brown, Luciano Berio, Karlheinz Stockhausen, and (back row, left to right) Henk Badings, André Boncourechlier, Bruno Maderna, Henri Pousseur, Mlle. Seriahine, Luc Ferrari, and Pierre Schaeffer. Photo Faider, Brussels.

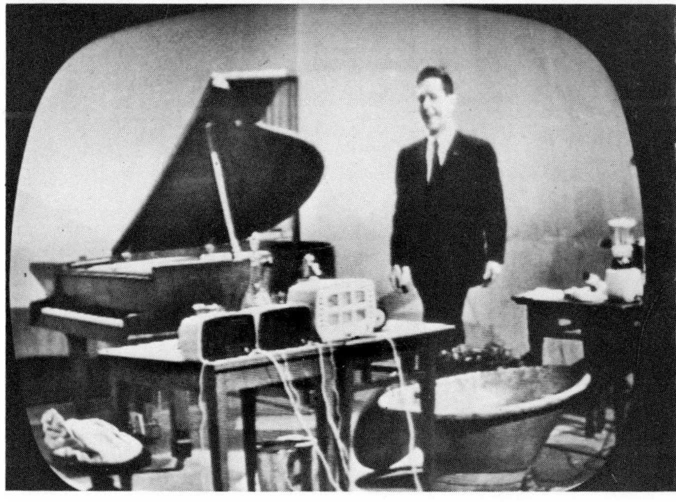

39, 40. On Italian TV, 1958. *Above:* On the quiz show *Lascia o Raddoppia* (Double or Nothing), where he won $6,000 by answering questions about mushrooms; *below: Première* of *Water Walk.*

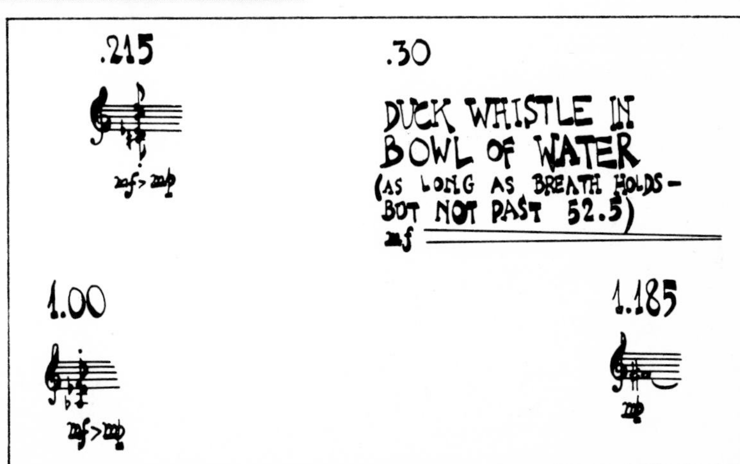

41. Excerpts from *Water Music,* 1959. Copyright Henmar Press, Inc., New York.

118 34

David Tudor and I went to Hilversum in Holland to make a recording for the Dutch Radio. When we arrived at the studio there was a ~~15 minute~~ short delay. To pass the time, we chatted with the engineer who was to work with us. He asked me what ~~sort of~~ kind of music he was about to record. Since he was a Dutchman I said, "It may remind you of the work of Mondrian." When the session was finished and ~~we~~ the 3 of us were leaving the studio, I asked the engineer what he thought of the music we had played. He said, "It

22 reminded me of the work of Mondrian."

42. Manuscript page from "Indeterminacy," 1959.

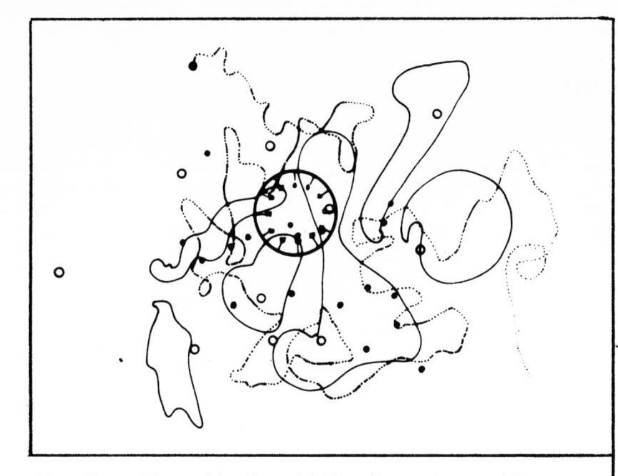

43. *Cartridge Music*, 1960. Superimposition using page 6. Copyright Henmar Press, Inc., New York.

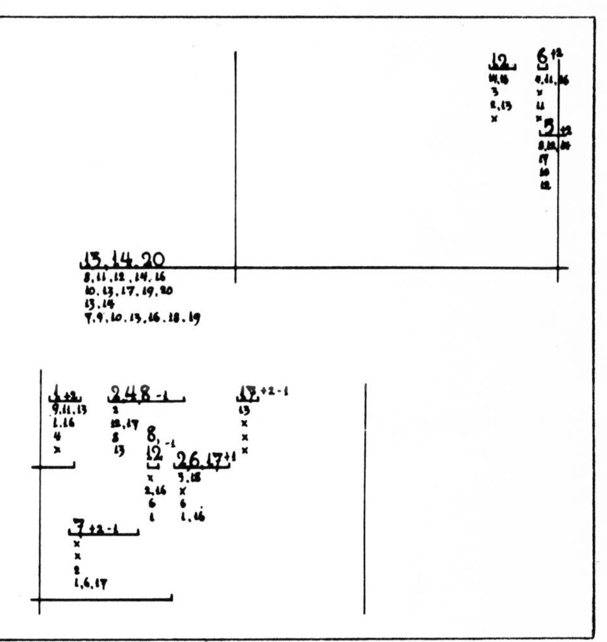

44. *Theater Piece: Part IV*, 1960. One of eighteen unnumbered pages. Copyright Henmar Press, Inc., New York.

45. *Music for Carillon, No. 4*, 1961. Page 5 of score. Copyright Henmar Press, Inc., New York.

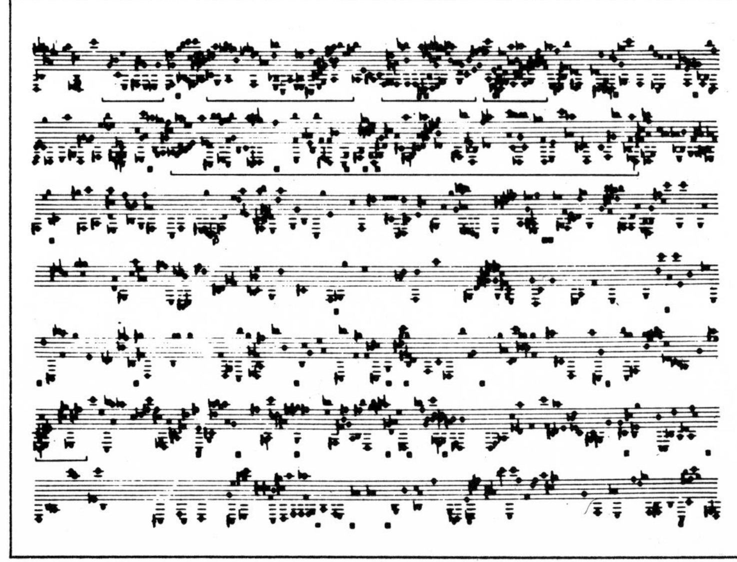

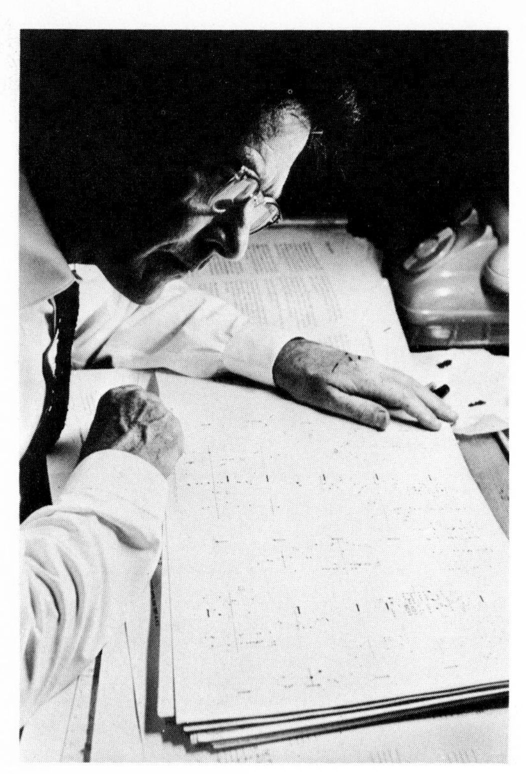

46. Cage in Japan, early 1960's, with the score of *Atlas Eclipticalis.* Copyright 1969 by Henmar Press, Inc., New York.

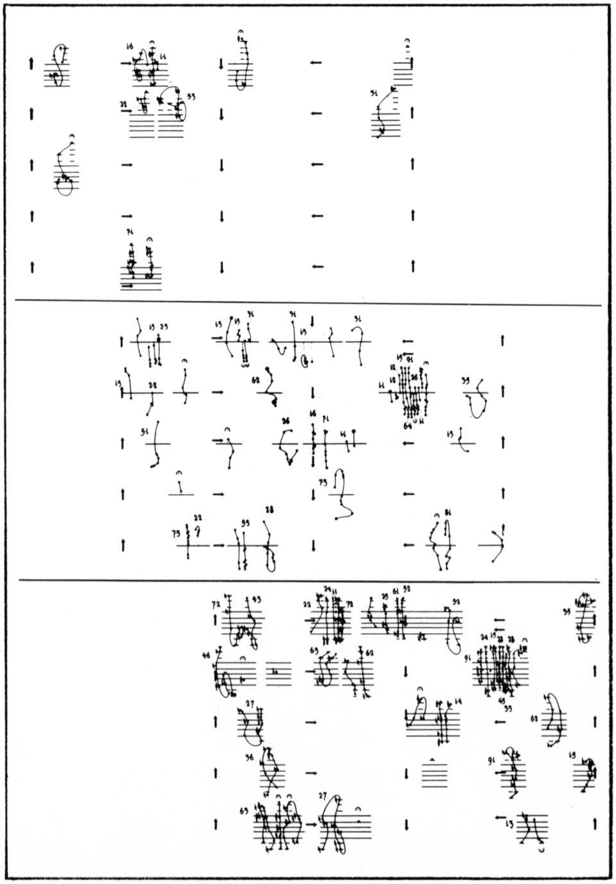

47. *Atlas Eclipticalis: French Horn 5, Percussion 4, Cello 7*, 1961–62. Pages 245, 309, and 157 of score. Copyright Henmar Press, Inc., New York.

48. Cage in Japan, early 1960's, with D. T. Suzuki, the Zen philosopher with whom he studied at Columbia in the late 1940's.

49, 50. Cage in Japan, early 1960's. *Above:* With score of *Winter Music* (1962; for four pianos); *below:* Conducting.

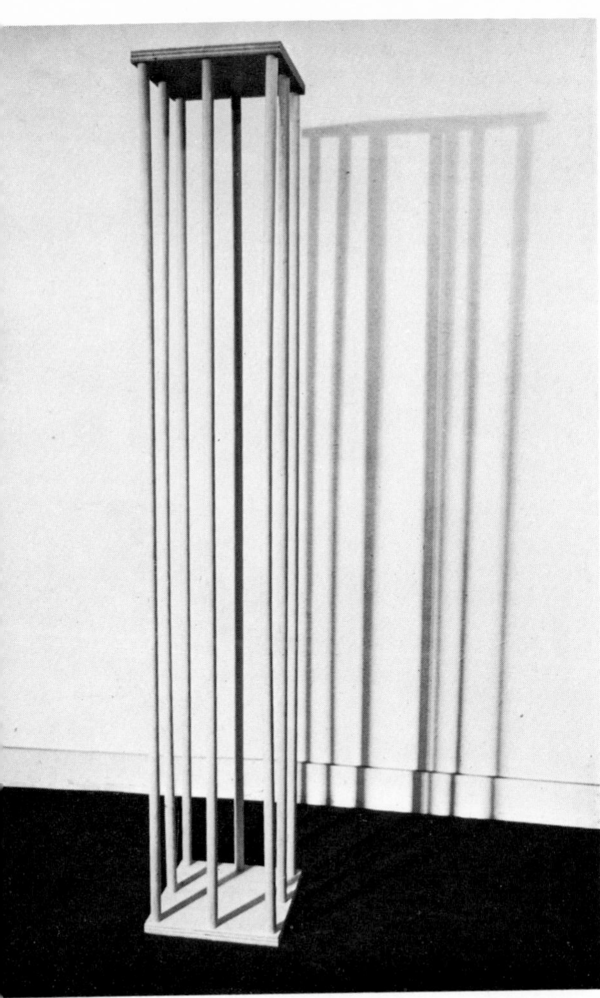

51. *Statue of John Cage*, exhibited 1963, by Walter de Maria, with letter to subject from the artist.

Jan. 2, 1963

Dear John Cage,

I think that it is only fair that I tell you that I have made a statue of you. Like the other sculptures and boxes that I am showing in this show, the sculpture was made about a year ago. It is 7 feet one inches tall. I do hope that this does not offend you.

Should you not be able to see the show, I am enclosing a photo of the statue, which I would like you to keep.

Walter De Maria

SOUND-SYSTEM (A) HAVING CONTINUOUSLY OPERATING (TAPE MACHINES (6+), SHORT WAVE RECEIVERS (6+), OSCILLATOR(S) (B)) AND, OPTIONALLY, NON-CONTINUOUSLY OPERATING (ELECTRONIC PERCUSSION DEVICES (B)(6+)) SOUND-SOURCES.

AUDIBILITY OF SOUND-SYSTEM DEPENDENT ON MOVEMENT OF DANCERS (C), THROUGH INTERRUPTION OF LIGHT BEAMS (D)(6+), PROXIMITY TO ANTENNAS (B) (4+).

.PERFORMANCE WITHOUT SCORE OR PARTS.

TELEVISION (PREFERABLY CLOSED WITH IMAGE DISTORTIONS (E)) AND/OR FILM (PREFERABLY MULTIPLE) PROJECTION OF DANCE AND OTHER IMAGES (F).

VARIATION: PLACEMENT OF PHOTO-ELECTRIC CELLS ON THE IMAGE SCREEN.

AS THOUGH THERE WERE A DRAWING OF THE CONTROLS AVAILABLE AND -ON A TRANSPARENCY- TRANSCRIPTION FROM ASTRONOMICAL ATLAS WHICH (WERE IT SUPERIMPOSED) WOULD GIVE SUGGESTIONS FOR USE OF CONTROLS.

RELAYS (D) PERMITTING AUDIBILITY OF SOUND-SOURCES TO CONTINUE FOR A PERIOD VARIABLE BY DIAL CONTROL FROM 0 TO 2½ MINUTES.

(A) DESIGNED BY DAVID TUDOR.
(B) DEVISED BY ROBERT MOOG.
(C) CHOREOGRAPHY BY MERCE CUNNINGHAM.
(D) PHOTO-ELECTRIC DEVICES DEVISED BY BILLY KLÜVER.
(E) DESIGNED BY NAM JUNE PAIK.
(F) FILM BY STAN VANDERBEEK.

52. *Variations V*, 1965. Page 1 of "thirty-seven remarks re an audio-visual performance." Copyright 1965 by Henmar Press, Inc., New York.

53. *Variations V*, 1965, performance with dancers Merce Cunningham and Barbara Lloyd in background. In foreground (left to right) are Cage, David Tudor, Gordon Mumma. Photo Herve Gloaguen, courtesy The Cunningham Dance Foundation, Inc.

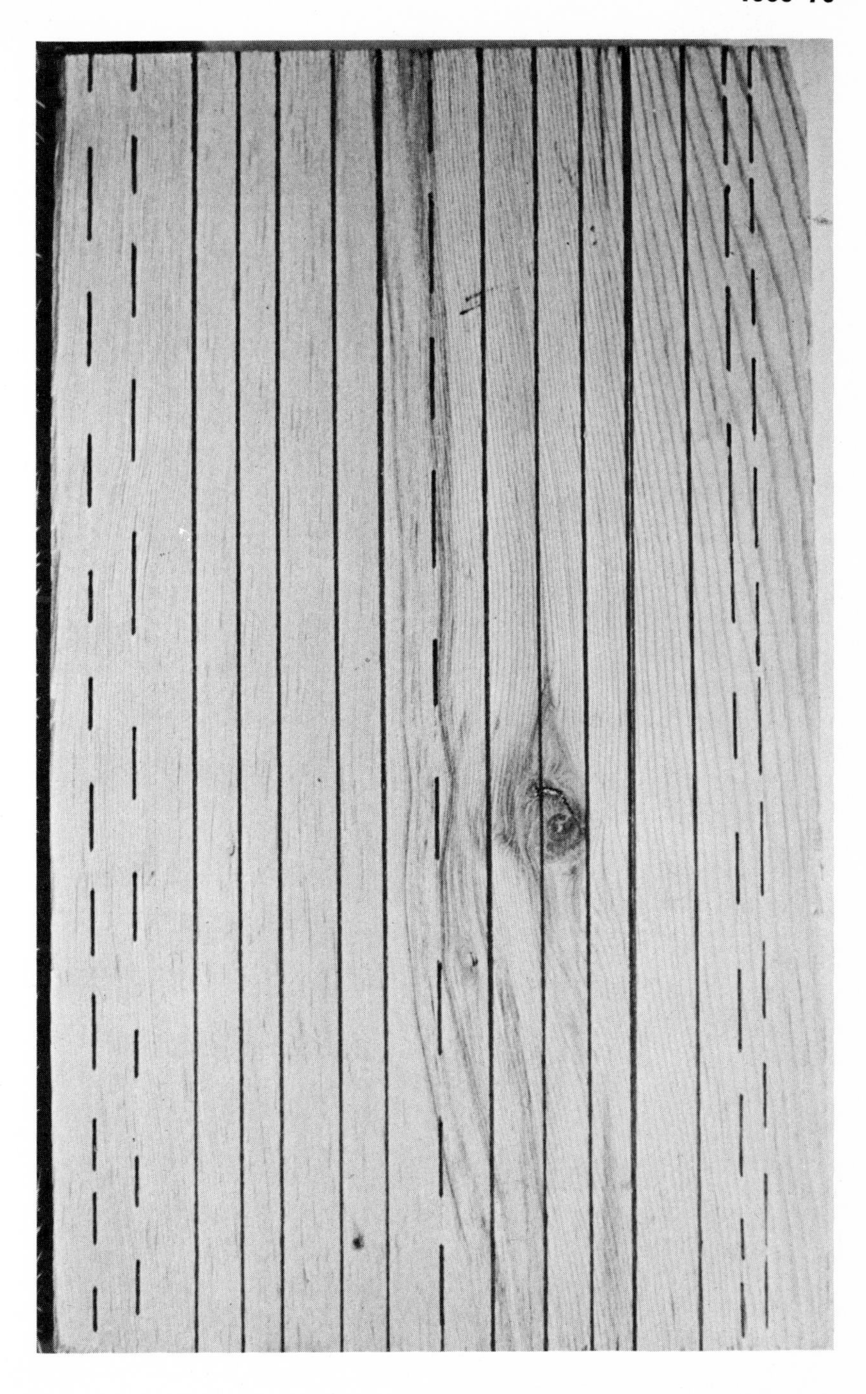

54. *Music for Carillon, No. 5*, 1967. Page 3 of score. Copyright Henmar Press, Inc., New York.

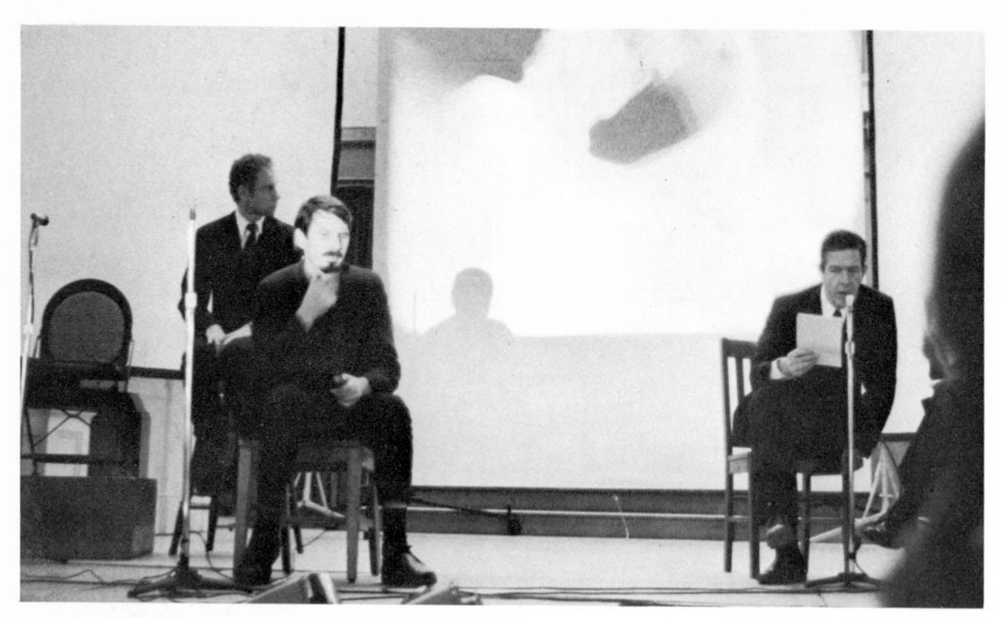

55, 56. "Contemporary Voices in the Arts" series sponsored by the New York State Council on the Arts, early 1967. The series consisted of seven performances held on campuses in upstate New York and concluding with an evening at the 92nd Street YM-YWHA, New York City (in cooperation with the Poetry Center). On each campus, the artists held discussions and demonstrations of their work, their own concept of their art, the interrelationships of various art forms, and the creative process in general. Participants from the seven art media were: electronic composer John Cage, poet Robert Creeley, choreographer and dancer Merce Cunningham, engineer Billy Kluver, kinetic sculptor Len Lye, painter Jack Tworkov, and film-maker Stan VanDerBeek. *Above:* Union College, Schenectady, New York, January 27, 1967, with (left to right) Cunningham, Creeley, Cage, and, on screen, a film by VanDerBeek; *below:* 92nd Street YM-YWHA, February 25, 1967. On stage, a five-course dinner was served, during which the performers' voices and sounds of the silverware were electronically amplified. Photo Adelaide de Menil. Photos and descriptions courtesy Withers Swan Public Relations, New York.

57. Cage with longer hair, 1969. Photo Bruce Bacon Studio.

58. *HPSCHD*, Champaign, Ill., 1969. Photo Bruce Bacon Studio.

59, 60. *Not Wanting to Say Anything About Marcel*, 1969, two parts of a plexigram multiple by John Cage and Calvin Sumsion. Letters were selected and arranged by aleatory operations and imprinted on eight parallel sheets of Plexiglas (each 20″ x 13½″), mounted on a wooden base. The complete work consists of four such constructions. Published by EYE Editions (Box 30216, Cincinnati, Ohio), 1969, and printed under the supervision of Hollanders Workshop, Inc., New York, with each edition limited to 125 numbered and hand-signed copies.

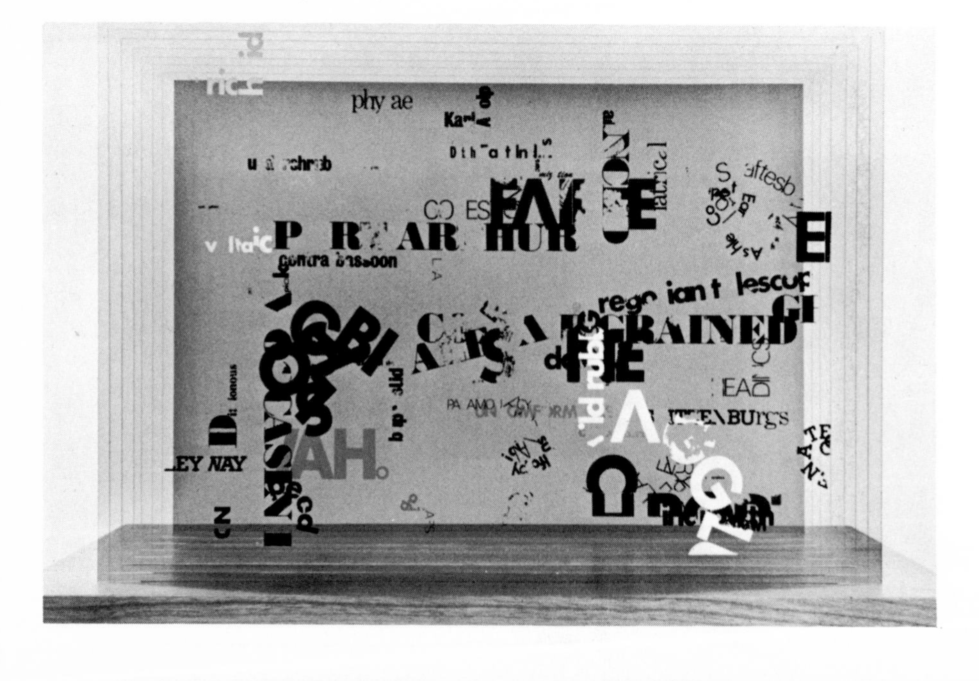

part, for any duration, by any ensemble, chamber or orchestral drawn from an eighty-six-part orchestra of conventional instruments with miscellaneous unspecified nonpitched percussion instruments.

The title, *Atlas Eclipticalis,* is taken from a book of astronomical maps Mr. Cage used in composing. This involved chance operations, including the placing of transparent templates on the pages of the atlas and inscribing the positions of the stars. There is no score in the conventional sense, Mr. Cage informs us, since the work is an example of "indeterminacy."

It is also an example of what may be called "live" electronic music. Most electronic music is dependent on magnetic tape for its performance and so becomes a recording. This music uses electronic circuits (microphones, amplifiers, loud-speakers) in connection with musical instruments.

I wrote *Winter Music* for piano(s) in the winter of 1956–57. This was accomplished quickly. *Atlas Eclipticalis* required some nine months. I began it, being commissioned by the Montreal Festivals Society, in 1961, while I was a Fellow of the Center for Advanced Studies at Wesleyan University in Middletown, Connecticut. The writing of the eighty-six parts was completed early in 1962, but performances of ensembles of the already finished parts took place earlier. It has been choreographed by Merce Cunningham and then has the title *Aeon.*

In 1954, while in Europe, I met the Japanese musicologist, Hidekazu Yoshida, who gave me his notion of the three lines of haiku poetry, the first line referring, he said, to nirvana, the second to samsara, and the third to specific happening. I thought, in writing *Atlas Eclipticalis,* of the first line and of the stars as nirvana. And I had the intention of writing two other works, that would complete the trilogy. This I did in 1963 with *Variations IV* and *0'00".*

I am particularly indebted in my work to my teachers, Richard Buhlig, Adolph Weiss, Henry Cowell, and Arnold Schoenberg; to many composers with whom I have been closely associated, Lou Harrison, Alan Hovhaness, Virgil Thomson, Morton Feldman, Christian Wolff, Earle Brown; with two others whom I never knew except through their works, Anton Webern and Erik Satie. I am devoted to the works of Edgard Varèse. Without close association with David Tudor, the pianist, my recent work, that of the past fifteen years, would be unthinkable. And there are many people not actually in the field of music who have influenced me. This would be a long list, but includes particularly the artists Robert Rauschenberg and Jasper Johns, the sculptor Richard Lippold, the philosopher Daisetz Suzuki, and the botanist Guy G. Nearing. And of course my father, the inventor John M. Cage. And Merce Cunningham, dancer and choreographer. And now the young composers, particularly Toshi Ichiyanagi who helped me in some of the manuscript work of *Atlas,* George Brecht, and La Monte Young.

[Cartridge Music] *John Cage*

This note appeared in the 1962 Time recording of Cartridge Music (*1960*).

The title *Cartridge Music* derives from the use in its performance of cartridges, that is, phonograph pick-ups into which needles are inserted for playing recordings. Contact microphones are also used. These latter are applied to chairs, tables, wastebaskets, etc.; various suitable objects (toothpicks, matches, slinkies, piano wires, feathers, etc.) are inserted in the cartridges. Both the microphones and cartridges are connected to amplifiers that go to loud-speakers, the majority of the sounds produced being small and requiring amplification in order to be heard. The dials of the amplifiers affecting volume and tone are controlled by the performers.

Each performer makes his own part from materials supplied. These materials (made Stony Point, N.Y., July, 1960), all but one sheet of which are on transparent plastic, may be superimposed in any position. One then sees a complex of points, circles, biomorphic shapes, a circle representing block time, and a dotted curving line. Readings are taken, which are useful in performance, enabling one to go about his business of making sounds, generally by percussive or fricative means, on the object in a cartridge, changing dial positions on the amplifiers, making "auxiliary sounds" by use of the objects to which the contact microphones are attached, removing an object from a cartridge and inserting another, and, finally, performing "loops": these are repeated actions, periodic in rhythm. The term "loop" is borrowed from tape-music terminology. It describes a circle of magnetic tape, which permits repeated playing of the material recorded on it.

The sounds that result are noises, some complex, others extremely simple, such as amplified feedback, loud-speaker hum, etc. (All sounds, even those ordinarily thought to be undesirable, are accepted in this music.)

By giving the readings meanings in reference to subject matter, the material of *Cartridge Music* was used to write several texts, among them: "Where Are We Going? and What Are We Doing?" and "On Robert Rauschenberg, Artist, and His Work" (both of which are included in *Silence,* Wesleyan University Press, 1961).

These objectives were uppermost in my mind when I supplied the material for *Cartridge Music*. First, to bring about a situation in which any determination made by a performer would not necessarily be realizable. When, for instance, one of the performers changes a volume control, lowering it nearly to zero, the other performer's action, if it is affected by that particular amplification system, is inaudible. I had been concerned with composition, which was indeterminate of its performance; but, in this instance, performance is made, so to say, indeterminate of itself.

Second, to make electronic music live. There are many ways to do this. The one I here chose was to make a theatrical situation involving amplifiers and loud-speakers *and* live musicians. The theatrical aspect is, of course, missing on the present record, a certain quality of mystery (since one cannot see how the sounds are being produced) taking its place.

Following the suggestion of David Tudor, the recording is the superimposition of four performances by the two of us. This is within the spirit of the directions given, which accompany the material supplied ("there may be any number of performers equal at least to the number of cartridges"), and it takes advantage of physical possibilities in a recording studio that are not available in concert performance.

There Is No Silence Now *Jill Johnston*

The most extended and perceptive review of Cage's first book came not from a musician but from Jill Johnston, the dance critic of The Village Voice *(November 8, 1962).*

Silence is the book by the man who might qualify for "best known, least understood" of contemporary artists. The collection of lectures, essays, and anecdotes by John Cage, if read both freely and carefully, should provide an experience of the man, his ideas, and inventions, that could be an occasion for expanding discoveries. Cage has pushed contemporary art beyond its thinkable limits by the breadth and strength of his intellect and the daring of his imagination, so much so that those who read *Silence* should find it difficult to curl up inside any comfortable box made before picking up the book. If that sounds discouraging I would add that John

Reprinted by permission of The Village Voice. Copyrighted by The Village Voice, Inc. 1962.

Cage is a cheerful existentialist and as such he suggests a view of the landscape more varied and changing than any afforded by squinting through the peepholes of a box.

For those who may not know, the title of the book is not a joke. In some important sense, Cage has reversed all traditional practices of composing music by making silence the material of music as well as sound. This seeming contradiction in terms is made possible by redefining the nature of silence. In the past, silence served music only to punctuate a phrase; it was, in other words, the invisible servant in the form of a pause that gave dramatic emphasis to an otherwise constant stream of sound (the ever-present directives of the master) or provided the space in that stream between the melodically continuous notes. It is well known that Cage has been prominent in upsetting this traditional practice (of melodic and harmonic structures) by working directly with sound—letting sounds be themselves, as he has often said, so that each sound may be heard only as itself and not depend for its value on its place within a "system" of sounds. It is not so well known that the key to this revolution is silence. Cage may be the first composer in history to say that there is no such thing as silence. He quotes, as personal proof, an experience in an anechoic chamber, a room made as technologically silent as possible, in which he heard two sounds: his nervous system and his circulatory system. In terms of music, this means that the conventional "pauses" of the past are as filled with sound as the music made by performers from a notated score. This sound is what happens to be in the environment, and it is "called silence only because it does not form part of a musical intention."

Silence means the whole world of sound, Life; and its entrance into the world of music means the end of that exclusive activity called Art whereby the composer makes a separate act meant to "illumine the darkness" of the chaos of everyday life. What is our life that it must be so informed by these rarefied man-made structures?

The admission of life into music originally meant noise, and, in a short article on Edgard Varèse published in 1958, Cage describes the present nature of music as "arising from an acceptance of all audible phenomena as material proper to music." (I note the parallel to the "found object," or "ready-made," in painting and construction.) Cage has extended this acceptance by making himself, so far as possible, like a man who might do nothing more (as a composer) than give a slight initial impulse to a stack of blocks, stones, cards, and watch the resulting configuration with the pleasure of experiencing something new. "Form is what interests everyone and fortunately it is wherever you are and there is no place where it is not."

One might also imagine how the same man could mastermind the most complex conjunction of events enacted by a number of people without knowing in advance what those events would be and how they would converge or separate in space and time. Such a situation is precisely what preoccupies Cage at the present time. In 1950, as a result of his already advanced ideas and actions, as well as his studies in Zen, he moved into an era of "chance operations" by implementing methods established in the *I Ching (Book of Changes,* a Chinese Book of Oracles dating from pre-Christian times), establishing sounds and continuities by tossing three coins six times. Any such method, though leaving a wide margin for the occurrence of events outside the intention of the composer, is still the "work" of that composer and permits little determination by the performer. By 1955, Cage had launched new techniques designed to eliminate this dictatorship over the performer and make him the creator of what he does (under the most fragmentary specifications), thus introducing what Cage calls indeterminacy—a truly experimental state of mind and action because it produces events "the outcome of which cannot be foreseen."

One of the most difficult lectures in *Silence* is "Indeterminacy" (given in Germany in 1958), set, like his other lectures, in a unique structure and typescript (in this case, "intentionally pontifical": small print) and examining in concise detail the degrees to which he finds each of several compositions (by Bach, Stockhausen, Earle Brown, Christian Wolff, Morton Feldman, and himself) to be "indeterminate with respect to its performance."

Cage's heresy, of course, is his partial, sometimes total, abdication of will. The pride of the West is bound up in the "profundities" resulting from the application of mind over the brute forces of nature. Now that this pride has been shattered by so many instances of irrationality in human nature and by discoveries pointing to the finitude of human knowledge, the most advanced thought and art of our time brings man back to his proper situation within nature. Cage achieves this position through external (as distinct from subconscious or "automatic") techniques—methods of chance and indeterminacy—which release him from his own psychology, taste, and permit the natural flow of impermanencies as they impress themselves on a mind empty of memories, ideas, and preconceptions; in short, empty. "If one maintains secure possession of nothing (what has been called poverty of spirit) then there is no limit to what one may freely enjoy."

Cage views the tradition of art in the West as an imposition on the viewer—forcing him to respond in a special way rather than making a situation of many possibilities. Particular emotional responses are inevitable, and, when the situation is indeterminate, each viewer will make his own experience out of it. The question, as always, arises: What is the point of making anything at all, since at any moment the world is teeming with possibilities for experience? For Cage, the answer is that there is no point, it is simply something to do, which means that living and making a thing are not two separate acts. And if everybody can do it, then let everybody, "for the more, as is said, the merrier."

Cage's adventurous intellect has brought him beyond the necessity of doing anything (in the Western sense of "striving"), and, in some sense, his music propounds the necessity of doing nothing. His silent piece, *4′ 33″*, is an expression of that necessity. It is a piece "in three movements during all three of which no sounds are intentionally produced. The lengths of time were determined by chance operations but could be any others." In this piece, Cage makes everybody present (audience) the creator and the performer. It is doubtful that too many people would be interested in paying their money to listen to themselves (coughing, chair-creaking) for an entire evening. But Cage made an important point about the nature of the "new music" that must have been well taken, by some at least, at the performance of his silent piece. Regarding the extreme result of silence in music, Robert Ashley, a composer, made a striking statement at an interview with Cage in Ann Arbor, Michigan. He said: "It seems to me that your influence on contemporary music, on 'musicians,' is such that the entire metaphor of music could change to such an extent that—time being uppermost as a definition of music—the ultimate result would be a music that wouldn't necessarily involve anything but the presence of people. That is, it seems to me that the most radical redefinition of music that I could think of would be one that defines 'music' without reference to sound."

The influence of John Cage, in the thought and action of many corners of contemporary art, is immense. One reason for this influence, I'm convinced, is his command of language. He has spoken eloquently for advanced music, his own ideas, and methods; for dance; for those who also enjoy life and like to hear somebody like Cage talk about it; for those who are also stimulated by the Eastern philosophies, Zen in particular; and for those who also sense the need for a life based on experience rather than judgment. There is no logic in Cage's lectures (unless it be the logic of style, which is everywhere in evidence); he merely describes situations, or gives spontaneous voice to convictions and insights, or rambles coherently about nothing, as he does in "Lecture on Nothing"—and, in so doing, he brings us some of the most crystal-cut prose of contemporary writing; that which comes close to, if it is not, poetry, because of its lucid condensation, its quicksilver transaction between thought and word.

[Poem for Edwin Denby] *John Cage*

Cage thinks this birthday poem for the poet and dance critic Edwin Denby was written in 1963.

rEmembering a Day i visited you
seems noW as I write that the weather theN was warm
i recall nothing we saiD—nothing wE did.
eveN so (perhaps Because of that)
that visit staYs

By permission of John Cage.

[The Arts in Dialogue] *John Cage*

This brief statement, entitled by the editor, was written for an exhibition of graphic music notation at the Honolulu Academy of Art, April, 1964.

The material of music, sound, is now understood not as a limited number of conventional pitches (those of the major and minor European scales) but as a field phenomenon. This understanding has introduced new kinds of notations. Some are graphic in character.

The arts are not isolated from one another but engage in "dialogue." Much of the new music (composing means that are indeterminate, notations that are graphic) is a reply to modern painting and sculpture (Marcel Duchamp, painting on glass, which is not separate from its environment; the "found object"; the dropped

Reprinted by permission of John Cage.

strings). However, each art can do what another cannot. It is predictable therefore that the new music will be answered by a new painting—one which we have not yet seen.

[Review of *Variations IV*] *Eric Salzman*

This review of Variations IV *(1964), in the second volume of the Everest recording (S–3230), originally appeared in* Stereo Review *(May, 1969). The reviewer, Eric Salzman, is a composer, a critic, and the musical director of WBAI, the Pacifica Foundation's radio station in New York.*

I put this record on right after listening to the Schumann *Carnaval,* and had a real start. There, cutting through the Cagean garble, was *Carnaval*, loud and clear. Well, thought I, either Schumann has gotten stuck in the speakers or my mind has finally been blown. It was neither, of course, just part of *Variations IV*. It is such coincidences that make Cage's nuttiest freakouts somehow relevant to a nutty world scrambled by a technology we hardly yet understand. Well, dig it, man, dig it!

As the totally unnecessary spoken introduction (it could have all been put in the liner notes) informs us, this is a portion of a six-hour performance in a Los Angeles art gallery, another segment of which had been released earlier by Everest. The sound sources include street noises, sounds in the gallery (audience noises, glasses tinkling at the bar, etc.), and radio broadcasts, as well as tapes and records of what not all put through a stereo mixer in various changing proportions. Talk about "information overload!" Language records, Oriental music, antique recordings, bits of pop, laughing records, news broadcasts, church bells, medical lectures, and Lord knows what. One of the parlor games of the future will be "Catch that Quote" in the John Cage *Variations IV*. I spotted *Carnaval*, the *Symphonie fantastique*, the Mozart *G Minor Symphony*, the Beethoven *Third*, *Fifth*, *Sixth*, and *Ninth*, the *Hallelujah Chorus*, the *Anvil Chorus*, the *March* from *Aïda*, bits of the *Barber* and *Boris*, *Bolero*, the *"Trout" Quintet*, the *Nutcracker*, the Bach *D Minor Toccata*, the *Hora Staccata*, and lots more!

This is, in short, the kitchen-sink sonata, the everything piece, the minestrone masterpiece of modern music, the universe symphony of everybody and everything. This is the world that tech-

Reprinted from Stereo Review, May 1969. © 1969 by Ziff-Davis Publishing Company.

nology offers us: instant communication with the entire experiential world, including the complete musical expression of the race and the entire possible aural universe (well, almost). In McLuhan's imagery, our nervous systems are extended around the world and receiving messages from every corner of the global village. Cage and Tudor just make it actually all audible to us for a certain length of time. This record is an excerpt, but so is the whole performance an excerpt; indeed the piece is an excerpt . . . from everything. It begins nowhere and ends nowhere. It has always been in progress; it is only that it became audible just recently. It is, in fact, still in progress; are you listening out there?

New York Mycological Society *John Cage*

Mycology has always been one of Cage's major enthusiasms, only partly because, as he pointed out, the words "mushroom" and "music" appear adjacent to each other in most dictionaries. For a short spell in the early 1960's, he supplied a posh New York restaurant with choice edible fungi. Following the short introductory note on the mycological organization he helped to form is a "walk-schedule" prepared by Cage for the 1965 season.

With Guy C. Nearing and Lois Long, I shared my interest in mushrooms with students at the New School by offering a class in "Mushroom Identification." This class was always very attractive to city-dwellers who wanted an escape from cement. There were for each session thirty or forty students. We have now organized the New York Mycological Society, and many of the former students are members. We have winter meetings with lectures by authorities in the field at the Bronx Botanical Gardens, and we have study meetings at the New York Academy of Sciences. Summer and fall, we roam the hills of Rockland and Westchester Counties.

New York Mycological Society: 1965 Walks
Secretary: Laurette Shapiro

Field trips at 10:00 A.M. (Note exceptions.) Guy Nearing, leader, unless stated otherwise. Time estimates from N.Y.C.

* = with Torrey Club.

Sunday, May 9, Katonah, N.Y., Art Bailie, leader. Meet at his home or RR Station. Rt. 35 off Saw Mill Parkway. 1½ hrs. by auto or train.

Sunday, May 16, Katonah, N.Y. See May 9.

Saturday, May 22, Albany, N.Y., Stanley Smith, leader. Go up New York Thruway. Meet at 2nd Albany exit (Washington Ave.) 3 hrs. by auto.

Sunday, June 6, Port Jefferson, Long Island, Euell Gibbons, author *Stalking the Blue-eyed Scallop,* leader. Food to be found & cooked on seashore. (Fungi too?) Meet at pking lot on waterfront, Pt. Jefferson, Rt. 25A, 1½ hrs.

Sunday, June 27, Southfields, N.Y. Meet on W. side Rt. 17 at Bramertown Rd. just North of Big Apple. 1½ hours by auto, bus, or train.

Sunday, July 4, Blue Lake. Meet at Sloatsburg RR Station, Rt. 17. 1½ hrs by auto/bus/train.

Sunday, July 11, Black Rock Forest. Meet at Cornwall on the Hudson Bus Station, Rt. 218 East of 9W. 2 hours by auto or Mohawk bus.

Sunday, July 18, Pine Meadow Lake. Meet at Sloatsburg RR Station. See July 4.

Sunday, July 25, Gate Hill. Meet at Suffern, N.Y. Opp. Bus Station, Junction Rts. 202 & 59, 1½ hrs.

Sunday, August 1, Arden, N.Y. Meet as on June 27.

Sunday, August 8, Ringwood Manor State Park. Meet at Sloatsburg RR Station. See July 4. Alternative Weekend, August 6–8, Londonderry, Vt. Details will be mailed on request to Secretary. Travel by auto Friday 5–7 hours.

Sunday, August 15, Stony Brook. Meet as on July 4.

* *Sunday, August 22, Southfields.* See June 27.

* *Saturday, August 28, Cold Spring, N.Y.* Stanley Smith, leader. Meet at RR Station 11:32 A.M. (10:05 from Grand Central). Junction Rts. 9D & 301.

Sunday, August 29, Blue Lake. See July 4.

Weekend, September 3–6, Maine coast, Euell Gibbons, leader. Details mailed by Sec'y. Alternative Local Walk: Southfields, Sept. 5. See June 27.

Sunday, Sept. 12, Pine Barrens, Atsion, N.J. where RR tracks cross Rt. 206. 2–2½ hrs. by auto.

Sunday, Sept. 19, Catskills. John Speziali, leader. Rt. 17 to Liberty, Rt. 55 to Curry. Meet at diner in Curry. 3 hours by car.

* *Sunday, Sept. 26, Stony Brook.* See August 15.

Sunday, October 3, Southfields. See June 27.

* *Saturday, October 9, Stissing Mtn.* Stanley Smith, leader. Meet at Pine Plains, N.Y., at 10:30 A.M. Taconic Pkway to Rt. 199, E to Pine Plains.
Sunday, October 10, Pine Meadow Lake. See July 18.
Sunday, October 17, Southfields. See June 27.
Sunday, October 24, Ringwood Manor. See August 8.
Sunday, October 31, Blue Lake. See July 4.
Sunday, Nov. 7, Pine Meadow Lake. See July 18.
Sunday, Nov. 14, Arden. See Aug. 1 & June 27.
Sunday, November 21, Southfields. See June 27.

> When *Tricholoma personatum* becomes known to the collector, either in the field or on the table, it is sure to become a favorite. It is fleshy, rotund, stocky, moist, and smooth, with a tendency in its cap to be wavy-rimmed and jauntily cocked in wet weather. It grows singly or in troops, occasionally in tufts of from five to six individuals. A patch of it is valuable and worth husbanding with covering of fine straw. . . . The common name of *T. personatum* in England is Blewits, which translated into understandable English is believed to be "blue-hats." It is everywhere eaten, being of substantial substance, good flavor, and cookable in any way. It is especially fine in patties, stews, and croquettes. McILVAINE, *One Thousand American Fungi*, 1900

Note: Nonmember Attendance on Walks—$2.00.

A Second Fame: Good Food *Ninette Lyon*

This reportage appeared originally in Vogue *(October 1, 1965). The author has written widely on cooking.*

In the artists' community at Stony Point, New York, where John Cage lives, nothing reveals the presence of a musician. The only melodies in this American composer's sparely furnished two-room cabin are the creaking of a big white hammock, the muffled sound of bare feet on cocoa matting. "We'll have a very simple lunch," he said when I arrived. "We'll pick it. I don't believe in cultivating things but in getting them where they grow naturally." We went off to gather watercress by a brook, and Cage offered it to me as if it were a bouquet of flowers. I was about to eat some when he stopped me. A digression from the pastoral: The streams are polluted by chemicals, and the salad must first be disinfected in water mixed with halazone.

Reprinted by permission.

In the house, John Cage prepared our meal with his own hands. His fingers pressed a lemon more efficiently than an electric squeezer. Friends from nearby joined us. A music teacher. A sculptor. They seemed to come down from the trees, so high on the woody hill do the community's houses stand. We ate lunch sitting on the floor, without cutlery, off big wooden dishes—cress salad with a dressing of mushroom catsup, cream, and lemon juice; organic bread, cheese, homemade jellies, and, to drink, retsina. As we ate, we talked—mostly about mushrooms. I knew John Cage was a famous mycologist, that he had won, in 1958, a television contest in Italy as a mushroom expert. I asked him when it had all started.

"During the Depression, in California," he said, "I had no money. I was living in Carmel and around my shack grew mushrooms. I decided they were edible and lived on them. After a week of this, I was invited for lunch by friends who had a house about a mile away. I found I no longer had the energy to get there. Mushrooms are so arranged chemically that we are incapable of absorbing their proteins. We can only use the minerals, the vitamins, and the water, which is not sufficient. But they taste so good they increase our ability to digest other things; our stomachs are so happy.

"I prepare them often just with butter, salt, and pepper. What you want first of all is the taste of mushroom. Each species has its characteristic. When I pick different varieties, I bake them in separate small dishes in the oven with butter and I watch them closely, as the tender ones get done first. When I have a lot of the same mushroom, I sauté them on top of the stove. You must always add salt later. Cooking is a question of principles: salt brings out the juices, and mushrooms are mostly water. For instance, the inky caps (*Coprinus micaceus*) have a great deal of liquid, black as ink. They are better fried on a high flame, and as you cook them, you tip the pan to get rid of the liquid. The French have many fine ways of cooking mushrooms: *cèpes à la Bordelaise, morelles à la crème,* artichokes filled with sautéed mushrooms and served cold as hors d'oeuvre. . . . Sometimes I experiment with new ways of serving mushrooms.

"I may have discovered this one: I broil under the grill, until they are quite crisp, caps of 'masked tricholoma' (*Tricholoma personatum*), these are also called blewits. Then I fill them with their stems chopped and sautéed with another species, the 'fairy rings' (*Marasmius oreades*). Delicious. Unfortunately these can't be found on the market: you have to hunt them.

"I have hunted mushrooms in many countries—Italy, Finland, and behind the Iron Curtain, in Poland, where the best are, and in Czechoslovakia, where I am a member of the Czechoslovakian mushroom society."

I asked him if there was any food he disliked. "I find it difficult to eat a fish that is fishy," said John Cage. "I love Japanese raw fish, but there you have the flavor of the hot radish served with it. The worst meal ever offered to me was in New Delhi: bad English hotel food, grey meat, watery vegetables. . . . I plainly refused to eat it. There are mushroom dishes in India, but few; the Indians associate mushrooms with filth. Also, one of the stories about the Buddha is that he died from a mushroom. This was unlucky because, out of three thousand mushrooms, only three or four are deadly. About twenty or thirty can make you violently sick.

"That is why you have to study and read so many books. I have about three hundred such books. But authors disagree, and you have to decide what you are willing to try. Charles McIlvaine, who wrote, in 1900, the mushroom 'Bible,' *One Thousand American Fungi,* did more for the eating of wild mushrooms than anyone else, but he must have had a very strong stomach.

"In France, there is an antidote against the 'destroying angel,' that white mushroom with a ring around its stem and a cup at the base (*Amanita verna*); the only trouble is that you have to take it before you even know you are sick. Later it has no effect. There was a well-known series of French murders by mushrooms. The man who collected them was deaf and dumb; he was instructed to gather only those with rings and cups. But not all such mushrooms are poisonous. When the man who wanted the murder done went to get the insurance, there had been no death. . . .

"Now, would you like more salad?" And as John Cage looked at me and laughed, his face crinkled and laughed with him.

Here, four recipes from John Cage.

Mushroom Dogsup

John Cage once read in a book that "catsup" is a thin liquid. So, as he likes it thick, he calls his recipe "dogsup." This can be done with any kind of edible mushroom and must be kept at least a year before being used.

Mushrooms
Salt
Ginger root
Mace

Bay leaf
Cayenne
Black pepper
Allspice
Brandy

Break the mushroom caps in small bits; slice the stem. Place in an earthenware jar with an ounce and one-half of salt for each quart of mushrooms. Let stand in a cool place for three days, stirring and mashing several times a day. On the third day, put over a low fire, in an enamel or Pyrex pan, until the juices flow freely. This takes about one-half hour. At that moment, a "catsup" is strained through a sieve; the "dogsup" is just mashed. Simmer for 20 more minutes. Measure the mash, add to each half pint: 1 ounce ginger root, chopped or grated; a blade of mace; a bay leaf, broken up; a pinch of cayenne; 1 ounce each of black pepper and allspice. Boil down to half the quantity. Add, for each half pint, a teaspoon of the best brandy. Bottle, cork, and seal. 20 quarts of mushrooms, he adds, will produce 4–5 quarts of "dogsup."

Wild Grape Jelly

As given by John Cage:

"You get a bushel basket full of wild grapes from the woods. Then you discard the stems and put the grapes over low heat to extract the juices. Then you put everything in a pillowcase and strain it overnight. As little sugar as possible must be used, to keep the jelly tart. Measure the juice, add half its quantity of sugar, and boil down slowly until a little jelly dropped on a plate keeps the shape of a pearl. Put in jars and let it cool before sealing."

Note: The jelly is very good with meat, and John Cage serves it with turkey on Thanksgiving, instead of cranberry.

Mushroom Salad Dressing

Juice of 1 lime or ½ lemon
2 tablespoons mushroom "dogsup"
Black pepper, freshly ground
Kosher salt
A pinch of cayenne
¾ cup heavy cream

This is served with a salad of peppergrass, watercress, chopped horseradish leaves, catbrier, and bitter cress.

Morels *à la* John Cage

A bottle of flat champagne is the origin of this dish: John Cage suggested serving it either as an entrée with croutons, or with *veau en cocotte* with dill and fresh noodles. He explained: "In the States, morels grow plentifully in the Midwest, but we also find a few around New York. They need sand, apple trees, and seem to like to be around farmhouses. You can never eat enough morels, so the quantity you give each person depends on what you have hunted."

For 1 pound mushrooms:
⅓ cup sweet butter
½ cup champagne
½ cup heavy cream
Salt and pepper

There is much sand in morels and they must be carefully cleaned with soft paper and a fruit knife.

Place the mushrooms and butter in a baking dish, cook in a moderate oven (350-375°F) for 20 minutes. Add champagne and continue cooking for a quarter of an hour. Season, cover with cream, and put back in the oven until the cream is bubbling.

* * *

And here is a fifth, transcribed by this book's editor in 1969.

Take the stems of *Agaricus Campestris* (the field mushroom) and chop them finely and flavor them as it pleases you—with fresh herbs, for instance, though I would avoid onions—and sauté them in plenty of butter with a little olive oil. Then stuff the caps with this mixture. Meanwhile, prepare a dish of soy sauce mixed with wasabi to taste. Take seaweed, approximately six inches by three inches and draw it through the mixture so it is dampened by the sauce, and wrap this around the broiled mushroom caps.

VII 1966–70

I hope that it is true, as Marshall McLuhan says, that the power of the arts to anticipate future social and technological developments, by a generation and more, has long been recognized; and that this concept of the arts as prophetic contrasts with the popular idea of them as mere self-expression.—EARLE BROWN, "Form in New Music" (1965)

A Lethal Measurement *Michael Zwerin*

This report of a conversation originally appeared in The Village Voice *(January 6, 1966), to which the author regularly contributes. Cage's own letter to the editor appeared two weeks later.*

"I don't think about jazz, but I love to talk, so by all means, come on up." That's what John Cage said to me last August when I telephoned to ask if he would be interested to talk to me about his thoughts on jazz.

We had trouble getting together because of busy schedules. After some weeks of futile attempts at making an appointment, I stopped trying and forgot about it. Then, a few weeks ago, he sent word to me through a mutual friend that he was now quite interested in discussing jazz. I called him and we made a date for the following Saturday afternoon.

At three o'clock sharp, my doorbell rang.

Looking at my watch, I said, "you're right on time."

"It's music," John answered.

He took off his coat, parked his attaché case, and asked me if I had some cheese, or something like that, to eat. We looked in the refrigerator and there was none, but he enthusiastically accepted some Swiss Familia cereal. When he had finished eating, we started to talk.

JOHN CAGE: "In the first place you should know that I am very critical about jazz. But, there are also many things about it for which I am grateful. One is the general involvement with the rhythmic structure. I do not refer to the regular beat. The regular beat is one of the things I am very critical of. I mean the phraseology, the rhythmic structure—a division of the whole into parts. Another thing I am grateful for is the timbre—in the great variety possible. Not only the many kinds of sounds which can be gotten from one instrument, but also the differences between the sound of one combo and another; whereas one symphony orchestra felt that it was perfectly proper for it to sound, generally speaking, like another symphony orchestra. This is one thing which made nineteenth-century music eventually so boring. It is what makes jazz interesting. That I am grateful for—that and the rhythmic struc-

Reprinted by permission of *The Village Voice*. Copyrighted by The Village Voice, Inc. 1966.

ture. Almost everything else I am not grateful for. I find it so tedious that I spend no more time than circumstances provide for listening to jazz.

"The form of jazz suggests too frequently that people are talking —that is, in succession—like in a panel discussion or a group of individuals simply imposing their remarks without responding to one another. If I am going to listen to a speech then I would like to hear some words.

"There is a form developed by Japanese poets, called 'waka.' Getting together for an evening, one of them would produce two lines and the next, in responding, would not be stimulated to do, as it were, likewise, but rather his intention would be to make what followed as different as possible from what had just preceded. In jazz, the succession seems to me relevant. For that reason, because of the closeness of reference, I find it just imaginatively unstimulating.

"Recently I watched a rehearsal of Charles Ives's *Fourth Symphony* on Channel 13 [New York's National Educational Television station]. Ives is a composer whose ideas would suggest some kind of relationship to the practices in jazz. One of the girls in the orchestra was interviewed, and she said 'It doesn't resemble music as much as it resembles life.' Now, this tendency toward blurring the distinction between art and life is the concern of much modern painting now, and much modern music. It was certainly the concern of Ives. It doesn't seem to me, in most cases, to be the concern of jazz. It seems—jazz does—to cling to the fact of art more than to the fact of life."

MICHAEL ZWERIN: "But jazz is still young, and still evolving. It came out of work songs and parades where keeping the time was essential to the purpose of the music. Anyway, the steady beat is exactly what I like in jazz—the excitement, the tension, that this can build."

JC: "Is tension really something that you want to have? Take the aesthetic traditions in India. I don't wish to imply that I like classical Indian music, but nevertheless there the nine classical emotions proper to a work of art are given as four white ones, four black ones, and one in the middle—tranquility. That is the thing to be aimed for, not the tension you speak of."

MZ: "You object to the lack of conversational quality in jazz. There is supposed to be conversation in jazz—the dialogue between the soloist and the rhythm section. It goes on simultaneously and its content is one of the key things in the music."

JC: "The person responsible for keeping the beat in jazz does not slow it down or speed it up, does he? Now, when we have something, do we always have to have this measurement of it? I think that, if you examine these things, which you think you like about jazz, and then apply them to your daily life—that is to say outside the field of jazz music altogether—you will discover that they are things you really have no use for."

MZ: "Does every work of art have to contain all of the emotions? I don't get—or expect to get—a complete experience from jazz."

JC: "The essential thing, surely, about a work of art is that it somehow be useful to us in connection with our daily lives. Now if this notion of measurement—that someone is ahead of the beat or behind the beat—is essential to our lives, it means we mustn't do anything without this lethal measurement going along with it. I myself revolt against this notion of measurement. I'm just as cross about this with Bach as I am with jazz. The similarity is very clear now that we have the jazzing up of Bach."

MZ: "I find that jazz, for better or for worse, reflects an important part of our age. For instance, it is very industrial."

JC: "But our age is far better reflected by Charles Ives."

MZ: "Yes. So?"

JC: "If one is true, how can the other be true?"

MZ: "Ives is definitely much more complicated than most jazz. But jazz has something different—not better nor worse—just different from Ives. It is more physical. The finger snapping; the goose pimples. Jazz combines the physical and the cerebral. It can interest your mind and your feet. But more than anything, it means to me an individual—a personal—form of expression. It is a man talking, as they say, off the top of his head, rather than someone like Ives planning and constructing an intellectual machine—a 'work' of art."

JC: "It seems to me that, given Ives, and given the great exploratory nature of jazz, they should explore other things which would be so much more interesting—things that are suggested by Ives."

MZ: "They are beginning, now, to get at that sort of thing."

JC: "Yes, possibly. What is involved with Ives, it seems to me, is the suggestion that not one thing is happening at a time, but rather that everything is happening at the same time. They simply are. We are living in a period when our nervous systems are being exteriorized by electronics, so that the whole glow is happening at once. There is no need to minimize the complexity of the situation, but rather a great need to make this complexity something we can all enjoy. If our arts introduce us to it, then I think they are performing a useful function. But if they continue—as so much jazz seems to me to do—to provide an escape from the actual complexity in which we live, then I think they are to be avoided.

"I could like a great deal of jazz if we had a great deal of it at one time. Say for instance that we had twelve machines here; we could put on twelve records and immediately get a situation reminiscent of Ives."

MZ: "Jazz is getting freer. Tone-rows and modes are now standard forms. They are even getting away from the time dependence —inferring it rather than clobbering you with it all of the time."

JC: "But what is free about a tone-row? You have to run up and down that row as though you were a mouse in a trap. Why do we need anything like what you call form? It is not easy to do anything. What one falls into at that point is taste and memory. What is really difficult to do is 'anything' free of taste or memory."

MZ: "Free of memory? In other words, you think there is no necessity to remember something improvised earlier and then come back to it—expand it, invert it, or generally work it over in some manner? This sort of thing is very important to me in listening to jazz."

JC: "No, this is long past in terms of serious music."

MZ: "Isn't this what art is all about, though—to inject a structure, no matter how free—any structure: your own structure, no matter how obscure? Isn't the idea to make the random things around us less random—clearer?"

JC: "This was the notion of art, but I think that has been changed. We are living in a period of great change; I think that you would agree. And, I think that this is one of the things that is being changed. We are not thinking in a Renaissance way any more."

At this point, my Cairn Terrier, Maisie, overturned a glass. As I cleaned up the mess, I asked John if he would like to hear a record of which I am particularly fond. He agreed. I put John Coltrane's "A Love Supreme" on the turntable and we listened to it.

JC: "Well, that music doesn't interest me at all. Why should it?"

MZ: "Because it interests me."

JC: "But what interest does it have for you?"

MZ: "It excites me; physically, mostly."

JC: "But this can be done in many ways."

MZ: "Sure, but that's his way. Does the regular time bother you, even when it's kept so subtly?"

JC: "Oh yes."

MZ: "To me, the main premise of jazz is the regular time—swinging."

JC: "If that is true, then I don't want any of it because I don't see it as relating to anything I can use. I don't mean use in music, I mean use in my life. The clock is okay ticking away second by second: It is useful if I have to catch a train, but I don't think that catching a train is one of the most interesting aspects of my living. I think times that I am most full with the enjoyment of life are precisely those times when the ticking of the clock, the passing of time, is forgotten. So, likewise with measurement. This reiterated beat in jazz reminds me of all those aspects of my life which don't seem to me to be the most interesting."

MZ: "Recently, I heard a rock and roll band called The Teddy Boys, and I was amazed at some of the things they did with the time. They were bending it all over the place—speeding it up; slowing it down. This was not 'art' either—they were playing in some tourist spot on Eighth Street, for people who I am sure didn't notice anything strange about the music. It worked too: musically as well as commercially."

JC: "Rock and roll is more interesting to me than jazz. It is more contemporary. The impression it gives is not of discourse but of everybody in agreement; doesn't it?"

MZ: "Yes, I suppose so. I like rock and roll too, but really, they are in agreement on a fairly low level!"

JC: "They are at least in agreement; hmmm? There is no discussion. This business of one thing being free while something else is not being free bothers me. Everyone seems to be together in rock and roll music. With it! Another thing which is quite fascinating is its use of electronics. This makes it extremely pertinent to our daily experience. And this is what Ives, among other things, felt that art should do. That is to say, it should make people stronger—and he meant stronger in every which way, including physically, including sense perceptions—to be able to perceive more than one had perceived."

There is a recording entitled *Indeterminacy* on which Cage tells many stories, each one varying in subject matter from the one before—(waka)—each story lasting about one minute. One of them is about a "silent chamber" at Harvard. When sitting in that room, he heard two sounds: a high one and a low one. Afterwards he asked the engineer why, if the room was so silent, he had heard two sounds. He described them. The engineer explained that the high sound was his nervous system in operation; the low one his blood in circulation.

Thinking of this story, I asked John why he liked the loudness of rock and roll.

JC: "Silence is all of the sound we don't intend. There is no such thing as absolute silence. Therefore silence may very well include loud sounds and more and more in the twentieth century does. The sound of jet planes, of sirens, et cetera. For instance now, if we heard sounds coming from the house next door, and we weren't saying anything for the moment, we would say that was part of the silence, wouldn't we? . . . But, I think that electronics now are essential, and I think this is what makes rock and roll so interesting."

MZ: "You said something before about our living in a period of great change. Music is changing now—it is unifying. Jazz, rock and roll, folk music, and serious music are all coming closer together, it seems to me."

JC: "I think as one goes on with sound systems in relation to sound sources, that music in this area could interest me very much. I agree with you, in other words. I would like—if anyone wanted to satisfy me—a little more complexity. You spoke, for instance, about rock and roll being on a low level."

MZ: "I meant that it was relatively uncomplex."

JC: "Exactly. Now this ought to suggest to someone in the field that something could be done that was complex."

MZ: "But then you come right back to the beat. You have to have that or it's not rock and roll."

JC: "It's a curious thing, but the reason the beat doesn't oppress me as much in rock and roll as it does in jazz, I think, is because the volume is so high. In other words, one's attention is taken away from the beat by the amplitude. The volume of sound is so great that it blurs, as it were, the fact of the beat. Any other ways that one might discover to blur the fact of the beat would increase, actually, the rhythmic interest, at least as far as I am concerned, of the music that was being made, whether it was jazz or not. Take as an example of rhythm, anything which is irrelevant. This refers back to what I said earlier about waka—the poet trying to make his remarks as irrelevant as possible to the ones that had preceded. Then if you notice your perception of sounds as you walk down the street—that is when you are in life, as it were, not in art—the things which interest you and surprise you are precisely those things that are irrelevant, and they bring to your notice the fact of time. Now, when time is organized by the regular beat, we lose, actually, the experience of irrelevance and, I would think, lose essentially the rhythm."

We ended at this point, as it was now after five and John had to leave. Before he arrived, I had been listening to some jazz records which I am to review for *Down Beat* magazine. After he left, I listened again, and found that I heard them through changed ears. As a matter of fact, most of the jazz I have listened to since then sounds different to me. I listen more critically to the music—and I see more possibilities in it.

Electronic Souls

Dear Sir:

Michael Zwerin writes well. I enjoyed reading his article, . . . which reports our meeting and conversation. Since I was hungry, his offer of Bircher Muesli was welcome. But he didn't mention that after our talk he offered me a drink, which I declined.

He also omits a specific suggestion I made with regard to liveliness in the field of rock 'n' roll: to do what Ives does in his *Fourth Symphony:* have three groups playing simultaneously in three different tempi. When this is done, I hope I'm around to hear it. I suggest (and there's no reason to stop with three) a complex starting and stopping process both during and at the beginning and end of the performance, like Ives, that is, rather than influenced, say, by Meister Eckhardt's notion that the soul is so simple it attends to only one thing at a time. Nowadays everything happens at once and our souls are conveniently electronic (omniattentive).

JOHN CAGE

Cagean Poetry *Richard Kostelanetz*

Only within the past few years has Cage been publicly accepted as a *poet,* although his witty and distinctive writing has long earned the admiration of literate people. In the introduction to my selection of recent American verse, *Possibilities of Poetry* (1970), I judged, "In fact, some of the most adventurous extensions of [Charles] Olson's method have come from writers outside his immediate camp. The composer John Cage, a sometime colleague at Black Mountain, has developed in several word-pieces entitled *Diary* a stylistically inventive shorthand for miscellaneous remarks." The first three Diaries have been reprinted in *A Year From Monday* (1967), as well as translated into other languages and included in anthologies. The worksheet reproduced below outlines the constraints Cage followed in writing the 1967 version, officially entitled: "Diary: How To Improve the World (You Will Only Make Matters Worse) 1967." The roman numerals identify the stanzas, the arabic numbers the amount of words permitted to each typeface, the symbols refer to results derived from chance operatings, as translated into terms suitable for consulting the *I Ching*. "I then write these diaries as quickly as I can," Cage told me in 1969, "and I notice it takes me a year to finish each one. I try to keep only those things that are of general use."

Regarding his own position as a poet, Cage frequently tells the following story:

> London publisher sent blank ("Fill out") so I'd be included in survey of contemporary poets of the English language. Threw it out. Week later urgent request plus duplicate blank arrived. "Please return with a glossy photo." Complied. July, August, September. Publisher then sent letter saying it'd been decided I'm not significant poet after all: If I were, everyone else is too.

And poets of note have taken to working their own versions of Cagean language—the Scottish poet Edwin Morgan in "Opening the Cage," quoted earlier as an epigraph, or the young American poet Ted Berrigan in "Really the Key," included in *Bean Spasms* (1967):*

> I dug up some hog photos and boiled them with butter, spoons, and sculptmetal for Bob Rauschenberg and Jasper Johns. I was anxious to know what Jasper Johns meant because I knew he invented boiled significance. I was curious to know whether he would find a bond of sympathy between boiled hogs and hog photos. Most gallery-goers in the North have no experience at all of boiled artifacts. People who've photographed hog boils speak the language of the pork and bean. Anyway, Jasper Johns said they were very disgusting but that they didn't taste particularly like boiled hogs. Then he painted South Carolina for a few weeks in November. When I saw him after he got boiled, he said he hated boiling them again and that they'd melted him down very much like Rauschenberg's hog had.

In parody, of course, is as much flattery as satire.

* "Really the Key" was first published in *Bean Spasms* by Ted Berrigan, Ron Padgett, and Joe Brainard (Kulchur Press, 1967).

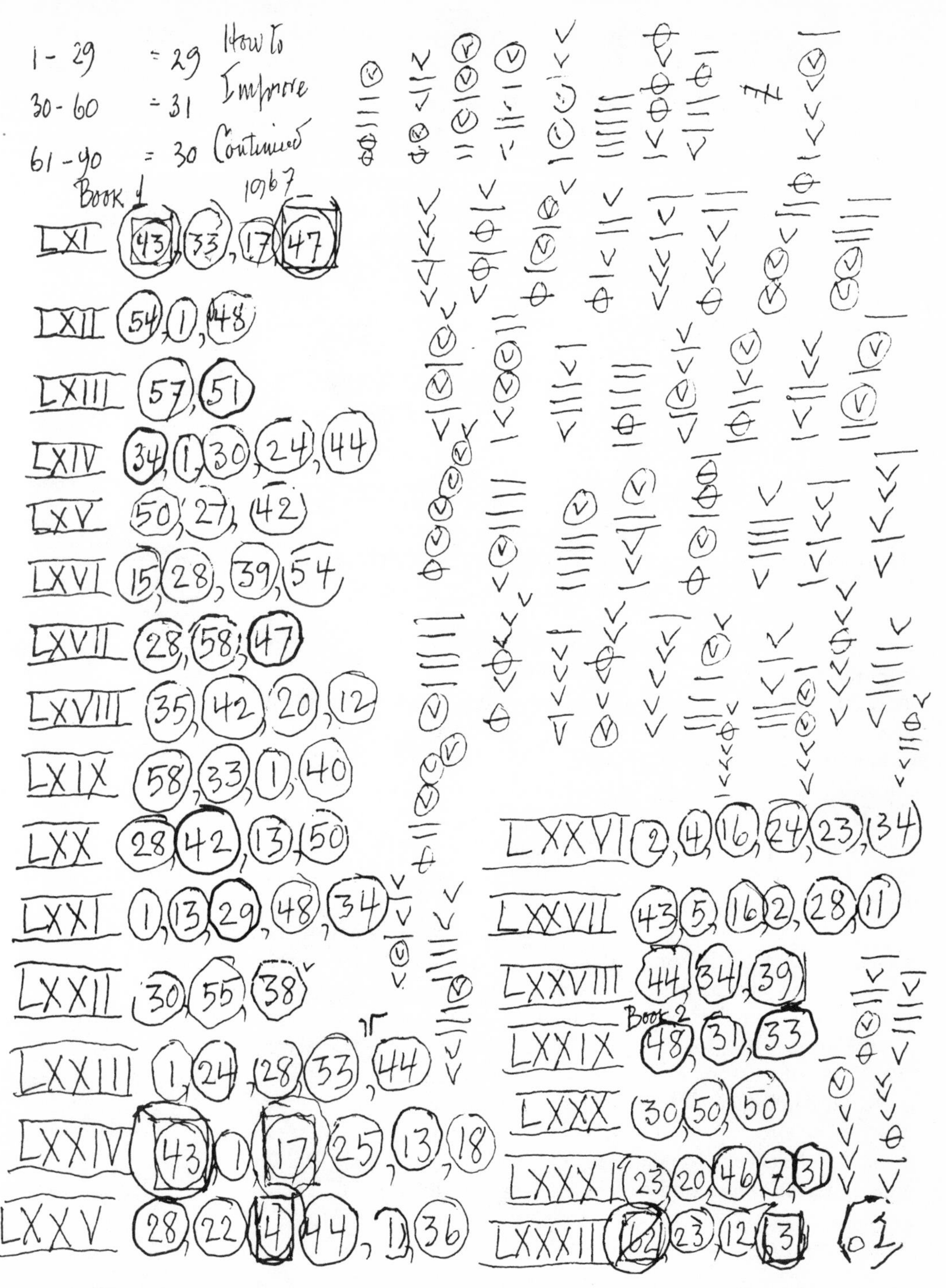

Worksheet for *Diary*, part II.

McLuhan's Influence *John Cage*

This essay was written in Cincinnati, Ohio, on January 11, 1967, in response to a request from Ralph Thomas of the Toronto Daily Star.

Much of twentieth-century art and music has been untraditional. To people satisfied with conventions, many artists have appeared as willfully irresponsible members of society. Where these same traditionalists demanded the latest models for home appliances, automobiles, etc., they ridiculed the newest forms of art. Critics reinforced these conservative attitudes.

Marshall McLuhan, by showing that society is undergoing a profound change, greater even than that from the Middle Ages into the Renaissance, and that this change is happening regardless of one's willingness to accept it or knowledge that it's happening, has greatly influenced many artists simply by encouraging them to continue their work. He has given a dramatic cause (the effect of electronics as opposed to the effect of print on sense perceptions) for the present social change. Art and now music in this century serve to open people's eyes and ears to the enjoyment of their daily environment. We are now, McLuhan tells us, no longer separate from this environment. New art and music do not communicate an individual's conceptions in ordered structures, but they implement processes which are, as are our daily lives, opportunities for perception (observation and listening). McLuhan emphasizes this shift from life done for us to life that we do for ourselves.

When, in 1961, I wrote my lecture *Where Are We Going? and What Are We Doing?,* which is four lectures heard at one and the same time, it was in awareness of McLuhan's point that nowadays everything happens at once, not just one thing at a time. I believe, as he says, that we do not live in the day of the invention of the wheel (which extended one's ability to get from one place to another), but we live as the effect of electronic inventions by means of which our central nervous systems have been exteriorized. This means, for me, that where, formerly, by disciplines of yoga, zazen meditation, the arts, and other fully engaging activities, one could make life endurable by changing his mind, now that change of mind is socialized and is taking place inevitably and can be sped up comprehensively by thinking and designing, as does Buckminster Fuller. The world we live in is now a global mind. There

By permission of John Cage.

is the possibility that that mind will come to utopian terms with itself. Using that common head, we can become people devoted to life rather than to competitiveness and the killing of one another. The problem, Fuller insists, is technological, specifically, to triple the effectiveness and to implement the distribution of the world's resources so that there will be enough to go around and that it will get around. At the beginning of this century, only 7 per cent of the world's peoples had what they needed; the rest were have-nots. Now nearly 47 per cent have. By 1972, Fuller says, it'll be 50-50. If we do not destroy ourselves as we continue changing, Fuller prophesies that, by the year 2000, everyone in the world will have what he needs. There will then be no rational reason for war. If, at that time, people want to hate one another, they may, but on an individual, rather than international, level. The middle, as Edgar Kaufmann, Jr., says in an article on design in the September, 1966, *Architectural Forum,* will have dropped out, and, having an organization, as it were, high above us, comprehensive and global, individuals—at the extreme remove from this technological order—will have available greater differences of how to spend their lives than ever before. A victory for humanity.

I have written three texts on world improvement. They would have been unthinkable without the previous work of McLuhan, Fuller, and Norman O. Brown and Marcel Duchamp, to name two others who deeply influence my thinking. Marshall McLuhan suggested that I write some music using the Ten Thunderclaps from Joyce's *Finnegans Wake*. His son Eric McLuhan is writing a book showing that the Thunderclaps give poetically a history of civilization's changes. I have taken McLuhan's suggestion and am about to write the music. Therefore, not a moment passes without my being influenced by him and grateful to him.

Re *Musicircus* *John Cage*

Cage's major recent pieces have been environmental extravaganzas, where many unexpected events occur within a delimited space. A letter written in 1969 to the book's editor describes Musicircus *(1967), done at the University of Illinois. The second selection, the editor's review of HPSCHD —performed at that campus in May, 1969—appeared, slightly abridged, in* The New York Times *(May 25, 1969).*

By permission of John Cage.

The Stock Pavilion, not "Stockyards Pavilion," is a building used for showing cattle. The arena floor is covered with a soft earth and a carpetlike material—a kind of amplified sawdust, but of a dark red-and-black color. The bleachers are cement. The structure itself is reminiscent of the turn-of-the-century exhibition buildings or, say, those in Paris of that time. (Metal structural members visible, plus glass.) *Musicircus* was done on November 17, I believe, in 1967. It consisted simply in inviting those who were willing to perform at once (in the same place and time). There were: the composer Salvatore Martirano, who, like the others, used a group of performers and gave a program of his own; Jocy de Oliveira (Carvalho) who gave a piano recital including Ben Johnston's *Knocking Piece,* music by Morton Feldman, etc.; Lejaren Hiller; Herbert Brün; James Cuomo and his band; another jazz band; David Tudor and Gordon Mumma; Norma Marder giving a voice recital sometimes accompanying a dancer, Ruth Emerson; the mime Claude Kipnis, who responded with a whole sound environment; perhaps others I don't remember—and my notes and papers regarding it are packed now. In the center of the floor was a metallic construction upon which the audience could make sounds. (This is actually someone's composition—but I don't now remember whose.) No directions were given anyone. I connected contact mikes to the light switchboard, changing the lights and, at the same time, producing sounds of the switches. At either end of the Pavilion but beyond screens, were places to buy apple cider and doughnuts, popcorn, etc. (A reference to Ives.) Ronald Nameth arranged the play of films and slides. And also obtained dark light and large balloons. We advertised it with the remark: You won't hear a thing; you'll hear everything. No admission was charged. Jack McKenzie, who was coordinator, estimated that five thousand people attended. The various musics each had a stage or platform near the bleachers so that the floor was free for use by the audience. The general sound was of a high volume, though not everything was amplified. Loudspeakers were high up around the perimeter. The general shape of the building is rectangular but with rounded ends.

Environmental Abundance

Richard Kostelanetz

Flashing on the outside underwalls of the huge double saucer Assembly Hall, at the University of Illinois's Urbana campus, were an endless number of slides from fifty-two projectors; and, inside, between 7:00 P.M. and just after midnight Friday evening, May 16, 1969, was a John Cage–Lejaren Hiller collaboration, *HPSCHD,* (1967–69) one of the great artistic environments of the decade. In the middle of the circular sports arena were suspended several parallel sheets of visquine, each 100 by 40 feet, and from both sides were projected numerous films and slides whose collaged imagery passed through several sheets. Running around a circular ceiling rim was a continuous 340-foot screen, and, from a hidden point inside, were projected slides with imagery as various as outer-space scenes, pages of Mozart music, computer instructions, and nonrepresentational blotches. Beams of light were shrewdly aimed across the interior roof, visually rearticulating the modulated concrete supports. In several upper locations were spinning mirrored balls reflecting dots of light in all directions—a device reminiscent of a discotheque or a planetarium; and the lights shining directly down upon the asphalt floor also changed color from time to time. There was such an incredible abundance to see that the eye could scarcely focus on anything in particular; and no reporter could possibly write everything down.

The scene was bathed in a sea of sounds, which had no distinct relation to each other—an atonal and astructural chaos so continually in flux that one could hear nothing more specific than a few seconds of repetition. Fading in and out through the mix were snatches of harpsichord music that sounded more like Mozart than anything else; this music apparently came from the seven instrumentalists visible on platforms raised above the floor in the center of the Assembly Hall. Around these bases of stability were flowing several thousand people, most of them students at the University, some of whom came from far away—the museum directors from Chicago and Minneapolis, the writers, artists, and film crew (doing a profile of Cage) from New York City, students who hitchhiked from all over the Midwest, and the not-young lady harpsichordist who first commissioned *HPSCHD,* all the way from Switzerland.

Most of the audience milled about the floor while hundreds took seats in the bleachers. All over the place were people, some of

© 1969 by the New York Times Company. Reprinted by permission.

them supine, their eyes closed, grooving on the multiple stereophony. A few people at times broke into dance, creating a show within a show that simply added more to the mix. Some painted their faces with Dayglo colors, while, off on the side, several students had a process for implanting on white shirt a red picture of Beethoven wearing a sweatshirt emblazoned with John Cage's smiling face. As in the Central Park be-ins, I met friends from various places I had not seen in ages, and other people I knew before only by mail.

While co-composer Hiller officiously checked on the machinery and its upkeep—though it scarcely mattered artistically if a few channels were lost—John Cage glided around the hall beaming beatifically. Altogether, the sound was rather mellow and nonclimactic, except for occasional blasts of eardrum-piercing feedback that became more frequent toward the end. Just after midnight, the electronic sound machinery was turned off, the mix ran down into silence, the house lights turned on, and the elated audience drifted out. At parties that night and the following day, people contrasted perceptions; and, while everyone saw the same things in general, each one registered a specific experience particularly his own.

The sounds came from fifty-eight amplified channels, each with its own loud-speaker high in the auditorium. Fifty-one channels contained computer-generated music composed in octaves divided at every integer between five and fifty-six tones to the octave (five tones, six, seven, eight, up to fifty-six, except number twelve); and since all these channels were going at once, with each operator of the four assembled tape recorders permitted to adjust their respective volumes, the result was a supremely microtonal chaos in which, as Cage's Illinois colleague Ben Johnston put it, "It was insured that no order can be perceived."

On top of this mix, one could hear seven amplified harpsichords, for *HPSCHD* is that word reduced to the six characters necessary for computer transmission. Three were playing fixed versions of Mozart's late-eighteenth-century "Introduction to the Composition of Waltzes by Means of Dice," in which the performer is allowed to play sections in any order he wishes. With computer assistance, Cage and Hiller realized three different fixed versions of the fragments, two of which incorporated other passages from Mozart. Two more harpsichordists, Neely Bruce and Yuji Takahashi, played through differing but individually fixed collages of harpsichord music from Mozart to the present, while David Tudor played "computer print-out for twelve-tone gamut." The seventh keyboard operator, Philip Corner, had nothing more specific than blanket permission to play any Mozart he wished; and every instrumentalist received this further instruction: "In addition to playing his own solo, each harpsichordist is free to play any of the others."

In sum, then, above the microtonal din were references to Mozart, a favorite classic composer of both Cage and Hiller. "With Bach," Cage explained, "there is a tendency to fixity and unity; in Mozart, there is scalar diversity and abundance. I used to think of five as the most things we could perceive at once; but the way things are going recently, it may be in a sense of quantity, rather than quality, that we have our hope. When you use the word 'chaos,' it means there is no chaos, because everything is equally related—there is an extremely complex interpenetration of an unknowable number of centers." For all its diffusion, therefore, *HPSCHD* was an indubitably organic piece, where every element contributed its bit to the whole and which successfully established a unique and coherent ensemble of interrelated parts.

So the aural content of the work—what one should hear—is literally fifty-eight channels of sound, even though most of us can scarcely separate more than one or two from the others at any time. "You don't have to choose, really, but, so to speak, experience it," Cage added between puffs on his filtered and mentholated cigarette. "As you go from one point of the hall to another, the experience changes; and here, too, each man determines what he hears. The situation relates to individuals differently, because attention isn't focused in one direction. Freedom of movement, you see, is basic to both this art and this society. With all those parts and no conductor, you can see that even this populous a society can function without a conductor." Cage characterized *HPSCHD* as "a political art which is not about politics but political itself. As an anarchist, I aim to get rid of politics. I would prefer to drop the question of power, whether black power, flower power, or student power. Only by looking out the back window, as McLuhan says, do we concern ourselves with power. If we look forward, we see cooperation and things being made possible, to make the world work so any kind of living can take place."

The visual material was compiled under the supervision of Ronald Nameth and Calvin Sumsion, both connected with the university; and Robert Frerck supervised the use of films. There was no dress rehearsal, nor did the piece really need one. Forty-eight people, in sum, contributed to the performance. In the course of gathering equipment, Cage persuaded an awed official of the GAF

Corporation to lend eighty Sawyer projectors ("He wanted not a few but eighty!"), just as he earlier persuaded other companies to lend fifty-two tape recorders and all the amplification machinery; and art students were enlisted to paint innumerable slides. NASA lent 40 films and 5,000 slides (explaining the abundance of outerspace imagery), and the Museum of Modern Art extended a print of George Méliès's *Trip to the Moon* (1902). And so on and so on, all to fill up the Hall with an indeterminate chaos of images, all to complement the indeterminate chaos of sounds.

Work on *HPSCHD* (pronounced either Hip-see-kid, H-P-S-C-H-D, or as Cage prefers, "harpsichord") began nearly two years ago, just after Cage arrived at Illinois as Visiting Research Professor in the School of Music and Associate of the Center for Advanced Study; on hand, he already had a standing commission from the Swiss harpsichordist Antoinette Vischer. Wanting to "make with the computer an art that has not been possible before," he sought out Lejaren Hiller, who pioneered computer-assisted composition; and together they worked out the fifty-two tapes, many of which were composed with the *I Ching* randomizing procedures Cage has long favored. "Every single note was a mutual decision," Hiller declared. "It's a rather unique instance that two composers' endeavors are so intertwined that you cannot tell them apart." Nonetheless, the piece's total conception seems more distinctly Cage's than Hiller's, whose reputation stems from the use of computers rather than a distinct style; and, within the extant repertoire of electronic music, these tapes sound rather simple and repetitious. Cage's regular music publisher, C. F. Peters, plans to release a 631-page "score," and "a particular condensation of the piece," as Hiller puts it, has just been released by Nonesuch Records (H-71224). Although only three of the harpsichord parts are included, the record offers a more intensified (and, shall we say, artful) aural chaos than the diffuse original; but that perhaps is precisely what a recording should do. Each album also includes computer-printed instruction that, to quote Hiller, "tells the listener how to turn the volume- and tone-controls every five seconds to hear the piece properly. Every sheet is different, so you can trade it off like baseball cards." Although recording is not an appropriate medium for this aleatory and spatial art, this remains, in my opinion, the best (and most) Cagean record ever made.

HPSCHD was not just a musical light show or an extravagant multi-media display but a masterful example of that peculiarly contemporary art, the kinetic environment, or an artistically activated enclosed space. In this respect, *HPSCHD* extends Cage's continuing interest in filling huge spaces with a lifelike chaos of sounds and sights, or building an artful universe within the larger world. Here, as before, Cage prefers nontheatrical spaces, like a gymnasium or a "stock pavilion" (scene of a 1967 Urbana piece), for his multiringed, highly theatrical artistic circus. Who would believe, before Cage arrived, that Urbana's Assembly Hall itself could be transformed into a work of art? Whereas *Variations VII*, by all counts the best piece at the 1966 Theater and Engineering Festival, filled up the cavernous 69th Regiment Armory, *HPSCHD* tackles an even larger space, for an even larger audience, and makes it succumb to his environmental art.

HPSCHD is a Universe Symphony in the distinctly American tradition dating back to Charles Ives, who spent the last forty years of his life on a similarly all-inclusive but unfinished work. As Ives imagined his *Universe Symphony,* groups of musicians would be distributed around the countryside—up the hills and in the valleys; and they would sound a joyful disorder similar to the last movement of his *Fourth Symphony* (1910–16). However, thanks to technological progress, Cage and Hiller can use facilities Ives never had—tape recorders, amplifiers, motion-picture and slide projectors—to distribute their chaotic art all over an enormous space; and, in the increased quantity, was a particular kind of quality never before experienced in either art or life. In the future, let *HPSCHD* turn on even larger spaces, like Madison Square Garden, the Astrodome, or even the Buckminster Fuller dome that someday ought to be constructed over midtown Manhattan. Wish you were, or could be, there.

These Days *John Cage*

This essay was written in 1968 in response to an invitation to contribute to a symposium on "Alternatives to Violence," but the book's publisher decided against including it.

Parallels may now be drawn between individual experience and social experience, for we have, through electronic technology, extended the central nervous system (Marshall McLuhan). Mind, formerly housed in each person's head, is now also exteriorized, at home outside (nature, society) globally, and, more and more,

By permission of John Cage.

outerspatially, that is, universally ("God" made "definite"—Buckminster Fuller).

Searching for alternatives to world violence, we can therefore take as directives proven means used now or formerly by individuals to "pacify" their minds. What were and/or are they?

Self-discipline. That is to say: self-alteration, particularly with regard to ego likes and dislikes, ego memory and resultant fixed habit ("Leave thy father and mother and follow Me." Disciple. Yoga: yoking or, rather, making nonexistent the ego. Cf. the ten ox-herding pictures of Zen Buddhism. Once caught, the ox [the ego] is no longer visible. What happens? The ox-herder, fat, smiling, [Cf. Konrad Lorenz, conclusion of *On Aggression, re* laughter, humor], returns to the village bearing gifts). The ego can act as a barrier to daily experience (the senses) by cultivating its judgment-making faculty and as a barrier to nocturnal experience by paying no attention to the poetic warnings given by dreams. Disciplined (by means, traditionally, of myth, religion—e.g., meditation, sitting crosslegged, philosophical exercises—e.g., koan, Wittgenstein, arts, crafts—when these are not self-expressive, ego-flattering activities, the sciences—e.g., Thoreau: "I am sorrel; I am ice," whatever to which one gives oneself away), the ego is no longer a barrier. One's attention is placed so that "ego" is open, fluent with its experience—dream or received through the senses; it doesn't sit in judgment, but joins in service to others—whether sentient or nonsentient (I'll go along, he said, with the here and the now).

Say one doesn't have the "strength" to discipline (change) himself. Then there are teachers. (The world is never left without them. "I am with you always.") And there are chemicals, electrodes. We may be put away, changed in hospitals, or put ourselves away (drop out, depend on drugs).

Enough for the instance of the individual. Time passes. What of all Mankind and the Earth he inhabits? Global (at least) Mind must be pacified. This will not be accomplished by means of politics: Buckminster Fuller points out, "Take away the energy-distributing networks and the industrial machinery from America, Russia, and all the world's industrialized countries, and, within six months, more than two billion swiftly and painfully deteriorating people will starve to death. Take away all the world's politicians, all the ideologies, and their professional protagonists from these same countries, and send them off on a rocket trip around the sun and leave all the countries their present energy networks, industrial machinery, routine production and distribution personnel, and no more humans will starve nor be afflicted in health than at present." But it could be accomplished (Buckminster Fuller) by means of unemotional (cf. zazen, yoga) problem solving (comprehensive design science), relating world resources to human needs, so that, A.D. 2000, 100 per cent of humanity will be "haves." Nations (i.e., ego) removed, regenerative—constantly accomplishing more with less—fluency of man and world as a university from which no one graduates. Organization not for control of others, but for implementation of fullest life for others (e.g., air travel, telephone, water that's not polluted, air that's fit to breathe, clothing that suits whatever climate, absence of hunger)—Fuller: "As long as one human being is hungry, the entire human race is hungry," the home (currently being Russia-U.S.A. designed as space-ship, wireless, and free of utility pipes) placed wherever one wishes to live or move, population stabilized (birth and death rates changingly balanced) and upgraded (eugenics), *use* instead of ownership, property globalized through electronics (there is only one Person, the One we are), etc.

We have, that is, nothing but alternatives to violence, things to which Global Mind may give attention. Time-consuming things rather than humanity-destroying ones: Otherwise, Fuller warns, "Oblivion." Nothing's accomplished in the way of Global Discipline by being angry because the world's angry (i.e., protest against war), or, rather, what's accomplished is to give further lease on life to divisive structures (nations, politics, finance) that would otherwise die a natural (i.e., technological) death. Recent instance: French riots; de Gaulle's position subsequently strengthened. Divisiveness is being weakened by technology: Electrical power, by means of new dielectrics permitting 1,500-mile radius of transmission, now exceeds national boundaries.

We don't vote. Why? The election was national, concerned with power. Our attention's on the world. Concern is service, not power.

We cultivate getting things done by as many people as are interested in doing them without any one person's telling the others what to do.

We renounce laws that protect those who "have" from those who "have-not." If forced to obey them, we do so unseriously.

Substitute for laws: systems intelligently set up so that they work for all, e.g., utilities.

There'll be violence (we're in the midst of what Fuller calls the critical period; at present, 47 percent have and 53 percent don't; by 1972, it'll be 50-50—end of critical period), but attention placed elsewhere will minimize it (Daniel in the Lions' Den).

[Cunningham Stories] *John Cage*

These stories were scattered through an issue of Dance Perspectives *(Summer, 1968) especially devoted to Merce Cunningham; and Cage sometimes declaims selections from them during performances of Cunningham's* How To Pass, Kick, Fall, and Run *(1966).*

At the age of twelve, Merce Cunningham went to study dancing with Maude Leon Barrett. She was not his first instructor. He had performed in public a "sailor's hornpipe" at the age of eight. Mrs. Barrett used to say she had one foot in the grave and jiggled the other in order to stay out.

One day early in summer, Mr. Cunningham drove over to Mrs. Barrett's to pick Merce up. Mr. Barrett was on the roof doing some shingling. Lucille was in the living room pumping the player piano. Leon was in the dining room practicing basketball. A dog that was out of his mind was running in circles chasing his tail from one room to the other. Merce and Margery Barrett were with Mrs. Barrett in the kitchen practicing a tap routine. Instead of making his presence known, Mr. Cunningham turned around and went home alone.

After he was grown up a little, Merce's mother told him that, when he was a baby, he fell out of a car and that a passerby, noticing what had happened, thought he was a bundle.

Once, when he was lighting the candles before mass in St. Mary's, Merce set his surplice on fire.

Joyce Wike and Merce Cunningham used to save enough money by not eating for three days so that, on the fourth day, they could dine in Seattle's finest restaurant.

When the information was released that Merce Cunningham had been awarded a Guggenheim Fellowship, someone asked him what

Copyright 1968 by Dance Perspectives Foundation. Reprinted by permission.

he was going to do with all that money. His reply was one word: Eat.

After a solo recital, which I accompanied at a university in Oregon, Merce went to the office of the Women's Physical Education Department to pick up the check. The head of the department had not been pleased with the program. She asked whether Merce actually insisted on receiving payment. A discussion followed: We needed the money in order to get to the next engagement, which was in Columbus, Ohio, where the stage was small and the proscenium was low. Each time Merce jumped, his head disappeared from view.

Merce Cunningham phoned his mother in Centralia, Washington, to say that, after the dance program in Cheney, Washington, he and his company were to be entertained in the home of one of her friends, Mrs. So-and-So. Mrs. Cunningham said, "Oh! Put your best foot forward." When we got to the party, it turned out that the principal guest was the local distributor for the Chevrolet Company and that our hostess was the wife of the Ford Company's agent. None of the people there had come to the dance program. However, there was very good food and drink and we stayed fairly late. As we were leaving, Mrs. So-and-So, speaking to Merce Cunningham, said, "Thank you for coming and fitting in so well."

Merce Cunningham's doctor used to be Dr. Lawton. Dr. Lawton's the one who prescribed Merce's vitamin pills and breakfast powders. He told Merce to sit when he didn't have to stand, to lie down when he didn't have to sit, and to sleep whenever he could sleep. Possessed of an active disposition, Cunningham keeps busy even when he's sitting. With pen or pencil he makes calendars, circling the days involving performances or other engagements. One calendar finished, he starts another. For years, sitting at the breakfast table, he taught himself Russian. This enabled him to speak in their language to members of the Bolshoi Ballet before performing with his company for them. Formerly, using tweezers, he filled baskets with webs of many differently colored threads, colored toothpicks suspended in them by means of glue. Having learned to knit, he knitted the many-colored costume he wears in *Lavish Escapade*.

The Cunningham Company used to make transcontinental tours in a Volkswagen Microbus. Once, when we drove up to a gas station in Ohio, and the dancers, as usual, all piled out to go to the toilets and exercise around the pumps, the station attendant asked me whether we were a group of comedians. I said, "No. We're from New York."

Cunningham is, by inclination, a soloist. When the studio roof leaks, as it always does and has after heavy rain or snow falls, he puts pails and saucepans at strategic points, dresses up in a black or white mechanic's zippered jump-suit, gets out a bucket of roof-coating and a scrub brush with a handle like that of a broom, goes up on the roof, and works there until the job is done. Recently, professional repairmen did this work following pre-Christmas rains. When Cunningham was telling Viola Farber how much more effective his roof-tarring was than theirs, she said, "But you've had more experience."

One day while he was sweeping the Fourteenth Street studio, Merce heard a knock at the door. After he opened it, one of the two men in the hall explained they were city inspectors and wanted to see the man in charge. Merce said, "I can't help you." One of them asked, "Well, who are you?" "Oh," said Merce, "I'm just the fellow who cleans up around here."

Merce was upstairs teaching. I was downstairs chatting with David Vaughan, the studio secretary. A young man came in at 11:30 expecting to take the class. Mr. Vaughan said, "You're too late. You are permitted to be five minutes but not half an hour late. You know, don't you, what Mr. Cunningham would do if I let you enter the class at this time?"

Mr. Sarabhai from Ahmedabad in India, after seeing a performance by the Cunningham company, asked Merce whether his dancing was popular in the United States. Merce explained that programs were given principally in universities and colleges. Mr. Sarabhai said, "That isn't what I mean. Do people do it after dinner?"

Unchallenged by the physical difficulties of dance technique, Merce Cunningham spent many months doing the same exercises except for his arms. His arms, held in the air above his head, supported a cast-iron automobile brakedrum.

Every morning Merce Cunningham does his yoga. He is self-taught by means of books he collected on the subject. Aware of the intimate connection of body and mind, and not having a yogi's assistance, he proceeds with caution. Once, while breathing deeply in the lotus position, he noticed that an unfamiliar force seemed to be rising up his spine. He changed his mind and very shortly was standing on his feet.

Among the Cunningham company's performances in India was one in Chandigarh. This city, north of Delhi, is the capital of the Punjab. Le Corbusier designed the three large state buildings there and also did the city planning. Our Indian friends didn't want us to miss seeing Chandigarh, so an arrangement was made that we would perform there without fee, that the local sponsors would take care of our travel to and from Delhi, and that they would also provide a place for us to stay. Our transportation was by bus, a bus that picked up other passengers and moved up and down more than it moved forward. We arrived at our destination late at night. But it was an abandoned multiple-dwelling with toilet facilities unfamiliar to us, and rooms with built-in concrete beds without anything on them. Our sponsors said we should have brought bedrolls with us. With some delay and difficulty and at our own expense, we changed to a more or less regular hotel. The rehearsals the next day in the theater were not easy. Equipment we'd requested was not available. Electricians, instead of using plugs, simply inserted bare wires in sockets. At the last minute, two small thin boys, having heated over charcoal heavy slabs of iron fitted with wooden handles, pressed the delicate, white nylon veils for *Nocturnes* better than they'd ever been pressed before. At the performance, the house was full and the audience was at all times delighted. The manager of the theater came backstage afterward and asked us to remain in Chandigarh and perform for several days on a percentage basis. He said, "If we'd known how good you were, we wouldn't have treated you so badly."

[European Influences]

Daniel Charles and Eric Salzman

These two essays, written several years apart, indicate Cage's immense influence upon contemporary European composition. Daniel Charles has taught philosophy at the University of Aix-en-Provence, France. His remarks are excerpted from a longer essay included in Paul Henry Lang and Nathan Broder's Contemporary Music in Europe *(Schirmer, 1965); Eric Salzman's review of Karlheinz Stockhausen's* Hymnen *(1968) originally appeared in* Stereo Review *(September, 1969).*

Entr'acte: "Formal" or "Informal" Music*

Daniel Charles

One of the possible criteria by which to characterize the different avant-garde composers in France is their attitude toward John Cage's music.

Xenakis is doubtless the most favorably inclined; in an article published in 1962, he criticized the poetics of the "open work" developed by the "neo-serialists" in recent times. However, he took care to add the following paragraph:

> Still, this meaningless attitude can only be valid in one case. To destroy consciousness and let the deeper strata of the psyche emerge in unreasoned acts is a fascinating thing, which, however, ought to be supplemented by yoga conceptions on the mastery of the reflexes, etc. This path, which John Cage, Earle Brown, and David Tudor have opened up in music, is related to the attempts in certain paintings and poems. It is fraught with promises for a future that will have to produce the integration of conscious and subconscious reason into a harmonious whole that has been lost.

But this paragraph disappeared when the article was reproduced, and considerably enlarged, in *Musiques formelles.* Apart from Xenakis (and Messiaen, a prudent admirer of the prepared piano), French musicians have reacted to Cage with little more than a mass of indignation, not to say hostility.

Boulez was the first to react, in *Aléa*, against what he called "chance by inadvertence." Since then, his stock of denigration has not run dry; I have seen him lead a riot, at Darmstadt, against a piece by La Monte Young. And, in the work he recently published under the title *Penser la musique aujourd'hui*, one may find a little anthology of his recriminations.

In 1958 I went to Brussels, in connection with the Exposition ("the shop window of the universal economy," as Heinz-Klaus Metzger put it), to accompany Pierre Schaeffer in my capacity as member of the Groupe de Musique Expérimentale ("musique concrète") of the French radio and television network. I had been at a Cage concert, after which the Canadian composer Gilles Tremblay and I had the misfortune of manifesting our approval of *Winter Music.* "You must choose," Schaeffer immediately exclaimed, "between Cage and the Studio."

Finally, in a recent polemic that appeared in the *Mercure de*

* Copyright *The Musical Quarterly.* Reprinted by permission.

France, Gilbert Amy (who speaks the language of orthodox neo-serialism pretty accurately) and François Mâche (a fugitive from "musique concrète" who nevertheless claims to adhere more or less to Xenakis) were able to agree on one point alone: that the primacy of writing, or "graphisme," as conceived by Cage is unacceptable.

Even if all this mistrust does fluctuate—*Music of Changes* has been given a hearing at the Domaine Musical, and François Bayle has done a great deal to keep Cage's ideas from being ignored in Parisian musical life—the general climate until now has been one of hostility.

It is not my intention to go into the reasons why this ostracism has taken root and, on the whole, maintained itself. I have only mentioned the matter the better to obtain a detached view of recent musical mores in France. One may nevertheless say that each man's conception of music history—and of the role he would like to play in it—is the factor that determines his reactions to Cage. The latter's works are only known very imperfectly, but their reputation appears to be established: Their composer is thought a visionary, and his productions are considered teratological in that they blindly deny, or seem to deny, all historicity, all relationships to contemporary musical "evolution."

This situation has not escaped Cage himself. No doubt the average avant-garde musician in France resembles his Dutch confrère—as least, if one is to believe this passage from *Silence:*

> Once in Amsterdam, a Dutch musician said to me, "It must be very difficult for you in America to write music, for you are so far away from the centers of tradition." I had to say, "It must be very difficult for you in Europe to write music, for you are so close to the centers of tradition."

In Boulez, the master of the evolutionary mode of thinking, one finds this concern over loyalty to the Western heritage developed to the highest degree, in the guise of an irrepressible penchant for craftsmanship, for the finely wrought work, for the severity of the finished product. It is as though he had taken an ethical vow, intrinsic to his aesthetics; he has often admitted to it. Everything must be structured, everything is finely chiseled in the end: That is why his writings allot so much space to technique and risk being mistaken for catalogues of recipes, if the reader is not on his guard. That is also why, until recently, they manifested such reserve regarding form: Before arriving at a renewal of form, it was necessary, after all, to erect a morphology, to build a syntax—so that the forms themselves were craftsmanlike, the direct results of technical manipulations; it is no insult to the composer of *Marteau sans maître* to state that in *Structure 1 a,* for example, form as such does not exist, that it is nothing more than an assemblage of parts, that it is simply the result of a handling of parameters. Similarly, Boulez's writings remained reticent on the question of form—almost in the manner of the most "Oriental" of French musicians, Messiaen—up to *Sonate que me veux-tu?*, where one learns that "music is at present in possession of a wide range of means, of a vocabulary that once more attains a universality of conception and of understanding"—which ought to make it possible to tackle "a considerable need: that of thinking through the whole notion of form again."

* * *

In this one sees the fundamental difference that is doubtless at the root of Boulez's mistrust for the procedures of a man like Cage. "The European works present a harmoniousness, a drama, or a poetry, which, referring more to their composers than to their hearers, move in directions not shared by the American ones. Many of the American works envisage each auditor as central . . ." In Boulez's eyes, it would be inconceivable for the creator to descend from his pedestal; to be sure, his mailed fist will not relent with regard to the work, but it will (in a temporary way) with regard to the performer, whose duty it is to convey, as rigorously as before, what has once and for all been decided.

*Hymnen**

Eric Salzman

This work is a huge, monstrous tape fresco in an electronic junk-music idiom that one associates with certain new American, rather than European, music. The central materials of *Hymnen* (the German title) are national anthems and patriotic airs which, along with electronic and recorded sounds, various voices, and other more or less recognizable scraps (animal noises in one place), are mixed, modulated, and intermodulated, speed-changed, and otherwise mumbled, jumbled, rumbled, mangled, mashed, squashed, battered, bashed, torn, tattered, scratched, scribbled, and strangled, the whole alternating with black silences and fragments of spoken phrases in various languages. Stockhausen connoisseurs will recognize the master's voice as well as a big chunk of *Deutschland über Alles* (or, if you will, the *Emperor's Hymn,*

* Copyright *Stereo Review*. Reprinted by permission.

although Stockhausen clearly intends the other reference) that also appeared in the *Solo for Melody Instrument* recorded by the trombonist Globokar for Deutsche Grammophon (and which I guessed at the time was a spin-off from *Hymnen*).

It is worthwhile to compare this monumental work with the *Variations IV* of John Cage (to whom part of *Hymnen* is dedicated, the other dedicatees being Pierre Boulez, Henri Pousseur, and Luciano Berio). The Cage, portions of which have been issued on Everest, is less a work than a pattern for an event; it is a prototype of a kind of experience for which *Hymnen* is an (admittedly very different) interpretation. Cage also uses bits of familiar music—all the old favorites of the repertoire—and he cheerily transforms them, junks them, and/or mixes them with electronic sounds, other recorded sounds, as well as environmental noises. The whole is casual (in both senses), multifaceted, totally nonlinear; it is, in part or in whole, a relaxed, totally engaging, total, and even joyous experience. The Stockhausen, although its length is presumably variable, is far more organized. It has a cutting edge like a steel blade and a tense, nervous quality that never lets up. For all that goes on, it has a curiously flat, one-dimensional surface, across which patterns—simple, complex, familiar, unfamiliar, static, dramatic, dense, thin, electronic, recorded—are traced. The Cage is an experience and, even taken in big doses, an engrossing one. The Stockhausen is an ordeal—fascinating, disturbing, monumental, melodramatic, powerful, and exhausting.

The difference is, I suppose, the difference between a Rudi Dutschke and an Abbie Hoffman, between German SDS and the Yippies. Anyway, it'll give your equipment a workout; but don't expect to be able to detect any system distortion—you'll never be able to tell.

[*Not Wanting to Say . . .*] *Barbara Rose*

In Not Wanting to Say Anything About Marcel *(1969), an artistic multiple done on both Plexiglas and lithography paper in collaboration with the designer Calvin Sumsion, Cage pursued the suggestion mentioned a decade before in a letter to Hans G. Helms: "The application of some useful means, such as chance operations, to bring about the spacing so that the production of a form (in the sense of object) would only result in the case of a 'coincidence.'" The following essay by*

Copyright EYE Editions. Reprinted by permission.

the American art critic Barbara Rose originally appeared in the brochure announcing the work.

One can think of John Cage in many ways. More than a composer, he has been philosopher, poet, inventor, teacher, prophet (true or false, depending on one's viewpoint). Given his wide range of activity, the idea of John Cage as a visual artist does not seem so strange. Rather it seems merely another extension of a multidimensional personality defying the limitations of a one-dimensional world. One is not surprised to find Cage making graphics; the odd thing perhaps is to find him the last to use his own discoveries in creating an object. Since much of his activity has been directed toward breaking the hold of any elite, it is also logical that his first art objects should be multiples, editions available to the many as opposed to "the happy few."

That Cage has created revolution, not only in music, but in all the arts cannot be denied. He has formulated a new attitude toward the subject matter, content, composition, and function of art. When he advised artists to leave their ivory towers and look at the world around them again, he attacked the century-long alienation of the artist from society. When he refused to impose a set meaning to content, but left interpretation open to the psychology and experiences of the individual viewer, he destroyed the symbolic and metaphoric basis on which art since the Renaissance has rested. When he used chance as a means of composing, he undermined the traditional method by which Western art was structured. When he proposed that radical function was of greater significance today than a given radical form, he exposed the rhetoric of formalism as merely a revolutionary posture.

Of course, Cage would be the first to admit that he is not alone in making the revolution. But he has been especially effective in communicating his radical ideas through his music, lectures, and writing. Now he has begun to explore some of his own principles in a visual medium. Characteristically, he enlarges the occasion of making something beyond the object—to extend his thinking about art and life in general.

In making these lithographs and plexigrams, Cage explores specific problems. He is especially interested in the use of chance as a means of determining image, composition, and color, but he is also examining the problem of meaning and a way of behaving as well. By posing himself the problem of creating an homage to his late friend Marcel Duchamp without referring to Duchamp, he is asking what happens when one avoids something deliberately.

Among the things he is trying to avoid are conscious choice, taste, harmony, and quality as deliberately imposed elements.

The result of Cage's investigation surely proves that the artist asserts himself even in negation. For the lithographs and plexigrams he has produced have quality, harmony, order, and taste. Above all, they remind one of Duchamp—their suspended images creating a feeling of three-dimensional forms floating in free space reminiscent of Duchamp's experiments with perception and illusionism. Permitting a work to occur, as opposed to imposing an order, he has produced an extremely personal object, delicate in tone, original in color, excellent in workmanship.

Above all, Cage's graphics prove that artistic freedom is yet another illusion. Not even the artist is free of himself, his tastes, memories, and associations. The decision to avoid something is not enough, if the artist's individual sensibility asserts itself even in a situation determined by change. Cage's first visual works are proof of his original premise: We must accept, since we are not free to avoid anything.

VIII some random remarks

What I think is more important today than the accomplishment of an individual is social change. The meaning of something is in its use, not in itself. That is Wittgenstein's discovery, and this general climate of thought is also in Satie.—JOHN CAGE, in conversation (1970)

John Cage: Some Random Remarks

Richard Kostelanetz

The editor of this documentary monograph has written on Cage several times, in almost as many ways. The following essay, which represented his most extended critical reassessment, was originally published, in somewhat different form, in The Denver Quarterly, *III, 4.*

To be unpolitical does not mean to be without politics. Every attitude that is more than egoistic is to that extent social, and a social attitude is a political attitude.—HERBERT READ, "The Politics of the Unpolitical" (1943)

John Cage is one of these rare figures whom, if he did not already exist, the philistines would need to invent; for not only are his ideas so original that they all but beg to be misunderstood and/or misinterpreted, but his is the sort of eccentricity that unenlightened minds can smugly dismiss without a glimmer of revelation. It is true that some of his activities generate first-level newspaper copy, as well as arouse suspicions of fraudulence; however, many retrospectively unquestioned "breakthroughs" in all contemporary arts at first struck even the sophisticated intelligence as suspect, while, beneath Cage's comedy and his propensity for unprecedented actions, are eminently serious purposes. What makes uncomprehending criticism more irrelevant, if not more pernicious, than even undiscriminating adulation is that Cage, very much like two of his own gurus, Marshall McLuhan and Norman O. Brown, is a fount of richly imaginative ideas that cannot be rejected or even accepted whole cloth. Even though these ideas usually attract more comment than commentary, more rejection than reflection, he is, to increasingly common opinion, clearly among the dozen seminal figures in the arts today. Quite simply, much of what he says is valuable and digestible, though much is also chaff; yet the task of winnowing poses a multifarious critical challenge, which has not, in my memory, been too eagerly or thoroughly assumed. His new book, *A Year from Monday,* a second collection of fugitive pieces, provides a propitious occasion for more comprehensive scrutiny; and let me start by saying that this book is rich in ideas relevant to all sorts of artistic, philosophical, and social endeavors. He is so emancipated from professional conventions that he is free to follow his imagination into any medium and risk innovative work in areas other than music. Though his ideas invite philistinism, even from the sophisticated, I doubt if any open-minded and intelligent person would not be challenged—surely irritated, perhaps persuaded to change his mind—in the course of perusing this compendium of provocative aphorisms, intellectual absurdities, and formulations so original they will doubtlessly make sense to some, nonsense to others. However, just as Cage no longer finds himself able to write a linear expository essay (and the book itself cannot be "read" in the conventionally linear way), so I find myself unable to compose a traditionally structured critical piece about him. His book is so fertile and various that one must dip in, pick out, and think about whatever strikes the mind, and that process itself informs the structure of these miscellaneous paragraphs. A further truth is that an assignment to write on Cage brings out, for better and worse, one's courage for originality.

One must initially acknowledge Cage's indisputable originality in an age that suspects everything has already been done; for nearly all that he makes, whether in art or life, is riddled by idiosyncratic and imaginative touches. He talks like no one else, conducts his personal existence like no one else, composes performance pieces like no one else, and, as this book amply demonstrates, writes as no one else would dare. (Even its original price, $7.92, represents a minor innovation, which is perhaps part of a one-man campaign to induce 1% as an appropriate sales tax.) He takes even his most comic ideas very seriously and asks us to do so too, and laugh as well. His penchant for the unusual gives his writing the quality of constant surprise; and, for this reason, much of it evades immediate comprehension, though his thought is not particularly complex. Even at the beginnings of his artistic career, over thirty years ago, Cage managed to be ahead of the herds; and, as he continues to renounce past positions for new frontiers, even most of the aggressive younger bulls graze art-historically behind their aesthetic daddy. Although fashionable to a degree, Cage continually thinks *ahead* of current intellectual pieties, including those that are, to some extent, his own creation. True, his private enthusiasms have a way of becoming public fads, although he has no enterprise to sponsor them and collects no royalties. In contrast to Cage, transient fashion, in Alain Robbe-Grillet's phrase, "imitates the modern forms without feeling their necessity." Cage's essays and conversations are studded, for instance, with the names and remarks of intellectual celebrities, in addition to close friends (who are sometimes also intellectual celebrities) and several unfamiliar names; and since certain unknowns he enthusiastically quoted a few years ago are now universally familiar cultural figures—McLuhan, Jasper Johns, and Buckminster Fuller among them—touts on incipient intellectual fashion might be well advised to bet on Cage's new oft-dropped sources of wisdom. In this new book, the author of a revolution in music clearly wants to accomplish something similar for prose; and although the desired breakthrough still seems a few steps away, Cage is by now discernibly beyond literary conventions. "My pleasure in composition, renounced as it has been in the field of music, continues in the field of writing words; and that explains why, recently, I write so much." In his earlier collection of pieces, *Silence*, the more recent essays eschewed linear organization for the structure of random comments; and, in the new book, few collections of sentences are even as approximately linear as this paragraph. The discontinuous compositional style seems an appropriate vehicle for Cage's invariably unconventional thoughts, as well as an approximate literary analogy for his scrupulously discontinuous music, yet precisely because the style continually risks obscurity, it signifies that Cage is still more of an artist than a propagandist.

One radical artistic idea that Cage has pushed beyond its previous provinces is the work of art as *primarily* an aesthetic illustration. The illustrative point of *4′ 33″* (1952), which consists of four minutes and thirty-three seconds of David Tudor, an established musician, sitting silently at the piano, is that all the unintentional, random sounds framed within that auditorium and within that period of time can be considered "music," for "doing nothing," as the critic Jill Johnston notes, is clearly "distinct from expressing nothing." By investing a situation where music is expected with nothing but silence (and where, as in the original performance, the well-known performer three times moves his arms in ways that suggest the piece has three distinct movements), Cage implied that in the silence was "music" that could be heard; this polemical illustration is an example of "art by subtraction" to the point that negation produces addition—in Mies van der Rohe's felicitous phrase, "Less is more." Since Cage invariably takes the intellectual leaps his radical ideas imply, he subsequently concluded that not only were any and all sounds "music," but the time-space frame of *4′ 33″* was needlessly arbitrary, for unintentional music is indeed with us—available to the ear that wishes to perceive it—in all spaces and at all times. (*Variations III* [1964], he once told me over dinner, is so open, "We could be performing it right now, if we decided to do so"; and another time he mentioned juvenile pieces composed by mathematical rules that "I destroyed because they didn't sound musical to me then, though I would probably think differently now.") From this, too, would inevitably follow another thesis, which holds that just as one does not naturally discern why one period of "silence" is better than another, but rather perceives personal significances in chaotic experience, so it is likewise irrelevant to evaluate one conglomeration of noise against another. What mattered, quite simply, was what the perspicacious ear managed to apprehend, if not appreciate. "Value judgments are destructive to our proper business, which is curiosity and awareness," he often says. "How are you going to use this situation if you are there? This is the big question." However, Cage also realized that, rather than deduce himself out of a career, he as an artist could program sound-generating instruments to produce an aural experience as random and miscellaneous as the unintentional noise on the street; and most of his performance pieces since the middle 1950's have been unstructured, indeterminate, multifarious events. It is customary to call these works "chance" music; but since chance per se is not perceptible, I prefer to characterize them as musically chaotic. As artistic wholes, these works differ from life in expressing a heightened incoherence, an appropriate scale, an absence of visual and aural focus—an ordered disorder, which is perceptibly different from disordered disorder. (Thus does Cage allow his artistry to compromise his theoretical position.) Most are also flat in structure, thoroughly lacking climax, development, emphasis, pacing, contours, and variations; so that their components need merely be turned on until turned off by a formally irrelevant decision (for example, no more pages left in the score, the audience has completely departed, it's midnight, and so on). At the root of Cage's compositional principles is collage—the mixing of materials not normally heard together; but, because he is less interested in barbed juxtaposition than abundant mixtures, the result is less collage than something distinctly Cagean. That roughly explains why an experienced ear, though it may not have heard a particular piece or rendition before, can usually identify a certain unfamiliar piece as Cage's work and not another's. In *Theater Piece* (1960), he pursued an implication of *Music Walk* (1958) by suggesting that a plethora of physical actions could, by performer's choice, be substituted for randomly activated sound-generating procedures; and, since he has previously ruled that all sounds are music, this instruction eventually implied, by analogy, that "theater" could be said to exist as soon as the perceiver's mind wished to define it. "Theater takes place all the time, wherever one is," Cage wrote in *Silence,* "and art simply facilitates persuading one this is the case." Nonetheless, it is precisely in their realized inchoateness and, in Cage's phrase, "purposeful purposelessness," as well as extravagantly spectacular qualities, that his own recent theater pieces distinguish themselves from both ordinary life (merely the "model" for the art) and others' "happenings" theater. In retrospect, then, the primary significance of *4′ 33″* lies precisely in its inferences, which gave Cage and others "reason" or "permission" to create eventually a musical theater that is indeterminate not only in its composition but its performance, too—aleatory kinetic presentational structures that are chaotic in both structure and detail. What is most conspicuously lacking in *A Year from Monday* is an analogous path-breaking gesture that could command as much suggestive influence for literature as his earlier "musical" demonstrations. The blank piece of paper is by now too obvious, if not, as we would now say, "Mallarmé's piece"; and the inferential idea of cellophane as a frame, which is perhaps the closest analogue in the visible arts to silence in music, appeared as a passing remark in my introduction to *The New American Arts* (1965), although I then lacked sufficient courage and/or professional reputation to put it on display. Regrettably, Cage has not particularly developed his stunningly suggestive assertion in *Silence*: "I have nothing to say and I am saying it and that is poetry." Maybe such a radical printed literary work cannot exist—if I could conceive it, I might do it myself; but, in principle, I hesitate to make such blanket negative statements about the future of Cage, or literary art.

Adopting the musical notion of unashamedly artificial constraints to literary purposes, Cage posits unprecedented ground rules that serve to emancipate him from conventional ways of organizing and rendering words. An instance of this is "Indeterminacy" (1958), consisting of ninety funny stories, each of which, by self-imposed rule, will be a minute in length when read aloud. When Cage performs this piece on a Folkways record of that title (1959), while David Tudor makes random noises in another room, "Indeterminacy" is very much about variations in prose tempo, as well as the random interactions between musical sounds and verbalized words. Here the form of the work expresses part of its ultimate content, as a performance illustrates (as opposed to explains) the piece's declarative title and Cage's aesthetic position; therefore, the ninety funny stories, which are pleasurable in themselves and comic to various degrees, are just the surface occasion for less obvious, but more substantial, concerns. Here, as in much else of Cage, the unperceptive spectator can be deceived into accepting the surface as all of the point—as silence is simply no sound, so stories are just anecdotes; but more significant meanings are invariably implied or inferred, by the piece, the spectator, or both. However, to put these stories into conventional print, as Cage does in *Silence*, destroys much of their primary effect (corrupting their original purpose even more than recordings of Cage's recent pieces betray, as fixed renditions, their scored indeterminacy); and, in the traditions of *printed* literature, ninety funny anecdotes within a larger frame comprise no innovation at all. Similarly, another performance piece, "Juilliard Lecture" (1952), published in the new book, is in its printed form all but unreadable, as is "Talk I" (1965), which, as Cage's headnote reveals, was not intended to be understood anyway.

The major essays in *A Year from Monday* comprise a three-part "Diary: How To Improve the World (You Will Only Make Matters Worse)," its sections subtitled respectively the years 1965, 1966, 1967; and, in composing what he characterizes as a "mosaic of ideas, statements, words, and stories," Cage posits a system of compositional constraints and indeterminate procedures (which also constrain his expression) that his headnote describes as follows:

> For each day, I determined by chance operations how many parts of the mosaic I would write and how many words there would be in each. . . . I used an IBM Selectric typewriter to print my text. I used twelve different type-faces, letting chance operations determine which face would be used for which statement. So, too, the left marginations [*sic*] were determined, the right marginations being the result of not hyphenating words and at the same time keeping the number of characters per line forty-three or less.

In practice, these constraining procedures induce an original style with its own distinct tone and particular rhythms. The "Diaries" are "poetry," not because they manipulate poetic conventions, but because they cannot be persuasively classified as anything else. However, as a form suitable primarily for miscellaneous insights and connections, prejudices, and gossip (usually to an excess), anecdotes and speculations, it is also a rather needlessly limited vehicle for verbal expression. Although it enables Cage to note unusual analogies, make one-line suggestions, relate one kind of position to another, and provide reviewers with numerous quotable gag lines (that are not representative of the text as a whole), this note-making format discourages the elaboration and development of thoughts, as well as granting Cage an easy escape from the necessity of pursuing the implications of his more radical ideas. On the other hand, precisely in its disconnectedness, such prose demands that the reader make his own connections. Beyond that, the form here, unlike "Indeterminacy," suggests no conceptual content that I can perceive or infer (even though previous experience with both Cage and other avant-garde materials persuades me to add that I may well be missing the significance); therefore, the primary substance of these diaries lies not in the form but the quality of the commentary, which is inevitably erratic, instinctively radical, and often stimulating. Finally, as a literary form appropriate for random remarks, this compositional process represents a successful mating of man and his makings; nothing could be more suitable, if not congenial, to an artist on the move, as Cage (so the headnotes suggest) is most of the time, as distinguished from a contemplative thinker or a professional writer. Perhaps because Cage derived an expression appropriate in form to his personal style, *A Year from Monday* is a more readable, communicative, and artistically suggestive book than its predecessor.

A major theme of *A Year from Monday* is fortuitous happenstance, as the book is riddled with observations on how delightfully random both art and life can be; for, out of Cage's definition of environmental reality, comes his recent aesthetic bias. "We open our eyes and ears seeing life each day excellent as it is. This realization no longer needs art, though without art it would have been difficult (yoga, zazen, etc.) to come by." The theme of happenstance is implied in the book's title, whose spirit and significance Jill Johnston caught so well that quotation is appropriate:

> [It] refers to a projected rendezvous with friends in Mexico, but who could say what would happen a year from Monday, much less a year from Tuesday, another day of interrupted designs; and so of course nobody went to Mexico, but one day Cage and Merce Cunningham bumped into Bucky Fuller in an airport outside of Madrid, which has nothing to do with the title of the book, or everything from the viewpoint of unpredictability in an ambiguous reference to time.

In another way to elaborate the theme: Whatever someone plans for a year from Monday is not likely to happen, although something else will, which may be just as valuable, providing that the perceiver keeps his channels open to experience. "Only the unusual exists," runs a proverb from pataphysics, "and everything is unpredictable, especially the predictable." However, given the style of discourse established by Cage's philosophy and the book's title, it seems nothing but inappropriate that its pages should be chronologically numbered and then snugly bound, or that this hardbound edition is well beyond the budgets of most avant-garde readers, or that purchasers do not need to cut open the pages (perhaps to their own designs) to read them, or that the lectures and essays and such are reprinted in more or less chronological order (as if to demonstrate some fictitious development [!] in Cage's thought), or that a tape of Cage's inimitable voice is not included; but perhaps another implicit theme is that even those artists furthest out compromise with the conventions of familiar media.

Most of the prose pieces collected in *A Year from Monday* deal with varieties of coherence in intentionally unstructured (orderly disordered) prose; and, even though Cage is more imaginative than most authors, including many of those who consider themselves "avant-garde," he neglects all the leaps his bias suggests. First of all, the headnotes to each essay are written in expository vocabulary; but, even though these notes are doubtlessly intended to make more comprehensible the material that follows, their conventionally linear form seriously compromises the revolutions in printed communications that the essays themselves imply. Second, even though the "Diary" for instance, uses an engaging variety of typefaces (thanks to IBM ingenuity), all the print is approximately of the same height; and this limitation causes another restriction in the expressive possibilities of printed words. (All the print is black—another limiting convention—although the Something Else Press has issued the third diary in a two-color edition, and the S.M.S. Press has published the fourth, dated 1968 and not collected into *Monday,* in three colors.) Third, in all the essays, not only is the type laid out in horizontal lines, but Cage also usually composes in sentences, which, though often clipped short, similarly impose unnecessary restraints. Indeed, even though he must know that precisely in syntax and linearity is the inherent conservatism of language as an expressive medium, Cage still strives for aphorisms, which are, after all, linear *bon mots.* It seems apparent to me that, if only to follow his predilections (something he is wont to do), Cage might inevitably need to reject sentences entirely and experiment with expressively designed words, or pattern poems, which would draw upon those talents for visual composition and penmanship that are already evident in his exquisitely crafted musical manuscripts.* Nonetheless, *A Year from Monday* represents a clear stylistic progression beyond the prose in *Silence;* for, if an implicit motif of the earlier book was his quest for a literary style that would *both* express his thoughts and illustrate his aesthetic ideas, now Cage has so patently forged to the frontier that I for one can see distinct territory ahead.

In the history of contemporary art, Cage functions as an antithetical catalyst, who leaps ahead so that others may move forward by steps. Late in the 1930's, he suggested prophetically that all noises, including those electronically produced, would enter the domain of serious music; and, by his own use of sounds unfamiliar to concert halls, he helped establish precedents for all contemporary electronic composition. Indeed, by making art out of materials not usually familiar to art, Cage, along with his friend Marcel Duchamp, also provided antithetical precedents for pop art, found objects, industrial sculpture, and much else; and Allan Kaprow, a sometime painter who originated (and christened) that performance art known as happenings, testifies that, although he personally does not subscribe to all of Cage's radical innovations, "he taught us to be free." In this respect, another implicit theme of *A Year from Monday* is that all kinds of criticism and all kinds of fiction, including critical fictions and fictitious criticism, can be put on pages, intermixed, and bound between hard covers. Cage's impact upon artists working in the musical traditions can be perceived in all aleatoric composition—the works of Morton Feldman, Christian Wolff, Earle Brown, David Behrman, early La Monte Young, among many other Americans, in addition to such major European musicians as Pierre Boulez and Karlheinz Stockhausen. However, whereas all these composers adopt aleatoric techniques in various ways, only Cage holds to the extreme position that regards all sounds available to the ear as music (or all movement as theater). Still, no one dares *imitate* Cage's pieces, not only because they are in some dimensions so extreme, but also because, in the world of art, a certain kind of performance event is generally known as Cage's domain. ("Others could do them,"

* Cage has since done so, in *Not Wanting To Say Anything About Marcel* (1969), so, for once, the critic knew in advance where his avant-garde subject would go.

he once confessed, "but they won't.") Instead, his radical antitheses stimulate others to produce their own synthesis; for, without his radical leaps, historically there would not have been certain other steps ahead. Sometimes Cage creates radical antitheses for himself to synthesize—by acting in an extreme way, perhaps with a special kind of irony, an artist can force himself to entertain new thoughts; for the fact that Cage has formally presented *4′ 33″* scarcely a few times persuades me to believe that he knows, first, that this piece is an ironic gesture and, second, that he sometimes takes positions finally unacceptable to sensible human beings, a category that includes himself. For instance, the first performance of *4′ 33″* theoretically granted him permission to explore the fullest range of sounds, both intentional and nonintentional, yet, even though *4′ 33″* was in a fundamental sense artless, most of these subsequent works represent a synthesis. That is, they draw, if not depend, upon the posited antithesis, as well as, of course, Cage's disciplined cleverness and his mastery of aleatoric mixed-means dramaturgy. (A glint in his eye persuaded me to take the following statement ironically: "If you want to know the truth of the matter, the music I prefer, even to my own and everything, is what we hear if we are just quiet.") Similarly, although he deduces, as a radical antithesis to conventional practice, that he cannot, in principle, offer critical opinions on art or life, the synthesis is that in fact he is a very opinionated, if not dogmatic, propagandist for his idiosyncratic taste and radical aesthetic positions. In *A Year from Monday*, nonetheless, there are no discernible antithetical catalysts; thus, no new syntheses are likely to follow.

Critics and laymen are forever debating Cage's place in contemporary music, and part of his originality lies in continually defying the categories by which we talk and classify, if not demonstrating, by his practice, how inherently philistine might be the boundaries themselves. Historically speaking, he descended from several distinctly modern musical traditions. One was concerned with introducing sounds previously not in the language of music (for example, Edgard Varèse's *Ionisation* [1930]); a second emphasized the possible expressiveness of the theatrical space in which music was performed (for example, Charles Ives's *The Unanswered Question* [1908]); a third consistently eschewed classical tonality and structure, not for a new musical language with its own grammars of coherence, such as Schoenberg's twelve-tone system, but for more chaotic kinds of aural experiences. (Incidentally, Cage's relationship with Schoenberg, about which so much is often made, had less to do with artistic influence than personal contact.) As a developing composer, Cage posited a succession of path-breaking stylistic positions by logical—rather, paralogical—deduction. His first discrete style was percussion music that scrupulously avoided familiar pitches and rhythms (e.g., *First Construction* [*in Metal*] [1939]), and then he invented the prepared piano, which systematically perverted, in a minimally random way, the instrument's natural sounds for unusual aural effects. Particularly in the recorded *Sonatas and Interludes* (1946–48), however, Cage's pieces for his home-brewed invention suspiciously echo the piano music of Erik Satie, that Cage has publicly praised, confirming that even avant-garde art discernibly comes out of previous art. By the late 1940's, Cage introduced aleatoric techniques into the process of setting marks to paper, thereby abandoning premeditated control not only over the finished score but also, in some pieces, over how the score would eventually be performed. So far, Cage clearly remained within musical traditions, having pursued a more or less straight path from premeditated scores and fixed performance to chance composition and indeterminate performance. To my ear, the music so far is needlessly repetitious, limited in range and effect, and excessively dependent upon the kinds of surprise that can strike the sensibility only on first hearing. The turn-about year was 1952, in which he composed *Williams Mix*, a tape collage, which, I find, represents his most valuable purely aural endeavor; presented the *première* of *4′ 33″;* and staged an untitled mixed-means event at Black Mountain College in North Carolina—in retrospect, this seems the first happening in America. From here on, everything Cage did was, by his subsequent logical deduction, as much indeterminate theater as indeterminate music—*Radio Music* (1956) "for one to eight performers, each at one radio"; *Music for Amplified Toy Pianos* (1960); *Rozart Mix* (1965) for twelve tape machines, several performers, one conductor, and eighty-eight loops of tape; *Variations V* (1965), with Merce Cunningham and his dance company, films by Stan VanDerBeek, a sensitized electronic field; the supremely spectacular theatrical environment *HPSCHD* (1967–69); etc. His "scores" for these recent pieces, though published by a music company, offer not a precise plan for articulating sound but descriptive (often prose) instructions for generating activities that, like a football play, are likely to run out of intentional control—that produce "indeterminate" results. "I never imagine anything until I experience it," Cage once declared; but this is completely contrary to one of the basic tasks of musical training, *solfège*, which teaches one to regard a score and then imagine, or hear in one's head, the finished work. In *A Year from Monday* he acutely defines his current art as a "process set in motion by a group of people," a kind of activity that, in the history of human endeavor, seems closer to noncompetitive games than aesthetic artifacts.

Rather than, as some antagonists would have it, abandoning inept musical composition for "stunts," Cage became the true master of mixed-means musical theater, perhaps the most valid American species of "opera," which could be reviewed by the music critic or the dance critic, by the theater critic or the art critic, or, more usually, by none of them. To my sensibility, these recent pieces are far more interesting and valid as theater of mixed means, as I christened it in a book of that title (Dial, 1968), than as purely aural art; compared with Milton Babbitt's or Elliott Carter's music, they seem feeble indeed. For that reason, not only are records of certain recent Cage works, such as *Variations IV*, invariably embarrassing; but, in confronting a live experience of these pieces, one quickly discovers that purely musical values and categories do not provide satisfactory and/or relevant perceptual expectations or critical standards. (Also, if only to accept his pervasive Americanness, Cage ought to use the native spelling—theater—rather than, as he does, the European.) Indeed, in the history of theatrical events, Cage artistically descends not from literary drama but such American exemplars as vaudeville, *Hellzapoppin'*, the Marx Brothers, Ives's unfinished *Universe Symphony*, and the dance performance of Merce Cunningham.

Partly because of Cage's immense influence, there now exist in each of the nonliterary arts in America two avant-garde tendencies, both of which are clearly distant from nineteenth-century conventions and discernibly different from pre-1945 practice. One would isolate the intrinsic qualities of the art—serial music, minimal and optical painting, early Merce Cunningham; the second would, like Cage, miscegenate—mix in enough materials, aesthetic preoccupations and structural standards from the other arts to insure that something between or inter-media is created. Almost by definition, all miscegenated art ridicules the pigeon-holes of the current critical enterprise and the academic departmental system, as well as the parochial aesthetic values indigenous to each art; and, perhaps until periodicals recognize that they ought to sponsor critics of mixed-means work, artists such as Cage are less likely to be widely understood, let alone appreciated. On the other hand, there is some sense, as well as some irony, in Cage's radical suggestion that, "Now we have such a marvelous loss of boundaries that your criticism of a happening could be a piece of music or a scientific experiment or a trip to Japan or a trip to your local shopping market." Anything can be considered art, anything, theater; anything, criticism—although his commitments to Zen persuade him to oppose Western ideas of syllogistic logic, Cage consistently deduces an antithetical catalyst.

The news in *A Year from Monday* is that Cage has recently been renouncing music for social philosophy; but, just as he abandoned concert music for a mixed-means theater that subsumes his music, so he regards his music, which has always been about *changing peoples' minds,* as a springboard into political thought. In retrospect, we can see how much politics has always been present in his music. First of all, his music implies the abolition of archaic structures, as does his politics; and both his music and his social thought suggest that new forms ought to be built from the most essential materials:

> In music, it was hopeless to think in terms of the old structure (tonality), to do things following old methods (counterpoint, harmony), to use the old materials (orchestral instruments). We started from scratch: sound, silence, time, activity. In society, no amount of doctoring up economics/politics will help. Begin again, assuming abundance, unemployment, a field situation, multiplicity, unpredictability, immediacy, the possibility of participation.

In contrast to most modern artists, who have been pessimistic about both technology and the future, Cage has, perhaps because of his "sunny disposition," always taken the optimistic side—a position that is indicatively gaining more adherents nowadays; and his current social prophecies indicatively parallel his recent artistic predilections. Just as Cage's latest performance pieces shrewdly exploit various electronic media in an autonomous way, all to create a field of intentionally nonstructured activity, so Cage insists that technology can socially be considered more of a blessing than a curse. (His art is, after all, more appropriate for an age of television and take-home video tape, rather than radio and phonograph records.) In Cage's coherent web of related radical ideas, the major common theme is that, since great changes are still possible in both life and art, we should strive to achieve what has not already been done. Cage, in his social thought, concurs with good liberal prejudices—equality of opportunity, universal civil rights, equitable distribution of economic affluence, the elimination of prejudice and segregation, and so on; but, recognizing that liberal prejudice is not enough, he takes, as usual, several leaps ahead. As an instinctive anarchist, he favors less work, rather than more, or more unemployment rather than less, as well as a guaranteed annual wage to provide for those for whom no jobs exist. "Taxation could be augmented," he remarks in passing, "to the point where no one had any money at all." Similarly, he expresses the anarchist's negative reaction to comprehensively detailed planning, noting of Le Corbusier (and, implicitly, of much modern architecture), "Art this is called. Its shape is tyranny." (Yet, he refuses to acknowledge the totalitarian tendencies in Buckminster Fuller's thought.) For situations of too much order, such as programmatic architecture and organizational bureaucracy, he champions disorder; for situations of needless disorder, he supports overall ordering, such as centrally organized and universally free public utilities. He is enough of a McLuhanite to believe that a truly global voltage, as well as a universal design for plugs and jacks, could have a profoundly ecumenical effect. "Alteration of global society through electronics so that world will go round by means of united intelligence rather than by means of divisive intelligence (politics, economics)." Since automated technology promises more abundant leisure, if not the possibility of endless environmental pleasure, and the obsolescence of most social and aesthetic hierarchies, Cage wants to inculcate a psychology that will allow every man to appreciate the "art" constantly around him all the time; thus do the pedagogic purposes of his musical theater link to his optimistic visions for the future. I suspect that the final vision of his ecumenical anarchism would have all of us listening to *4′ 33″* together. Although his bias is "not fixing [society] but changing it so it works," what *A Year from Monday* does not offer is a politics —advice on how the golden age will come—perhaps because Cage believes that widespread mind-change *precedes* social change, and he senses, not untenably, that technological development itself will accomplish most of the transformations. "Once we give our attention to the practice of not-being-governed, we notice that it is increasing." This sense that the world is getting better largely on its own momentum may strike some political people as slightly naïve; but Cage's professional life exemplifies its own kind of radical activism. As a man who frequently commands audiences, spreading a certain gospel, reprogramming the heads of those who learn to appreciate his "music," offering images and proposals for a radically different future, exercising his almost Jesuitical persuasiveness—all at a time when most self-styled "radicals" offer merely negative criticisms—Cage is a harbinger-publicist for a new, necessary, comprehensive, unprecedented, unstructured, mixed-means revolution.

IX data

Computers are bringing about a situation that's like the invention of harmony. Subroutines are like chords. No one would think of keeping a chord to himself. You'd give it to anyone who wanted it. You'd welcome alterations of it. Subroutines are altered by a single punch. We're getting music made by man himself, not just one man.—JOHN CAGE, in a reading (1969)

History does not foretell the future, but study of the past may provide some keys to understanding. Above all, knowledge of history should liberate us from the past and enable us to be vividly contemporary.—LYNN WHITE, JR., "Science, Scientists, and Politics" (1960)

Within this collection of lists are five separate parts: a complete catalogue of John Cage's compositions to 1969; all compositions ever available on circulated recordings; Cage's own writings, including interviews; a selection of writings primarily on Cage's work; and books and essays relevant, in various ways, to Cage's endeavors. The present editor is indebted to Robert Dunn's compilations included in *John Cage* (Henmar Press, 1962) and emendations provided by Dick Higgins and Ellsworth J. Snyder. Information about any major omissions should be sent to the editor in care of the publisher, with their gratitude extended in advance.

Catalogue of Cage's Compositions
(by Instrument and Chronology)

The instrument in many of the following pieces is variable, so the list follows the classifications made by Cage himself for his publisher's catalogue of his scores (1962). 4′ 33″, for instance, though originally performed before a piano, is listed as "Instrumental Solo and Chamber Music (Various Ensembles)," because the score's instructions allow "any instrument or combination of instruments." All scores, except those marked with an asterisk (*), are available from Henmar Press, 373 Park Avenue South, New York, N.Y. Henmar intends to issue the remaining works; those with a # sign are, or were, available on commercial recording.

Piano

*Music for Xenia**	1934
*Two Pieces**#	1935
*Metamorphosis**#	1938
A Room	1943
Experiences I	1945–48
*Ophelia**	1946
*Two Pieces** #	1946
Dream#	1948
In a Landscape	1948
Suite for Toy Piano#	1948
Music of Changes	1951
For M.C. and D.T.	1952
Music for Piano 1	1952
Seven Haiku	1952
Waiting	1952
Music for Piano 2	1953
Music for Piano 3	1953
Music for Piano 4–19	1953
Music for Piano 20	1953
Music for Piano 21–36; 37–52	1955
Music for Piano 53–68	1956
Music for Piano 69–84	1956
For Paul Taylor and Anita Dencks	1957
Winter Music#	1957
TV Koeln	1958

*Electronic Music for Piano**	1964
Cheap Imitation	1969

Prepared Piano

*Bacchanale**#	1938
Amores#	1943
*Meditation**#	1943
*Totem Ancestor**	1943
A Book of Music	1944
The Perilous Night#	1944
Prelude for Meditation#	1944
*Root of an Unfocus**#	1944
A Valentine out of Season#	1944
*Daughters of the Lonesome Isle**	1945
*Mysterious Adventure**	1945
Three Dances#	1945
Sonatas and Interludes#	1946-48
Music for Marcel Duchamp#	1947
Two Pastorales	1951

Voice

*Twenty Years After**	1932
*Is It as It Was**	1932
*At East and Ingredients**	1932
Five Songs for Contralto	1938
Forever and Sunsmell	1942
The Wonderful Widow of Eighteen Springs#	1942
Experiences II	1945-48
A Flower	1950
Aria#	1958
Solo for Voice 1	1958
Solo for Voice 2	1960

Strings

*Nocturne for Violin and Piano**	1947
Six Melodies for Violin and Keyboard (Piano)	1950
String Quartet in Four Parts#	1950

Winds

Sonata for Clarinet (Solo)#	1933

Three Pieces for Flute Duet	1935
Music for Wind Instruments	1938

Harp

In a Landscape	1948

Carillon

Music for Carillon No. 1#	1952
Music for Carillon No. 2	1954
Music for Carillon No. 3	1954
Music for Carillon No. 4	1961
Music for Carillon No. 5	1967

Various Solos and Ensembles

Six Short Inventions#	1933
Solo with Obbligato Accompaniment of Two Voices in Canon, and Six Short Inventions on the Subjects of the Solo	1933
*Sonata for Two Voices**	1933
*Composition for 3 Voices**	1934
*Three Pieces for Flute Duet**	1935
She Is Asleep#	1943
Sixteen Dances	1951
4′ 33″	1952
59½″ for a String Player	1953
31′57.9864″ for a Pianist	1954
34′46.776″ for a Pianist	1954
26′1.1499″ for a String Player#	1955
27′10.554″ for a Percussionist	1956
Variations I	1958
Variations II#	1961
0′ 00″	1962
*0′ 00″ No. 2**	1968
*Sound Anonymously Received**	1969

Orchestra and Chamber Orchestra

The Seasons	1947
Concerto for Prepared Piano and Chamber Orchestra#	1951
Concert for Piano and Orchestra#	1957–58
Atlas Eclipticalis	1961–62

Percussion (and Electronic Devices)

*Quartet**	1935
*Trio**	1936
First Construction (in Metal)#	1939
Imaginary Landscape No. 1#	1939
*Living Room Music**	1940
*Second Construction**	1940
Double Music [in collaboration with Lou Harrison]#	1941
Third Construction	1941
Credo in Us	1942
March (Imaginary Landscape No. 2)	1942
Imaginary Landscape No. 3	1942
Imaginary Landscape No. 4 (March No. 2)	1951
Imaginary Landscape No. 5	1952
Speech	1955
Radio Music	1956
Cartridge Music#	1960
Music for Amplified Toy Pianos	1960
Variations III#	1963
Variations IV#	1964
Variations VI	1967
*Variations VII**	1967
*Variations VIII**	1968

Magnetic Tape

Williams Mix#*	1952
Fontana Mix#	1958
Music for "The Marrying Maiden"	1960
WBAI	1960
Rozart Mix	1965

Audio-visual

Water Music	1952
Music Walk	1958
*Sounds of Venice**	1959
Water Walk	1959
Theatre Piece	1960
Variations V	1965
*Musicircus**	1967
*Newport Mix**	1967
*Reunion**	1968
HPSCHD [with Lejaren Hiller]#	1969

Recordings

All compositions ever available on publicly circulated recordings, including those produced abroad and those currently out of print.

("Avakian" is a three-disc recording of the 25-Year Retrospective Concert of the Music of John Cage, which is available, as a package, only from George Avakian, 285 Central Park West, New York, New York 10025. Neither "Dial" nor "Disc" remain in business.)

Sonata for Clarinet (1933)
Philip Rehfeldt, clarinet — Advance 4

Six Short Inventions (1933)
Ensemble conducted by John Cage — Avakian

Two Pieces (1935)
Jeanne Kirstein, pianist — Columbia MS-7416

Bacchanale (1938)
Jeanne Kirstein, pianist — Columbia MS-7416

Metamorphosis (1938)
Jeanne Kirstein, pianist — Columbia MS-7416

Imaginary Landscape No. 1 (1939)
John and Xenia Cage, Doris Dennison, Margaret Jansen — Avakian

First Construction (*In Metal*) (1939)
Manhattan Percussion Ensemble, Paul Price, conductor — Avakian

Double Music [written in collaboration with Lou Harrison] (1941)
Manhattan Percussion Ensemble, Paul Price, conductor — Time 58000; 8000

The Wonderful Widow of Eighteen Springs (1942)
Arlene Carmen, contralto; John Cage, pianist — Avakian

Amores (1943)
Maro Ajemian, pianist (I and IV only) — Disc 875
John Cage, pianist; Manhattan Percussion Ensemble, Paul Price, conductor — Time 58000; 8000

She Is Asleep (1943)
Arlene Carmen, contralto; John Cage, pianist; Manhattan Percussion Ensemble, Paul Price, conductor — Avakian

Meditation (also credited as *Tossed as It is Untroubled*) (1943)
Jeanne Kirstein, pianist — Columbia MS-7417
Prelude for Meditation (1944)
Jeanne Kirstein, pianist — Columbia MS-7417
The Perilous Night (1944)
Jeanne Kirstein, pianist — Columbia MS-7416
Root of an Unfocus (1944)
Jeanne Kirstein, pianist — Columbia MS-7417
A Valentine Out of Season (1944)
Jeanne Kirstein, pianist — Columbia MS-7417
Three Dances (1945)
Maro Ajemian and William Masselos, pianists — Disc 643
Two Pieces (1946)
Jeanne Kirstein, pianist — Columbia MS-7417
Dance (1947)
Henry Jacobs, pianist — Folkways F-6160
Music for Marcel Duchamp (1947)
Jeanne Kirstein, pianist — Columbia MS-7417
Sonatas and Interludes (1946–48)
Maro Ajemian, pianist — Dial 19, 20
[Reissued CRI 199; and, in excerpt, Avakian]
Yuji Takahashi, pianist — [Sweden] Fylkingen FYLP X101–2
Dream (1948)
Jeanne Kirstein, pianist — Columbia MS-7417
Suite for Toy Piano (1948)
Jeanne Kirstein, pianist — Columbia MS-7417
Music for Keyboard (1935–1948)
Jeanne Kirstein, pianist — Columbia M2S-819
String Quartet in Four Parts (1950)
New Music String Quartet — Columbia MS-4495
Concerto for Prepared Piano and Chamber Orchestra (1951)
Yuji Takahashi, pianist; Buffalo Philharmonic Orchestra,
Lukas Foss, conductor — Nonesuch H-71202
Music for Carillon No. 1 (1952)
David Tudor, electronic carillon
[two-octave version] — Avakian
Williams Mix (1952) — Avakian
26′1.14499″ for a String Player (1955)
Bertram Turetzky, contrabass — Nonesuch H-71237
Concert for Piano and Orchestra (1957–58)
David Tudor, pianist — Avakian
Fontana Mix (1958) — Turnabout 34046

Aria (1958) with *Fontana Mix*
Cathy Berberian, mezzosoprano — Time 58003; 8003

Variations I (1958) — Heliodor 2549 009
Gerd Zacher, organ — [or Wergo 60033]

"Indeterminacy" (1959)
John Cage, speaker; David Tudor, pianist — Folkways FT-3704

Cartridge Music (1960)
John Cage and David Tudor, performers — Time 58009; 8009

Solo for Voice 2 (1960) in electronic version (1966)
Brandeis University Chamber Choir,
Alvin Lucier, conductor — Odyssey 32160156

Variations II (1961)
David Tudor, pianist — Columbia MS-7051
Two realizations (1967): Antonio Taurello and Gerardo Gandini, two pianos; Horatio Vaggione and Pedro Echarte, tape and unusual instruments — [Argentina] JME-ME2

Atlas Eclipticalis (1961–62), simultaneously with *Winter Music* (1957) and *Cartridge Music* (1960)
Ensemble Musica Negativa, Rainer Riehn, director — Deutsche Grammophon 137 009

Variations III (1963)
Gerd Zacher and Allende-Blin, percussion and wind ensemble — Deutsche Grammophon 139442

Variations IV (1964)
Excerpts I — Everest 6132; 3132
Excerpts II — Everest 3230

Fontana Mix-Feed (1958–65)
Max Neuhaus, percussionist — Columbia MS-7139
[Different performances: *Aspen,* 5–6 (1968); Massart M-133]

HPSCHD [written in collaboration with Lejaren Hiller] (1969)
Antoinette Vischer, Neely Bruce, David Tudor, harpsichordists — Nonesuch H-71224

Cage's Writings

Books

Virgil Thomson [in collaboration with Kathleen Hoover]. New York: Yoseloff, 1959.

Silence. Middletown, Conn.: Wesleyan University Press, 1961.

A Year from Monday. Middletown, Conn.: Wesleyan University Press, 1967.

Notations [in collaboration with Alison Knowles]. New York: Something Else Press, 1969.

Cage's music publisher, Henmar Press (New York), also issued, in 1962, *John Cage,* which is a heavily annotated catalogue of Cage's compositions and performances of them prior to 1962.

Booklets

Diary: Part III. New York: Something Else Press, 1967.

Diary: Part IV. New York: S.M.S. Press, 1968.

To Describe the Process of Composition Used in Not Wanting To Say Anything About Marcel. Cincinnati: EYE Editions, 1969.

Interviews

REYNOLDS, ROGER, in *Generation* (January, 1962). Reprinted in *John Cage*. New York. Henmar Press, 1962; and Elliott Schwartz and Barney Childs, eds., *Contemporary Composers on Contemporary Music*. New York: Holt, Rinehart, and Winston, 1967.

KIRBY, MICHAEL, and SCHECHNER, RICHARD. "An Interview," *Tulane Drama Review,* X/2 (Winter, 1965).

MIMAROGLU, ILHAN. "Interview with John Cage" [in excerpt], *Discoteca* (November, 1965).

ZWERIN, MICHAEL. "A Lethal Measurement," *The Village Voice,* XI/12 (January 6, 1966).

KOSTELANETZ, RICHARD. "John Cage," *The Theatre of Mixed Means*. New York: Dial, 1968. Abridged as "We Don't Know Any Longer Who I Was," *The New York Times,* Section II (March 17, 1968).

AUSTIN, LARRY. *"HPSCHD," Source,* II/2 (1968).

CHARLES, DANIEL. "Soixante réponses à trente questions," *Revue d'Esthétique* (Paris, 1968).

Shorter Pieces

(Those marked SIL are reprinted in *Silence;* AYM in *A Year from Monday;* and JC in this volume.)

"Goal: New Music, New Dance," *Dance Observer* (December, 1939). SIL

"Chavez and the Chicago Drouth," *Modern Music,* XIX/3 (March-April, 1942). JC

"For More New Sounds," *Modern Music,* XIX/4 (May-June, 1942). JC

"South Winds in Chicago," *Modern Music,* XIX/4 (May-June, 1942). JC

"Grace and Clarity," *Dance Observer* (November, 1944). SIL

"Summer Music: The Parks," *Modern Music,* XXI/1 (November-December, 1944). JC

"Dreams and Dedications of George Antheil," *Modern Music,* XXIII/1 (January, 1946). JC

"East in the West," *Modern Music,* XXIII/2 (April, 1946).

"Forerunners of Modern Music," *Tiger's Eye,* 7 (March, 1949). SIL Translated as "Raison d'Etre de la Musique Moderne," *Contrepoints* [Paris] 6 (1949).

"Contemporary Music Festivals Held in Italy," *Musical America,* LXIX (June, 1949).

"Satie Controversy," *Musical America,* LXX (December 15, 1950). JC

"A Few Ideas About Music and Films," *Film Music News,* 10 (January-February, 1951).

"Letters to the Editors: More Satie," *Musical America,* LXXI (April 1, 1951). JC

"Manifesto on Music," Living Theatre Program (New York, 1952). SIL

"Letter to Peter Yates," *Arts and Architecture,* LXX/11 (November, 1953).

"Manifesto on Painting of Bob Rauschenberg," incorporated into Emily Genauer's column, *New York Herald Tribune* (December 27, 1953). JC

"Music Lover's Field Companion," *United States Lines Paris Review* (1954). SIL

"Experimental Music," *The Score,* 12 (June, 1955). Reprinted in Gilbert Chase, ed., *The American Composer Speaks.* Baton Rouge: Louisiana State Press, 1966. SIL

"In This Day . . . ," *Dance Observer* (January, 1957). SIL

"2 Pages, 122 Words on Music and the Dance," *Dance Magazine,* XXXI/11 (November, 1957). SIL

"To Describe the Process of Composition Used in 'Music for Piano 21–52,' " [in German] *Die Reihe,* 3 (1957). Reprinted in English translation in the American edition of *Die Reihe,* 3. New York: Theodore Presser, 1959. SIL

"Morris Graves," introduction to catalogue, Museum of Art, Ogunquit, Maine (June 29, 1957). JC

"Erik Satie," *Art News Annual,* XXVII (1958). SIL

"Composition as Process: Indeterminacy," translated as "Uber Komposition deren Aufführung nicht Festgelegt ist," *Das Neue Forum* VIII 1, 4, 6, 8 (1958). SIL

"Composition as Process: Communication" [in excerpt], *The Village Voice* (April, 1958). Reprinted in Dan Wolf and Edwin Fancher, eds., *The Village Voice Reader.* New York: Simon and Schuster, 1963. SIL

Notes on various pieces, in the booklet accompanying the Avakian recording (May, 1958). JC

"The Future of Music: Credo," written in 1937, but not published until May, 1958, in the Avakian recording booklet. SIL JC

"Roster on Varèse," *Nutida Musik* [Stockholm] (Fall, 1958). SIL

"History of Experimental Music in the United States," *Darmstädter Beitrage zur neuen Musik,* IV (1959). SIL

"Unbestimmtheit," *Die Reihe,* 5 (1959). Translated as "Lecture 30′ 00″ " in the American edition of *Die Reihe,* 5 (1961). Subsequently incorporated into "How to Pass, Kick, Fall, and Run," in *A Year from Monday* (1967).

"Lecture on Nothing," *Incontri Musicali* (August, 1959). SIL

Preface to "Indeterminacy," in a booklet accompanying the Folkways Recording (1959).

"Lecture on Something," *It Is* (1959). SIL

Contribution to the Symposium "Form Is a Language," *Art News,* LIX/2 (April, 1960). JC

"On Robert Rauschenberg, Artist, and His Work," *Metro* [Milan] (May, 1961). SIL

"Where Are We Going? and What Are We Doing?" *Ring des Arts* (Summer, 1961). SIL

"Composition as Process: Changes," written in 1958, but not published until *Silence* (1961).

"Indeterminacy," written in 1959, excerpted in the Folkways booklet, but not published in its entirety until *Silence* (1961).

"Where Do We Go from Here?" *Dance Perspectives,* 16 (1962). AYM

"26 Statements re Duchamp," *Mizue* [Japan] (September, 1962). AYM

"Happy New Ears!" Sogetsu Art Center (1964). AYM

"Jasper Johns: Stories and Ideas," in Alan R. Solomon, *Jasper Johns*. New York: The Jewish Museum, 1964. Reprinted in Gregory Battcock, ed., *The New Art*. New York: Dutton, 1966. AYM

"Mosaic," *Kenyon Review* (Summer, 1965). Reprinted, revised AYM

"Nam June Paik: A Diary," Galeria Bonino exhibition catalogue (November, 1965). AYM

"Diary: Emma Lake Music Workshop 1965," *Canadian Art* (January, 1966). AYM

"Letters to the Editor: Electronic Souls," *The Village Voice,* XI/14 (January 20, 1966). JC

"Seriously Comma," *Preuves* [Paris] (March, 1966). AYM

"Rhythm," in Gyorgy Kepes, ed., *Module, Proportion, Symmetry, Rhythm*. New York: Braziller, 1966. AYM

"Diary: How to Improve the World (You Will Only Make Matters Worse) 1965," *Joglars,* I/3 (1966). Reprinted in *Link* (September-October, 1966); *Aspen* (Spring, 1967); Richard Kostelanetz, ed., *Possibilities of Poetry*. New York: Dell, 1970; and elsewhere. AYM

"Diary: How to Improve the World (You Will Only Make Matters Worse) 1966," *Paris Review* (Spring, 1967). Translated into Swedish, *Nutida Musik,* 3-4 (1966–67). AYM

"Diary: Audience 1966," in *The Arts: Planning for Change* (Associated Councils of the Arts, 1967). AYM

"Juilliard Lecture," written in 1952 but not published until AYM.

"Lecture on Commitment," written in 1961, published in AYM.

"Talk I," written in 1965, published in AYM.

"How To Pass, Kick, Fall, and Run," written in 1965, published in AYM.

"Miro in the Third Person: 8 Statements," written in 1966, published in AYM.

"Diary: How to Improve the World (You Will Only Make Matters Worse) Continued 1967," Great Bear Pamphlets. New York: Something Else Press, 1967 (Edition in two inks). AYM

"Afterword" (1967). AYM

Remarks about Merce Cunningham, *Dance Perspectives,* 34 (Summer, 1968). JC

"These Days," written 1968, published in JC.

"How to Improve the World (You Will Only Make Matters Worse) 1968 (Revised 1969)," *Tri-Quarterly,* 18 (1970).

Writings Primarily on Cage's Work

ASHTON, DORE. "Cage, Composer, Shows Calligraphy of Note," *The New York Times* (May 6, 1958).

AVAKIAN, GEORGE. "About the Concert," in the pamphlet accompanying the album, *The 25-Year Retrospective Concert of the Music of John Cage* (1959).

BARTSCH, WERNER, et al. *Die unvermeidliche Musik des John Cage*. Kolb, Switzerland: Druck, 1969.

BERGER, ARTHUR V. "*Imaginary Landscape No. 4 for 12 Radios* Heard," *New York Herald Tribune* (May 12, 1951).

BORETZ, BENJAMIN. "Music," *The Nation,* CXCIV (February 3, 1962).

BORTOLOTTO, MARIO. "Phantasiestucke après une lecture de Cage," *La Biennale* [Venice] (June, 1964).

———. "Un paradisus interruptus," *Avantguardia e Neoavantguardia* [Milan] (1966).

CHARLES, DANIEL. "Nature et Silence chez John Cage," *Le Langage* [Geneva], I (1966).

———. "L'Esthétique du 'non finito' chez John Cage," *Revue d'Esthétique,* 2–4 (1968).

COHN, ARTHUR. "The 25-Year Retrospective Concert of the Music of John Cage," *American Record Guide,* XXVI (August, 1960).

COPLAND, AARON. "The Music of Chance," *The New Music*. Rev. ed. New York: W. W. Norton, 1968.

COWELL, HENRY. "Current Chronicle," *Musical Quarterly,* XXXVIII/1 (January, 1952).

CURJEL, HANS. "Cage oder das Wohlpräparierte Klavier," *Melos* [Mainz], XXXII/4 (April, 1955).

DIBELIUS, ULRICH. "John Cage oder gibt es kritische Musik?" *Melos,* XXXV/10 (October, 1968).

EKBOM, TORSTEN. "En värld av ljud," *Nutida Musik,* 6 (1962–63).

"Fingersnaps and Footstomps," *Time* (July 29, 1940).

FINKELSTEIN, SIDNEY. "John Cage's Music," *New Masses,* LXII/2 (January 7, 1947).

"Fisch im Klavier," *Der Spiegel* (November 6, 1968).

FRANKENSTEIN, ALFRED. "In Retrospect—The Music of John Cage," *High Fidelity,* X/4 (April, 1960).

———. "Cage's Collected Essays," *San Francisco Chronicle—This World* (December 10, 1961).

GATTI, GUIDO. "Il Pardossale Caos di John Cage," *Tempo* [Rome], 3 (January 20, 1959).

GLANVILLE-HICKS, PEGGY. "John Cage," *Musical America* (September, 1948).

GOLDSTEIN, SIDNEY. "John Cage," *Music Business* (April, 1946).

GRUNFELD, FRED. "Cage Without Bars," *Reporter,* XXII (February 4, 1960).

GUSCHLBAUER, WILHELM. "John Cage—Genie oder Narr?" *Der Operfreund* [Vienna], VII/68 (May, 1962).

HAMBRAEUS, BENGT. "John Cage och gränserna," *Nutida Musik,* 3–4 (1966–67).

———. "Om Aria con Fontana Mix," *Nutida Musik,* 6 (1962–63).

HARRISON, JAY S. "John Cage Retrospective Is Presented at Town Hall," *New York Herald Tribune* (May 16, 1958).

HARRISON, LOU. "Recital at the New School," *Modern Music,* XXI/3 (March-April, 1945).

———. "Recital of Music for Prepared Pianos," *New York Herald Tribune* (December 11, 1946).

HECKMAN, DON. "The Sounds and Silences of John Cage," *Down Beat,* XXXI (May 7, 1964).

HELNS, HAMS G. "John Cage zum 50" [Broadcast]. Germany: Radio Bremen (October, 1962).

HERING, DORIS M. "John Cage and the 'Prepared Piano,' " *Dance Magazine* (March, 1946).

HILLER, LEJAREN. *"HPSCHD," Source,* II/2 (1968).

HOLLANDER, JOHN. Review of *Silence, Perspectives of New Music,* I/2 (Spring, 1963).

ICHIYANAGI, TOSHI. "John Cage," *The Ongaku Geijutso* [Tokyo], XIX/2 (February, 1961).

JACOBSON, BERNARD. Notes to *Concerto for Prepared Piano & Chamber Orchestra,* on the jacket of Nonesuch H-71202.

JAMES, PENCE. "People Call It Noise—But He Calls It Music," *Chicago Daily News* (March 19, 1942).

JOHNSTON, JILL. "There Is No Silence Now," *The Village Voice* (November 8, 1962).

———. "Poets and Kings," *The Village Voice* (October 15, 1967).

KOBLER, JOHN. "Everything We Do Is Music," *Saturday Evening Post* (October 19, 1968).

KOCHINSKY, LEON A. "The First Magian," *The Tiger's Eye,* I/1 (October, 1947).

KOSTELANETZ, RICHARD. "John Cage: Some Random Remarks," *The Denver Quarterly,* III/4 (Winter, 1969). Translated into Spanish, *Sur,* 322 (January-April, 1970).

———. "The American Avant-Garde, Part II: John Cage," *Stereo Review,* XXII/5 (May, 1969). Reprinted in Richard Kostelanetz, *Master Minds.* New York: Macmillan, 1969.

———. "They All Came to Cage's Circus," *The New York Times,* Section II (May 25, 1969).

———. Notes on the early piano music, included in Columbia MS 7416-7.

KUPFERBERG, HERBERT. "Audience Boos Add Flavor to John Cage Recordings," *New York Herald Tribune,* Section IV (February, 21, 1960).

LIST, KURT. "Rhythm, Sound and Sane," *New Republic* (December 24, 1945).

LYON, NINETTE. "John Cage: A Second Fame, Good Food," *Vogue* (October 1, 1965).

MCGARY, KEITH. "I Have Nothing," *Antioch Review* (Summer, 1962).

MAREN, ROGER. "The Musical Numbers Game," *Reporter,* XVIII (March 6, 1958).

———. Review of *A Year from Monday, Perspectives of New Music,* VI/2 (Spring-Summer, 1968).

MARKGRAF, BRUCE. "John Cage: Ideas and Practices of a Contemporary Speaker," *The Quarterly Journal of Speech,* XLVIII/2 (April, 1962).

METZGER, HEINZ-KLAUS. "John Cage o della liberazione," *Incontri Musicali* [Milan], 3 (August, 1959). Translated into Swedish, "John Cage/Frigiven musik," *Nutida Musik,* 3–4 (1966–67). Reprinted in the original German, "John Cage oder die friegelassene Musik," in Ulrich Dibelius, ed., *Musik auf der Flucht vor sich selbst.* Munich: Carl Hanser Verlag, 1969.

———. "John Cage," *Ruch Muzyczny* [Prague], VI/13 (1962).

———. "John Cage in Saint-Paul-de-Vence," *Melos,* XXXIII (December, 1966).

MONT, E. "Musiche de John Cage nel Ridotto dell'Eliseo," *Il Popolo* [Rome] (January 6, 1959).

MOORE, CARMAN. Review of *Notations, The Village Voice* (July 24, 1969).

MOULAERT, PIERRE. "Les Pianos Preparés de John Cage," *Dernière Heure* [Brussels], (November 7, 1954).

MUMMA, GORDON. "Four Sound Environments for Modern Dance," *Impulse: The Annual of Contemporary Dance* (1967).

"Percussion Concert," *Life,* XIV/11 (March 15, 1943).

"Percussionist," *Time* (February 22, 1943).

RINGO, JAMES. "The Lure of the Orient," *ACA Bulletin,* VII/2 (1958).

ROY, KLAUS GEORGE. "The Strange and Wonderful Sonic World of John Cage," *Hi-Fi/Stereo Review,* V/5 (November, 1960).

SALZMAN, ERIC. "In and Out the Piano with Cage," *The New York Times,* Section II (February 14, 1960).

SCARR, KATHLEEN M. "John Cage and 'Prepared Music,' " *Canon,* 8 (May, 1955).

SCHMITT, HANS-JURGEN. "Glückliche neuen Ohren," *Frankfurter Allgemeine Zeitung* (July 7, 1968).

SCHNEBEL, DIETER. "Das Aquarium der neuen Musik," *Frankfurter Allgemeine Zeitung* (March 15, 1969).

SLONIMSKY, NICOLAS. "If Anyone Is Sleepy, Let Him Go to Sleep," *Christian Science Monitor* (December 14, 1961).

SNYDER, ELLSWORTH J. *John Cage and Music Since World War II: A Study in Applied Aesthetics.* Ph.D. Dissertation, University of Wisconsin, 1970.

STUCKENSCHMIDT, H. H. "Die Dadaisten von Greenwich Village," *Frankfurter Allgemeine Zeitung* (March 17, 1960).

TEITELBAUM, RICHARD. Notes on *Variations II,* on the jacket of Columbia. MS-7051.

THIEMANN, SUSAN. "John Cage's *The Wonderful Widow of Eighteen Springs,*" *Notes,* XIX/2 (March, 1962).

THOMSON, VIRGIL. "Expressive Percussion," *New York Herald Tribune* (January 22, 1945). Reprinted in *The Art of Judging Music.* New York: Knopf, 1948.

———. "Atonality Today," *Étude,* 69 (November, 1951).

———. "The Abstract Composers," *New York Herald Tribune* (February 3, 1952). Reprinted in *Bulletin of American Composers Alliance,* II/2 (1952), and *The Score,* 12 (June, 1955).

———. "John Cage Late and Early," *Saturday Review,* XLIII (January 30, 1960).

TOMKINS, CALVIN. "Figure in an Imaginary Landscape," *The New Yorker* (November 28, 1964). Reprinted in *The Bride and the Bachelors.* New York: Viking, 1965; Rev. ed., 1968.

———. "Social Concern," *The New York Times Book Review* (January 21, 1968).

TRIMBLE, LESTER. "Music," *The Nation,* CLXXVI (May 31, 1958).
TYLER, PARKER. "Music," *View,* VII/3 (March, 1947).
WIDMER, URS. "Das Leben aus Probieren!" *Frankfurter Allgemeine Zeitung* (October 7, 1969).
WILSON, MILTON. "John Cage," *Canadian Music Journal,* IV/4 (Summer, 1960).
YATES, PETER. "Music for Prepared Piano," *Arts and Architecture,* LXIV/4 (April, 1949).
———. "Music," *Arts and Architecture,* LXX/7 (July, 1953).
———. "The American Composer," *Arts and Architecture,* LXX/11 (November, 1953).
———. "Two Albums by John Cage," *Arts and Architecture,* LXXVII/3–4 (March-April, 1960).
———. "*Silence* by John Cage," *Arts and Architecture,* LXXIX/2 (February, 1962).
———. "Cage's Weekend in Los Angeles," *Arts and Architecture,* LXXIX/5 (May, 1962).
———. "An Introduction to John Cage," *Twentieth Century Music.* New York: Pantheon, 1967.
———. Notes on *HPSCHD,* on the jacket of Nonesuch H-71224.
ZELLER, HANS RUDOLF. "Cage—wissenschaftlich betrachtet," in Konrad Boehmer, ed., *Zur Theorie der offenen Form.* Frankfurt: C. F. Peters, 1968.
ZILL, NICHOLAS, and ORME-JOHNSON, DAVID. "Cage in a Gilded World," *Jester of Columbia,* LXII/6 (March, 1960).
ZUECHERI, MARINO. "Hur Fontana Mix kom till," *Nutida Musik,* 6 (1962–63).
ZUMSTEIN, BRUCE. "*Musicircus* Rocks Stock Pavilion," *The Daily Illini,* XXIX/50 (November 18, 1967).

Books and Essays Relevant, in Various Ways, to Cage's Endeavors

AMES, VAN METER. *Zen and American Thought.* Honolulu: University of Hawaii, 1962.
AUSTIN, WILLIAM W. *Music in the Twentieth Century.* New York: W. W. Norton, 1966.
BATTCOCK, GREGORY, ed. *The New Art.* New York: Dutton, 1966.
———. *The New Music.* New York: Dutton, 1970.
BECKER, JURGEN, and VOSTELL, WOLF, eds. *Happenings.* Hamburg: Rowohlt, 1965.
BECKWITH, JOHN, and KASEMETS, UGO, eds. *The Modern Com-*

poser and His World. Toronto: University of Toronto Press, 1961.

BERGONZI, BERNARD, ed. *Innovations.* London: Macmillan. 1968.

BORTOLOTTO, MARIO. *Fase Seconda.* Turin: Einaudi, 1968.

BOULEZ, PIERRE. "Eventually . . . ," *La Revue Musicale* [Paris], 212 (April, 1953). Reprinted in *Notes of An Apprenticeship.* Translated by Herbert Weinstock. New York: Knopf, 1969.

———. "Aléa," *Perspectives of New Music,* III/1 (Fall-Winter, 1964). Reprinted in *Notes of An Apprenticeship.*

BROWN, EARLE. "Form in New Music," *Darmstädter Beitrage zur neuen Musik,* X (1965). Reprinted in *Source,* I/1 (1967).

BROWN, NORMAN O. *Love's Body.* New York: Random House, 1966.

CARDEW, CORNELIUS. "Notation—Interpretation, etc.," *Tempo* [London] (Summer, 1961).

CHARLES, DANIEL. "Entr'Acte," in Paul Henry Lang and Nathan Broder, eds., *Contemporary Music in Europe.* New York: Schirmer, 1965.

CHASE, GILBERT. *America's Music.* 2d rev. ed. New York: McGraw-Hill, 1966.

COPLAND, AARON. *Copland on Music.* New York: Doubleday, 1960.

COWELL, HENRY. *New Musical Resources.* Supplementary notes by Joscelyn Godwin. New York: Something Else Press, 1969.

CROSS, LOWELL. *A Bibliography of Electronic Music.* Toronto: University of Toronto Press, 1967.

———. "Electronic Music, 1948–53," *Perspectives of New Music,* VII/2 (Fall-Winter, 1968).

CUNNINGHAM, MERCE. *Changes: Notes on Choreography.* Edited by Frances Starr. New York: Something Else Press, 1969.

DE LEEUW, TOM. *Nittonhundratalets Musik.* Stockholm: Aldas/Bonniers, 1967.

DENBY, EDWIN. *Looking at the Dance.* 2d ed. New York: Horizon, 1968.

EDMUNDS, JOHN, and BOELZNER, GORDON, eds. *Some Twentieth Century Composers.* Introduction by Peter Yates. New York: New York Public Library, 1959.

EWEN, DAVID. *David Ewen Introduces Modern Music.* Philadelphia: Chilton, 1962.

FULLER, R. BUCKMINSTER. *Nine Chains to the Moon.* Philadelphia: Lippincott, 1938.

———. *No More Secondhand God.* Carbondale: Southern Illinois University Press, 1962.

———. *Untitled Epic Poem on the History of Industrialization.* Highlands, N.C.: The Nantahala Foundation, 1962.

———. *Education Automation.* Carbondale: Southern Illinois University Press, 1963.

———. *Ideas and Integrities.* Englewood Cliffs, N.J.: Prentice-Hall, 1963.

———. *Operating Manual for Spaceship Earth.* Carbondale: Southern Illinois University Press, 1969.

———. *Utopia or Oblivion: The Prospects for Humanity.* New York: Bantam, 1969.

HANSEN, AL. *A Primer of Happenings & Time-Space Art.* New York: Something Else Press, 1968.

HANSEN, PETER S. *An Introduction to Twentieth Century Music.* 2d. ed. Boston: Allyn and Bacon, 1967.

HASSAN, IHAB. "The Dismemberment of Orpheus," *The American Scholar,* XXXII/3 (Summer, 1963).

HELMS, HANS G. *Musik, Literatur, und Gesellschaft* [A series of broadcasts]. Germany: Radio Bremen, 1962.

———. "Von kritischer Kunst—Über Brecht, Schönberg, Cage, und Brown" [Two Broadcasts]. Germany: Bayerischer Rundfunk, August, 1963.

HIGGINS, DICK. *Postface.* New York: Something Else Press, 1964.

———. *foew&ombrwhnw.* New York: Something Else Press, 1969.

HILLER, LEJAREN A., and ISAACSON, LEONARD M. *Experimental Music.* New York: McGraw-Hill, 1959.

HITCHCOCK, H. WILEY. "Music," in A. N. J. den Hollander and Sigmund Skard, eds., *American Civilization: An Introduction.* London: Longmans, 1968.

———. *Music in the United States: A Historical Introduction.* Englewood Cliffs, N.J.: Prentice-Hall, 1969.

Huang-Po Doctrine of the Universal Mind. London: The Buddhist Society, 1947. Published in America as *The Zen Teaching of Huang Po.* Translated by John Blofeld. New York: Grove, 1959.

JOHNSTON, JILL. "Dance," in Richard Kostelanetz, ed., *The New American Arts.* New York: Horizon, 1965.

KAPROW, ALLAN. *Assemblage, Environments & Happenings.* New York: Abrams, 1966.

KIRBY, E. T. *Total Theatre.* New York: Dutton, 1969.

KIRBY, MICHAEL. *Happenings.* New York: Dutton, 1965.

———. "The New Theatre," *Tulane Drama Review,* X/2 (Winter, 1965).

———. *The Art of Time*. New York: Dutton, 1969.

KOHLER, OTTO. "Klamauk im Technischen Zeitalter," *Die Zeit* (January 25, 1963).

KOSTELANETZ, RICHARD. *Music of Today*. New York: Time, Inc., 1967.

———. "The Two Extremes of Avant-Garde Music," *The New York Times Magazine* (January 15, 1967).

———. "Modern Music Criticism and the Literate Layman," *Perspectives of New Music,* VI/1 (Fall-Winter, 1967).

———. *The Theatre of Mixed Means*. New York: Dial, 1968.

———. "Getting Cunningham Between Covers," *Ballet Review,* III/2 (1969).

———. "Inferential Art," *Columbia University Forum,* XII/2 (Summer, 1969). Reprinted in *Metamorphosis in the Arts*. New York: Abrams, 1970.

———, ed. *Imaged Words & Worded Images*. New York: Outerbridge & Dienstfrey, 1970.

LEUNING, OTTO. "An Unfinished History of Electronic Music," *Music Educators Journal,* CV/2 (November, 1968).

LIST, KURT. "A New American Music," *Listen,* IX/8 (June, 1947).

MELLERS, WILFRID. "The Avant-Garde in America," *Proceedings of the Royal Musical Association,* XC (1964).

———. *Music in a New Found Land*. New York: Knopf, 1965.

———. *Caliban Reborn*. New York: Harper & Row, 1967.

MEYER, LEONARD B. *Music, The Arts, and Ideas*. Chicago: University of Chicago Press, 1967.

NONO, LUIGI. "Geschichte und Gegenwart in der Musik von heute," *Darmstädter Breiträge zur neuen Musik*. V (1960).

———. "The Historical Reality of Music Today," *Score,* 27 (July, 1960).

PAULI, HANSJÖRG. "Musik im Fernsehen," *Melos,* XXXV/7–8 (July-August, 1968).

PECKHAM, MORSE. *Rage for Chaos*. Philadelphia: Chilton, 1965.

REYNOLDS, ROGER. "Indeterminacy: Some Considerations," *Perspectives of New Music,* IV/1 (Fall-Winter, 1965).

———. "Happenings in Japan and Elsewhere," *Arts in Society,* V/1 (Spring-Summer, 1968).

ROCHBERG, GEORGE. "Indeterminacy in the New Music," *Score,* 26 (January, 1960).

ROSE, BARBARA. *American Art Since 1900*. New York: Praeger, 1967.

SALZMAN, ERIC. "Music," in Richard Kostelanetz, ed., *The New American Arts*. New York: Horizon, 1965.

———. *Twentieth-Century Music: An Introduction*. Englewood Cliffs, N.J.: Prentice-Hall, 1968.

SCHAEFFER, PIERRE. *La Musique Concrète*. Paris: Presses Universitaires, 1967.

SCHWARTZ, ELLIOTT, and CHILDS, BARNEY, eds. *Contemporary Composers on Contemporary Music*. New York: Holt, Rinehart, and Winston, 1967.

SLONIMSKY, NICOLAS. *Lexicon of Musical Invective*. 2d ed. New York: Coleman-Ross, 1965.

SONTAG, SUSAN. "The Esthetics of Silence," in *Styles of Radical Will*. New York: Farrar, Straus and Giroux, 1969.

STOCKHAUSEN, KARLHEINZ. "Musik und Graphik," *Darmstädter Breiträge zur neuen Musik,* V (1960).

THOMSON, VIRGIL. *Music Right and Left*. New York: Holt, 1951.

———. "America's Musical Maturity: A Twentieth-Century Story," *Yale Review,* LX/1 (Autumn, 1961).

———. *Music Reviewed, 1940–54*. New York: Vintage, 1967.

WATTS, ALAN W. *Beat Zen Square Zen and Zen*. San Francisco: City Lights, 1959.

WILHELM, RICHARD, ed. *The I Ching, or Book of Changes*. Translated by Cary F. Baynes. New York: Bollingen, 1950.

WOLFF, CHRISTIAN. "New and Electronic Music," *Audience,* V/3 (Summer, 1958).

———. "Ueber Form," *Die Reihe,* 7 (1960). Translated as "On Form" in the American edition of *Die Reihe,* 7. Bryn Mawr, Pa.: Theodore Presser, 1965.

YATES, PETER. "Organized Sound: Notes in the History of a New Disagreement Between Sound and Tone," *California Arts and Architecture* (March, 1941).

———. "After Modern Music," *Location,* I/1 (Spring, 1963).

YOUNG, LA MONTE/ZAZEELA, MARIAN. *Selected Writings*. Munich: Heinar Friedrich, 1969.

index

Those titles of musical compositions, books, and essays that have no parenthetical attributions after them denote works by John Cage.